Travis Bradford
"Solar Revolution"

"The Hydrogen Economy"
Jeremy Rifkin

More Praise for
The Grand Energy Transition

"Robert Hefner's excellent book is an important contribution to today's historic debate on our energy future. It is even more valuable coming from a longstanding practitioner."

—JON M. HUNTSMAN, JR., Governor of Utah

"I first met Robert Hefner in 1994. We talked about his conviction that natural gas was the energy source of the future and that left a deep impression on me. It was then a minority view, one might even say, a fringe view. He has since been proved right. He saw ahead of most others a trend that has a far-reaching impact on how human society is organized. Like all living things, access to abundant energy and the efficient use of that energy decide which society will succeed in war and peace. Societies which respond earliest enjoy a major advantage."

—GEORGE Y.B. YEO, Minister of Foreign Affairs, Singapore

"How do we get from dirty, finite, and unsustainable fuels to sustainable life and growth on Planet Earth? Robert Hefner makes a fascinating and readable case for gas as our bridge fuel to a sustainable future. As he argues, energy use will bring civilization together or tear it apart."

—JOSEPH S. NYE, JR., University Distinguished
Service Professor, Harvard and author of
The Powers to Lead

"Robert Hefner has been right over the years on gas supply while many energy 'experts' have been suspicious, wrong, and not adequately attentive to the data and technical possibilities. Accordingly, his vision about the future role of natural gas deserves serious consideration. He is almost certainly right that natural gas will play a much larger role than previously thought."

—JOHN DEUTCH, Professor, Department of Chemistry, MIT;
and former director CIA, Deputy Secretary of Defense, and
Director of Energy Research, Department of Energy

"In *The Grand Energy Transition*, Robert Hefner describes how the world can make a one-time evolutionary step from the unsustainable current and projected global energy mix to 'virtually limitless clean gaseous energy sources.' Some energy experts might be dismissive about Hefner's vision, but this author did not arrive at his conclusion in a vacuum. A third-generation successful wildcatter and natural gas producer, Hefner has a history of proving the skeptics in the industry wrong. For decades, he argued against the U.S. government and industry pessimism about the future of U.S. natural gas production capacity and once again he has proved his critics wrong. I know of no other person who has consistently been so right about natural gas abundance. U.S. natural gas production has grown an astonishing 20 percent in the past five years due to the development of nonconventional natural gas at half the landed price of LNG in Asia. This well-written book, laced with interesting quotations from scholars, statesmen, and philosophers, should be read by open-minded energy experts, policy makers, and the public at large."

—**HERMAN FRANSSEN,** President, International
Energy Associates Inc; and past Chief Economist of
the International Energy Agency (IEA) in Paris

"*The Grand Energy Transition* is a timely and thoughtfully written book from one of the world's leading energy entrepreneurs. The first decade of the twenty-first century may go down in history as the moment when the world woke up to the fact that the political, economic, and environmental costs of its 150-year addiction to coal and oil could no longer be sustained and that a wholesale switch to an abundant and readily available alternative, natural gas, was the only viable way forward. This book provides the wake up call."

—**KISHORE MAHBUBANI,** Dean of the Lee Kuan
Yew (LKY) School of Public Policy, NUS and author of
The New Asian Hemisphere

The Grand Energy Transition

The Grand Energy Transition

*The Rise of Energy Gases,
Sustainable Life and
Growth, and the Next
Great Economic Expansion*

Robert A. Hefner III

WILEY

John Wiley & Sons, Inc.

For general information on our other products and services or for technical support, please contact our Customer Care Department within the United States at (800) 762-2974, outside the United States at (317) 572-3993 or fax (317) 572-4002.

Wiley also publishes its books in a variety of electronic formats. Some content that appears in print may not be available in electronic books. For more information about Wiley products, visit our Web site at www.wiley.com.

Library of Congress Cataloging-in-Publication Data:

Hefner, Robert A., 1935–

  The grand energy transition : the rise of energy gases, sustainable life and growth, and the next great economic expansion / Robert A. Hefner, III.

     p. cm.

  Includes index.

Summary: "A groundbreaking book on solving our growing energy problems. In this visionary book, leading energy industry executive Robert Hefner puts forth a convincing case about how the world can move beyond its current dependence on oil and toward a new era of clean, renewable energy. Written with the knowledge and authority of a major player in this industry, Hefner relates how misguided government policies and vested industry interests have contributed to our current energy problems and proposes a variety of measures that could encourage the use of natural gas, solar, wind, and hydrogen. Convincingly makes the case that natural gas is the essential bridge fuel to a new era of clean, renewable energy sources. Details how natural gas can help break our oil and coal dependency. Offers a sweeping, historic picture of the world energy situation. Presents a compelling and provocative case that natural gas is key to our short-term energy problems. A well-written and engaging book that mixes personal anecdotes and experiences with insightful analysis, The Grand Energy Transition is a powerful argument about how we can best solve our toughest energy problems"—Provided by publisher.

ISBN-13 978-0-470-52756-6

1. Renewable energy sources. 2. Energy policy. I. Title.

TJ808.H44   2009

   333.79—dc22   2009023129

Printed in the United States of America

10 9 8 7 6 5 4 3 2 1

I dedicate this book to my wife, MeiLi, who was the constant, driving force that propelled it to completion, and to my grandchildren, especially Steven, the scientist, and their generation, who must work to jet the GET.

Contents

Acknowledgments

First, this book would not have been possible without the tireless help of my trusted and superbly capable assistants, Jane Rider, for the transcription of innumerable drafts, and Janet Brewer, for research and accuracy, a particularly difficult job when dealing with energy statistics. Also, thanks to our GHK Team, who kept the company moving forward while I wrote about my life's work in energy and what I have learned.

Kurt Campbell, the co-founder of the Center for a New American Security, gave me important doses of encouragement, and two of his formidable associates, Sharon Burke and Christine Parthemore, helped me sort through and clarify decades of thoughts.

The Logistical Substitution Models for Energy Use, produced by my great friend and mentor Cesare Marchetti, and long-time energy associate Nebojsa Nakicenovic, were fundamental to the foundation of my GET hypothesis.

My friend and sometimes neighbor, Irwin Stelzer, was the first to encourage me to write. His encouragement led to a series of papers beginning in 1990 on energy and economics that I called the Hefner Reports and a series of papers called the Age of Energy Gases.

For more than 30 years, Amory Lovins has described to me the macroeconomic inefficiencies of energy use in the United States and proposed simple, profitable ways to wring these inefficiencies out of our economy. Amory's works have had a profound influence upon my thinking. I also wish to acknowledge my good friend Peter Krogh, who has always taught big ideas and pushed his students and friends to have big ideas and was the first person to use the motto of this book, "Jet the GET."

Andrew Cleary and Pat McGuigan provided great help with the manuscript. I must also acknowledge my first mentor, Ray Alf, who challenged me to go through life with a mind that always searched "beyond the limits," and Ed Schmidt and especially another friend and mentor Tommy Gold, who kept me on that path. Finally, Laurie Glover and David Kennedy, my first partners, who had faith in a very young man and helped jump-start GHK fifty years ago in 1959.

Introduction

The Inextricable Link between Energy and the Economy

This generation of Americans, led by President Barrack Obama, will have unprecedented challenges and opportunities. The challenges will be to resist overregulation of the banking and financial sectors and the constriction of free trade, both of which happened following the 1929 market crash and collapse of the banking system. The opportunities will be to use these times of great change to come together hand-in-hand with our government, just as we did following Pearl Harbor, to industrialize and produce the materials necessary to win World War II, this time to transform our energy systems, regain our energy independence, and lead the world toward the resolution of climate change.

We have overleveraged both our economy and our energy use. We are all now aware how U.S. banks and financial institutions overleveraged our financial system and have seen the costs of bailing out the system in daily headlines. But few people are aware that since the

1970s, we have also been leveraging our economic growth by consuming energy at less than the full-cycle cost. These often-hidden costs are the costs that economists call externalities. These include costs such as the largest part of our trade deficit, which is attributable to oil imports, the military costs of protecting the free flow of oil, the cost of oil-related wars, the cost of gasoline pollution in all our towns and cities, and the related health costs, and the near- and long-term costs of coal's toxic emissions, such as mercury, acid rain, and particulate emissions, with their related pulmonary health costs. Plus, the hundreds of billions of dollars or, if some scientists and economists are correct, multiple trillions of dollars of future costs attributable to climate change as a result of the buildup of CO_2 emissions in the atmosphere, mostly the result of energy consumption, 80 percent of which is from coal and oil use. When energy consumers don't pay these real full-cycle costs, we are sustaining economic growth by burdening the taxpayer, society, and future generations with these costs, which are eventually paid by the individuals directly affected, by the general taxpayer, or are accruing as additional government debt.

Our economic system and our energy system are inextricably connected because, unlike money, the expenditure (use) of energy is required for the production and consumption of all goods and services. Both our financial system and our energy system must now be deleveraged and rebuilt on sound economic principles. To do so in the energy sector, we can and must accelerate the Grand Energy Transition, the GET, so we can build toward an economic system of sustainable growth and, while doing so, unleash the next unprecedented economic expansion.

Our ongoing financial bailout is organized to create stability in the banking and financial system and is not a plan focused on the creation of sustained economic growth and new jobs. We need not freeze further government spending; rather, we must immediately eliminate all stupid spending. What is now needed is smart spending for an Energy and Industrial Recovery Plan financed and guaranteed by government, similar to the industrialization needed to win World War II. What is needed is a policy organized to restore America's confidence, regain our energy independence, and place us on the path not only to sustainable, clean energy consumption but to sustainable economic expansion. As the old saying goes, at this critical economic juncture in America's history, we must "spend money to make money."

President Obama has the bully pulpit and must use his abundant talent to rally the American people behind an Energy and Industrial Recovery Plan to, among other things discussed in this book, convert at least half of America's vehicle fleet to compressed natural gas (CNG) by 2015. To do so would reduce our oil imports by over 5 million barrels per day and save Americans tens of trillions of dollars in payments to foreign oil producers over the coming decades. To do so would ensure that when global "peak oil" occurs, America will have dodged that deadly bullet. To do so would unlock hundreds of billions of dollars in new capital expenditures by America's automobile and energy industries, as well as their collateral industries. To do so would result in tens of billions in new annual payments to American farmers and landowners as domestic natural gas producers develop and produce new natgas supplies. To do so could create a million new American jobs. To do so would regain our energy independence. And to do so would unleash America's next unprecedented and sustained economic expansion.

No one likes deficit spending, but a $1 trillion Energy and Industrial Recovery Plan, as presented in Chapter 12, to ensure America's economic resurgence is what is now needed to regain American confidence in our own economic system, to create new, well-paying jobs so Americans can begin paying off their personal debts, and to jumpstart the next sustained economic expansion so America can also pay off its national debt and put our government's financial house in order.

Some might fear that higher deficit spending could spur a run on the U.S. dollar, but I say no. I say no because a well-formulated Energy and Industrial Recovery Plan for the long-term, designed to regain our energy independence, significantly reduce payments to foreign oil producers, and stimulate domestic growth in our unprecedentedly powerful economic system, will show the world that America is back on track. I contend that no other policy could instill such confidence in our currency. The U.S. dollar would regain and maintain its status as the most important global currency. Global faith in the U.S. economy would be restored and the United States would once again become the "go-to" economy for global capital. And not least, the United States will have taken a giant step forward in restoring our global soft power.

I am the third generation in the energy business. I have spent my entire life exploring and producing natural gas and studying energy use in society. I have experienced firsthand the politics of formulating energy policy and the booms and busts that have come to America's domestic energy producers as a result of our past start-and-stop, largely erratic, and mostly short-term energy policies. This is why I took up the challenge to write this book, because I wanted to share with the American public, our Congress, and President Obama and his administration my own unique experience and theories on how we can and must move the GET forward.

This book describes my theory that we must think about our energy sources not as individual fuels such as coal, oil, or natural gas but rather by their state of matter, either as a solid, a liquid, or a gas. By doing so, the complexity of the energy sector is eliminated to reveal the elegant simplicity of our ongoing Grand Energy Transition. The GET is civilization's continuing technological energy evolution, which is leading us away from solid and liquid fuels and toward the Age of Energy Gases (natural gas, wind, solar, and hydrogen). This book shows how the GET is creating a clear and irrevocable energy path forward, and how the GET itself, driven by the developments of civilization, reveals the most likely energy winners and losers. This book makes the case that North America is blessed with abundant supplies of natural gas that can be scaled up in the near-term to become the bridge fuel to our energy-sustainable future and that these supplies, supplemented by Alaskan natural gas and the world's liquefied natural gas (LNG), are adequate to fuel at least half of our vehicle fleet for decades to come, as well as much of our existing power generation and all new electric power needs not met by wind, solar, and nuclear.

As I write this in the spring of 2009, America's natural gas exploration and production industry is once again going through a bust following a boom. This is because such large supplies of new natural gas have been recently developed that our domestic market has been overwhelmed. Over recent years, America's superbly capable independent natural gas producers have been so successful in deploying new technologies and innovations to produce America's natural gas supplies at prices about half that of oil that we have developed a supply glut, and once again, the bottom has dropped out of natural gas prices. For instance, in the Midcontinent and Rocky Mountain regions, natural gas spot prices have dropped from over $10 per Mcf ($60 per barrel oil equivalent) to, in some cases, less than $2 per Mcf ($12 per barrel oil equivalent). As a result, just as we are entering an economic downturn and are desperate for new economic growth and new jobs, tens of billions in annual revenues are being lost to millions of American farmers and landowners, independent natural gas producers, their shareholders, and energy service companies, unnecessarily adding to our ongoing economic contraction. Tens of billions of dollars of capital expenditure reductions have been announced, and multitudes of drilling rigs are stopping their work and their crews are being laid off. Tens of thousands of jobs are being lost once again, adding to America's joblessness and exacerbating the problem of people shortages in our industry, and all because America has no policy to use its clean, abundant natural gas instead of dirty coal and imported oil.

Without such an Energy and Industrial Recovery Plan, instead of the benefit of a million or more future new jobs in the energy and automotive sectors and the follow-on benefit of the economic multiplier here at home, Americans will go on sending to foreign producers trillions of dollars each decade for the oil to run our cars and trucks, all to the detriment of our economy and our trade deficit.

It is my belief that this book describes a clear energy path forward that can be accelerated by the policies I have recommended—policies that, if boldly embraced by the Obama administration and Congress, will not only accelerate our economic recovery but also lead to America's next great and unprecedented economic expansion.

Robert A. Hefner III
March 2009

Author's Note

This book was written over a period of two years; the ongoing 2008–2009 global financial crisis and its impact on energy and the economy may have altered some numbers.

Chapter 1

The Beginning

Sit down before fact as a little child, be prepared to give up every preconceived notion, follow humbly wherever and to whatever abyss nature leads—or you shall learn nothing.
—THOMAS HENRY HUXLEY

My long road to understanding the Grand Energy Transition, the GET, began on September 14, 1950. I was a 15-year-old student at Webb School in Claremont, California. On that day, my biology teacher, Dr. Ray Alf, changed my life forevermore. It was on that day that I had my first *Eureka!* moment. Dr. Alf took us out to a small pond on campus where we collected a bucket of pond water. He had said that a microcosm of all life was in one drop of pond water. We brought it into our basement laboratory where he taught how to make slides with one drop of his treasured *pond water* to view under high-powered microscopes. The depths of that life-changing experience evoked within me a message far beyond my 15 years. It has served to guide me in my quest for the understanding of energy within civilization.

That evening, I wrote the following in my biology notebook:

On Thursday, September 14, I reached a new pinnacle of experience. It was on this day that I bridged time and space with my microscope and saw with my own eyes a whole new world unfold before me. The hustle and bustle of the world we know was there. The age-old law of "survival of the fittest" was there also.

What was different about this tiny world, contained in one drop of pond water, was what made the 45 minutes so memorable to me. That difference was the amazing animal life, so small and every bit as capable to cope with the problems of its world as I am in mine. Here was a time for philosophical thought, for I had always considered myself superior to protozoa. What I had neglected to consider was the relativity of the protozoa to myself. It was not the mere view of this minute world that was amazing, but it was the questions it raised in my mind. Here among the parameciums, rotifers, and cyclops, I found what I considered a truly great experience and perhaps an answer to some of life's great problems.

In this book, you will see that the roots of my understanding of how energy evolves within civilization are grounded in the survival of the fittest and the natural selection of intelligent beings to seek growth within quality of life.

The man who opened my eyes to the mystery of energy and evolution, Ray Alf, was born in 1905 in Canton, China, to missionary parents. His second language was Cantonese, and he often recited the Lord's Prayer in Cantonese. He was a small, wiry man, full of energy and passion. One of his passions was to teach—particularly concepts about the origin of life, evolution, and how humans have only been around for the last few seconds relative to the history of life on Earth. He always believed that only through teaching could one leave behind a meaningful heritage for humanity. He certainly accomplished that with me.

At the time, he had a unique way of teaching evolution that has since gained much more scientific stature. He believed evolution would work through natural selection as Darwin taught, with small adaptations to local environmental changes over geologically long periods. But, as he was also a renowned paleontologist, he understood that evolution always seemed to suddenly make great leaps forward. He called this crisis "the crisis of change." Ray Alf became my first mentor and revealed to me the hidden universe that led me to a life in science. He was an unbounded thinker, and by example taught us to go beyond the limits.

Ray Alf opened the door through which I passed into a lifetime of energy exploration and thinking about energy, relativity, the origin of life, and evolution. It was from this foundation that I pushed myself forward, always keeping in my heart Ray's guiding principle to be an unbounded thinker and to go beyond the apparent limits.

It is my belief that it is humanity's God-given, inherent right to achieve sustainable life and growth on Earth. This book is about how I believe civilization will achieve this destiny.

Much of life takes place beyond our daily observation. In the quest for new ideas, it is necessary to move beyond the limits of conventional thinking and what can easily be seen. That is the basic premise we must keep in mind as we explore the past, the present, and the future of energy use, as Buckminster Fuller correctly said, on our "Spaceship Earth." Energy is everything, yet it cannot be seen. We can only see what happens as a result of its existence. Einstein's brilliant intuition that $E = mc^2$ says it all. Mass *is* energy; energy equals mass times the speed of light squared. Indeed, energy *is* everything.

Energy is a natural, hidden, and invisible system within civilization. Civilization cannot exist as we know it without the consumption of vast quantities of energy. Therefore, energy consumption is a moral good. It is fundamental to the creation and functioning of societies. Although economists argue with me, I believe energy is more fundamental to the functioning of an economy than is money. There cannot be an economic system without the consumption of energy. The production and provision of all goods and services and their consumption requires the use, or I would prefer to say *expenditure*, of energy. In economics, energy quickly exhibits fundamental pervasiveness, for it has a significant and continual relationship to all economic and demographic variables. The gross domestic product (GDP), employment levels, inflation, economic growth, and even the amount of spendable income available to the individual, the family, or local, state, and federal governments all relate to the use, availability, and price of energy.

Today, humanity is in an energy and climate crisis of our own making. We have altered and placed in grave danger our economy, environment, and the security of our societies by the energy we use. Indeed, the magnitude of the crisis—even the crisis itself—has been hidden from our view. The world does in fact operate as Ray Alf taught. There is always more going on than we can see or have yet envisioned. It will be the awareness of this economic, environmental, and societal crisis that will become the driving force of civilization's next evolutionary step, the one taking us to sustainable life and growth on Earth.

I hope this book about my concepts and ideas will add to energy solutions that will accelerate us through the Grand Energy Transition, the GET, to a sustainable destiny. This book is not intended to answer the millions of good questions about energy use and our energy future, nor is it a text about the details of energy production and consumption. Rather, it introduces a new way of thinking about energy and looking at the evolution of energy within civilization and, with this understanding, of forecasting the best possible comprehensive solution to today's formidable energy problems and a clear path forward to a new era of sustainable life and growth on Earth. So, most important in these times of limited monetary and human resources, the development of civilization itself and the evolution of the GET are showing us, our leaders, and policymakers the most likely energy winners and losers. At this point in history, we don't have time for the losers, so we all must take heed. Also, I am sure that along the way, this book will accomplish my other goal of sparking controversy and creativity that have always and will forevermore lead us forward.

Chapter 2

The Grand Energy Transition

The helmsman must guide the boat by using the waves, otherwise the boat will be submerged by the waves.

—CHOU EN-LAI

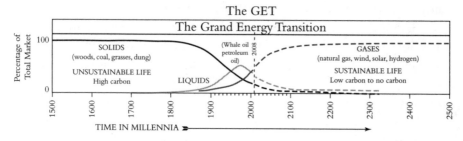

Robert A. Hefner III
© 2009, The GHK Company

The Grand Energy Transition (GET) is based upon my theory that in order to best understand humanity's energy past, present, and future, we must think about all the energy sources in their form of matter, solids, liquids, and gases, rather than individual fuels such as coal, a solid, oil, a liquid, or natural gas, a gas. By doing so, we see a natural evolution of energy within the development of civilization. What is revealed by this concept is a transition of elegant simplicity that cuts through the complexity of energy use, policy, and politics. The GET or, more accurately, civilization itself through trillions of energy choices based upon economic utility is showing us the way forward and determining the future's most likely energy winners and losers.

The GET should be understood as a one-time, evolutionary step forward for humankind. The GET is the liquid transition between the unsustainable solid energy sources of our past and the virtually limitless, clean, sustainable energy sources of our future. Energy gases will provide civilization with what I believe to be its destiny: sustainable life and growth on Earth. The GET will transform humanity's energy use from dirty, solid fuels to clean, environmentally sustainable gaseous fuels. The GET is the liquid transition; after all, liquid is a transitional state of matter, between these millennia-long solid and gaseous energy epochs of human civilization. The GET is a largely invisible transition that will have a larger long-term impact on how societies live on Earth than either the War on Terror, the Rise of Asia, World War II, or the Cold War. The acceleration of the GET will be civilization's most important challenge during the twenty-first century.

The GET is driven forward by the cumulative result of all human activities. It is derived from the natural human imperative to seek higher levels of economic standing and quality of life through creativity, innovation, and invention. The GET can be compared to Charles Darwin's theory of natural selection for the evolution of life. Just as Darwin compared natural changes in nature with societal changes within countries, I compare the energy changes of the GET to natural selection, driven by hundreds of trillions of individual energy choices each year.

The GET began near the middle of the 1800s, with liquids beginning to replace solids, and will take some 200 years to transition to its final stage: the Age of Energy Gases. Luckily, in the scale of history, most of the GET is behind us, so now all we need to do is finish the job. Setting politics aside, this could be achieved by 2050 because it does not require *Star Wars* technology. Indeed, most of the technology is in-hand and we live in the time of history's most rapid rate of technological accomplishment. By the middle of this century, most of the world's people, depending on their individual governments, can be living in an environmentally sustainable economy that is no longer producing increasingly intolerable pollution nor CO_2 emissions sufficient to drive global climate change. But in order to accomplish this goal in a timely way, we must come together as one human population behind energy-enlightened leaders and begin now to accelerate the GET. Our motto will be "Jet the GET."

Although the GET is the overarching liquid transition from unsustainable solid to sustainable gaseous fuels, within each transitional phase, cyclical energy substitutions also take place. For instance, within solids, coal displaced wood as a principal energy source; within liquids, whale oil was displaced by petroleum oil; and today, biofuels are being substituted for petroleum products. Although natural gas will continue to displace growing quantities of both solid and liquid fuels, it is already being challenged for market share by its sister fuels, wind and solar, in the wave of energy gases.

Civilization fueled its growing energy needs for millennia with solid fuels, mostly wood, grasses, dung, and coal. And just as the solid fuel era lasted for millennia, so, too, will the gaseous fuel era that I call the Age of Energy Gases that is the subject of Chapter 13. Let me say at the outset that, in addition to natural gas, the Age of Energy Gases includes all the energy gases—wind, solar, hydrogen, and, when it arrives, nuclear fusion, which is best described as the "sun in a box." The Earth's atmosphere is a gas, and wind is driven by the Earth's daily heat from the sun. The sun is mostly burning hydrogen gas (actually, the fusion of hydrogen), and each day the Earth is bathed in virtually limitless solar energy. The sun is our solar system's public power plant. Hydrogen itself is a gas and is the universe's most abundant element. On Earth, hydrogen is a potentially vast, virtually unlimited source of energy. When hydrogen is used as a fuel, it turns into heat and water and is, therefore, totally clean energy. So if hydrogen gas is separated from water by electrolysis or in other environmentally benign ways, it becomes a virtually limitless and totally clean energy that, in synergy with solar and eventually nuclear fusion energy, can sustain population and economic growth on Earth for millennia to come.

The final phase of the Age of Energy Gases will be the hydrogen-based economy, running principally on hydrogen, solar, wind, and eventually nuclear fusion.

Carbon-light natural gas, which contains only one carbon atom with four hydrogen atoms, is already growing to become our first major step toward hydrogen. Natural gas will continue to rapidly grow in the energy mix and become our principal bridge fuel to humanity's ultimate sustainable energy goal. You will see in Chapter 3 how the GET has been decarbonizing and cleaning up our energy system since it began over 100 years ago.

Throughout the history of civilization, each new fuel that has been introduced has been a better, more capable fuel that enhanced society in many ways. Each new fuel initially brings to society a large measure of new efficiencies and a burst of new technologies that lead to a new pulse of previously unimaginable economic growth, as well as environmental improvement and better quality of life in a more modern and sophisticated world.

But each new fuel also brings with it the seeds of its own demise. Each fuel is phased away not because we have run out, but because its costs to society as a whole, including economic, environmental, and security costs, become so high and bring risks so large that the fuel loses utility to consumers and the nations within which they live. In the case of carbon-based fuels, particularly carbon-heavy coal and oil, their very success created their own limits because the quantities of their use became incompatible with the growth of society. This is why our sustainable destiny must be the hydrogen economy, as hydrogen fuels create no limits to life and growth on Earth.

Civilization began around the wood fire, and wood and bronze-iron-based technologies, along with human and animal labor, remained our principal energy technology system for thousands of years until they began to be replaced by coal in the late 1700s. By the time coal got a foothold in the energy market and began its rapid growth, forests in England, Europe, and Asia had been ravaged. Initially, coal's more modern technologies not only improved energy efficiency many times and helped create economic growth never before experienced, but they also improved the quality of life for the general society. Even the environment improved as the use of coal slowed down the loss of great natural forests. Coal is a better fuel than wood because it packs a larger energy punch in a smaller and more transportable package. Coal was many more times efficient in providing heat for industrial uses, such as making steel.

Because each new fuel is in so many ways better, more versatile, and more efficient, each new fuel gives rise to a burst of new technologies that grow up around that fuel to power expanding innovation and new inventions. In 1769, James Watt invented the steam engine that, in turn, gave birth to an explosion of new and improved technologies. The coal-fired steam engine brought with it factories, mass production, and, because of coal's high energy mobility, manyfold improvements in the transportation sector, including larger and faster railroad engines and steam-powered ships. Trade and travel were greatly expanded and industrial production proliferated, such that together they brought the then-largest economic pulse ever experienced in human history, the Industrial Revolution.

The Industrial Revolution began in England, with its large coal deposits. England rode coal's energy and technology wave to the heights of the global British Empire upon which "the sun never set." But coal's success became its limits. At the height of the Industrial Revolution, the harmful side effects of dirty coal had affected everyone's life, rich or poor. Coal is dirty, mostly carbon, often radioactive, and when burned it emits CO_2, sulphur fumes, mercury, arsenic, and large amounts of heavy carbon dust and particulates. England, the very heart of the Industrial Revolution, became highly polluted, and homes, furniture, and clothes were coated in carbon dust. This became a significant factor in the nation's general health problems. Coal and all that surrounds its use became a principal contributor to the conditions of Charles Dickens's London. London's glorious buildings eventually turned black from so much carbon dust and particulates in the air. The heavy humidity of the British climate often turned this airborne pollution to dense fogs described at the time as being as thick as pea soup. These fogs were so dense that transportation slowed to a crawl during the fogs, which had the follow-on effect of a large negative impact on the economy. At the peak of the Industrial Revolution, coal had created the conditions of its own eventual demise—conditions that would impede Britain's technological progress for decades. Yet because an energy system is like one's life blood, its use goes on, and its vested interest in both industry and politics run so deep that it requires either a great, enlightened, and powerful leader; catastrophic disaster; or war to accelerate the evolutionary change to the next energy wave.

Although I do not say that the demise of the British Empire was entirely linked to the use of coal well beyond its most effective and efficient limits, I do believe the depth of the coal infrastructure, the size of its external costs to society, and its vested economic and political interests slowed England's economic and technological progress for decades during the twentieth century. Unfortunately, what was originally a better energy technology was left in place too long following the peak of the Industrial Revolution. Coal's deeply vested economic and political interests slowed the GET and impeded economic and technological progress. This is precisely what Harvard's renowned Austrian economist Joseph Schumpeter meant when he postulated that progress always requires "creative destruction."[1] Our energy system is deeply embedded within our economy and equally deeply vested within our political system. In order to overthrow the energy status quo and release the next burst of energy invention and innovation, large measures of creative destruction must take place.

Coal is a solid and is more cumbersome to transport than liquid oil and oil fuels that pack more energy punch per pound. By the beginning of the twentieth century, for both environmental and technological reasons as well as competitive prices, oil fuels were beginning to make headway by displacing coal. Oil, with less dirty carbon and more clean hydrogen, was a more efficient, more versatile modern technology. Oil soon began to command a larger share of the energy market. Winston Churchill had the foresight to see oil as a better, more mobile fuel with more bang for the buck for the British Navy in 1912,[2] but it was World War II that accelerated oil's use.

Still, coal's vested interests ran so deep that it took Lady Margaret Thatcher, the most powerful prime minister since Churchill, to break coal's ironhanded grip on the British economy in the 1980s. Since then, natural-gas–fired electric generation has grown from virtually nothing in the early 1990s to producing nearly one-third of the United Kingdom's 2006 output.[3] In an energy sense, England has leapfrogged the United States because it is farther along in the Age of Energy Gases. The pea-soup fogs that lasted well into the 1950s are now gone. London has since cleansed itself, and its glorious buildings are once again sparkling white. Today, London stands as one of the great jewels of global cities. By throwing off the coal yoke, London and the British economy transformed themselves, and the great city once again offers its citizens a world-class quality of life.

Oil became the next great energy wave and America rode oil's great wave to what some call the American Empire. Oil provided the life blood for post-war expansion to the modern economy and now the globalized, connected world. The transportation sector was revolutionized by the use of oil and its principal technologies, the automobile and the airplane. These two innovations of transportation radically changed how people lived and how far and fast they traveled. The turbine engine took air travel a step further, and airlines began carrying millions of people to all points of the globe. Oil's wave was accelerated by the necessity to pursue and win World War II. Great innovations came out of that effort—principally, the transport and chemical technologies surrounding oil and the development of the computer and the Internet that for the first time provided civilization with the ability to live in and benefit from a truly globalized economy and a globalized, modern transportation and communication system.

The tearing down of the Berlin Wall and the collapse of the Soviet Union, coupled with Deng Xiaoping's opening of China, created the political circumstances for civilization to become a global society for the first time, connected to each other and to virtually all of accumulated human knowledge at nearly the speed of light. But today, oil has also created its own limits. Coal's story of glory and decline is now being repeated by oil.

Several factors have resulted in a major reduction in the economic utility of oil:

- Oil contributes to pollution and global climate change.
- The oil industry's difficulties in meeting current and near-term consumer demand.

- Prices fluctuate wildly, sometimes rising rapidly. Recently, for example, they reached levels that brought the entire world great hardship and economic instability that exacerbated the ongoing global economic contraction.
- Building geostrategic tensions are often related to oil use, particularly for the United States, which bears the greatest burden in policing oil's free global flows.
- There are macroeconomic consequences to enormous, unbalanced concentrations of wealth in oil-rich countries, which contribute to U.S. trade deficits and diminished value of the U.S. dollar.

Oil has indeed begun its twilight years. In the long view of world history, liquid oil will become a short-term transition between the two-millennia-long energy epochs of unsustainable, finite solids and sustainable, virtually unlimited gases. This time, it is America's turn to deal with not only one but two deeply embedded, out-of-date energy technologies—coal and oil—that, barring enormous political will—tantamount to a "man on the moon" commitment to change—are likely to inhibit America's future for at least the first half of the twenty-first century. I fear that America's coal and oil infrastructure and their deeply embedded economic and political interests will again slow the GET within the U.S. economy and contribute to America's relative decline, as compared to the rise of countries already committed to major twenty-first-century energy changes. Those countries committed to the acceleration of the GET into the Age of Energy Gases and creative destruction in the energy sector will be the twenty-first-century winners.

Exhibit 2.1 puts the GET in the scale of history.

In Chapter 3, I will describe what brought me to conceive the idea of the GET and how it is driven by the evolution of civilization itself.

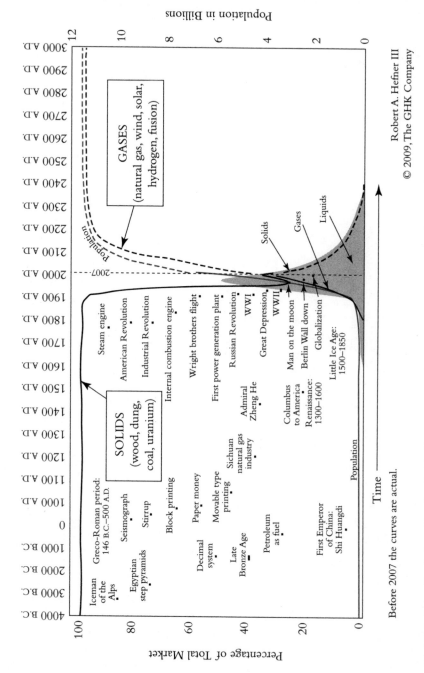

Exhibit 2.1 Earth Energies for the Millennia

Before 2007 the curves are actual.

Robert A. Hefner III
© 2009, The GHK Company

Chapter 3

The Conception of the GET and How It Works

To the extent humankind is eternal, resources are infinite.
—ROBERT A. HEFNER III

My views of energy are derived from being the third generation in the energy business, an education in petroleum geology, an early fascination with an underappreciated by-product energy source—natural gas, five decades of energy studies, a lifelong interest in Einstein and his intuition that $E = mc^2$, and chance but critical meetings and subsequent friendships with several of the world's most challenging out-of-the-box thinkers.

My father and grandfather (who started his career in 1903 at Spindletop, Texas's first giant oil field) taught me about the oil industry and much of its history. My education at the University of Oklahoma hooked me into a lifetime fascination with exploring the Earth's geology and a desire to learn more about how the Earth is "alive" with constant motion and change. Intensive study of natural gas led me to the realization that natural gas is not really part of the oil industry, but only a by-product of oil exploration. That forced me to think about why, how, and where natural gas (*natgas*, as modern traders call it) could be put to better use and achieve a price equal to oil, or even a premium based on its environmental superiority and its domestic security advantage.

My lifetime interest in Einstein has kept me asking, "What is energy?" Reflecting on $E = mc^2$ led me to the view that energy and matter have a distinct and special relationship. Mass *is* energy; energy equals mass times the speed of light squared. Therefore, energy is everything. This became the basis of my non-Malthusian belief that, to the extent humankind is eternal, resources are infinite. I embrace the view that humans have evolved to the extent that creativity, innovation, and invention will always surpass the finite limits of certain Earth resources.

My friendship with cosmologist Tommy Gold, one of those out-of-the-box thinkers, expanded my thinking beyond Earth and the solar system to the universe itself.[1] My later friendship with Cesare Marchetti and his associate Nebojsa Nakicenovic, at the International Institute for Applied Systems Analysis (a think tank located south of Vienna, Austria), introduced me to "the dynamics of energy systems and the logistic substitution model,"[2] upon which I have based much of my work on energy trends. Their work showed me that in order to best view energy trends, one must not look simply at past, present, and estimated future levels of consumption and potential energy resources, but, rather, at the percentage that each energy source is able to supply in the global energy mix over time. The next question is why each energy source gains or loses its percentage of the energy mix.

These decades of work led to another *Eureka!* moment, as I looked at energy in what may be a revolutionary way. Instead of attempting to think about each fuel source based upon its individual attributes, such as whether it is dirty or clean, domestic or foreign, renewable or not, virtually unlimited or constrained, or even at trends in its quantity of consumption, we must first look beyond each fuel, to reveal the elegant simplicity of transitions that I now call the Grand Energy Transition, the GET.

By viewing energy in its principal state of matter—either a gas or a solid or the transitional state of matter, a liquid—trends emerge that I believe clearly show how humanity has adapted energy sources for its needs through natural selection and how trends from the past show a clear way forward to our energy end goal for millennia to come. As Caltech's Carver Mead says, by "listening to the technology," we are pointed in a clear direction forward.[3] Human adaptation to daily life has created constantly changing, slow-moving, and powerful waves of energy consumption that always point us in the direction of a cleaner and greener environment, and enhanced economic efficiency for accelerating growth that is more affordable to society as a whole.

The GET is transforming energy use, its technologies, and fuels from:

- Solid and liquid sources to gaseous sources
- Dirty fuels to clean fuels
- Largely carbon-based to largely hydrogen-based fuels
- Chemically complex to chemically simple
- Inefficient technologies to highly efficient technologies
- Large, capital-intensive, centrally located energy plants and facilities to small, distributed facilities
- Nineteenth- and twentieth-century energy systems to twenty-first-century energy systems
- Low-tech dumb systems to high-tech smart systems
- Finite fuels to virtually infinite fuels

Exhibit 3.1 shows the elegant simplicity of the GET—the transition from high-carbon solid and liquid fuels to hydrogen-based gaseous fuels, from unsustainable to sustainable life and growth on Earth.

Global Energy Transition Waves

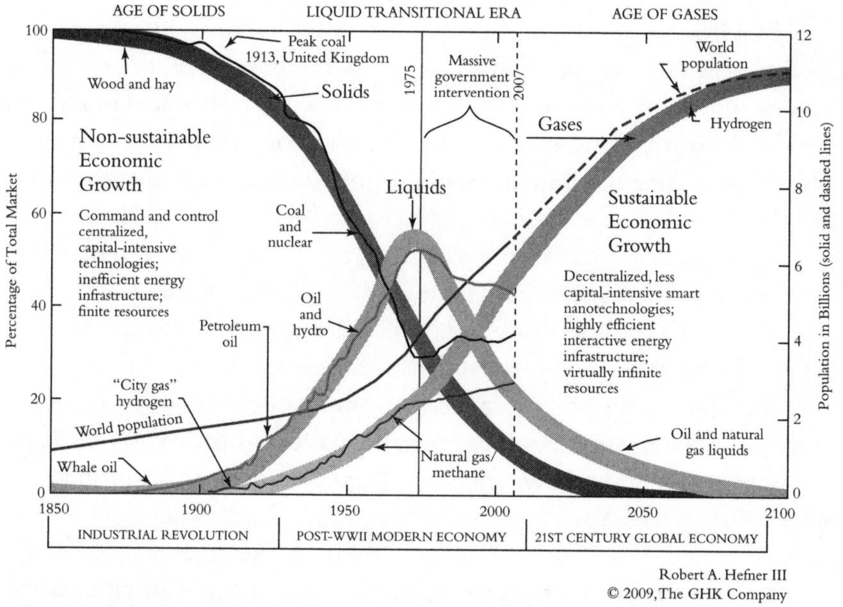

Robert A. Hefner III
© 2009, The GHK Company

Exhibit 3.1 GET Waves

Forces of Energy Transitions

Energy transitions are so powerful because they emanate from each individual, family, business, and government's daily energy consumption and are so slow moving because they are the net result of each individual's daily habits, and habits are hard to change. Energy transitions are moved forward by three forces, listed in order of their increasing importance:

1. Government intervention
2. Leadership
3. Individual behavior

The first and least powerful is government intervention that works well when policies are put in place that facilitate the direction of the GET. Unfortunately, because government policies too often are the result of deeply vested interests and effective lobbying, they often work in the opposite direction and slow down an ongoing energy transition. We see the result of a period of massive government intervention—largely in the wrong direction—beginning in the 1970s.

The second is leadership, which has often been a powerful force of change. However, no matter how charismatic, enlightened, and powerful a great leader may be, in the case of energy transitions, the timing of history must also work as a catalyst for such great change. Luckily for our world today, I believe the accelerating global awareness of our great energy and climate problems have brought humankind to that threshold through which such a leader or leaders may soon step.

The third and by far most powerful and fundamental driving force of an energy transition is each individual's actions and reactions to the perception of both the short- and long-term price of energy, its availability, and its effect on their standard of living and quality of life.

The forces that create energy transitions are incredibly complex, but when viewed in the context of energy's form of matter—gas, solid, or liquid—they reveal themselves in elegant simplicity, and in so doing have always carried us in the direction of a more sustainable energy future. Indeed, I believe that if we "listen to the technology," it will always point toward humanity's ultimate energy goal of sustainable life and growth on Earth.

Evolutionary waves of energy consumption are created by the cumulative choices and habits of each individual within the economy. There are energy expenditures imbedded in all goods and services. This process was best described in 1776 by the moral philosopher Adam Smith in his treatise *The Wealth of Nations*, as the working of society's "invisible hand." Our invisible hands drive the slow-moving, long-term process of energy evolution.

Each individual is continuously making either conscious choices about how to consume energy based on the momentary interaction of the price signal and human need, as well as a possible environmental or moral consideration, or largely unconscious energy choices based simply on daily personal habits. For example, how often one goes to the supermarket, whether one sleeps with the window open or the air conditioner on, whether one shops online or at the mall, drives oneself to and from work, carpools, or uses mass transit, and whether one drinks bottled water or tap water are all energy decisions. Human choices and habits are generally based on the classic economic definition of *utility* and are changed by the recognition that costs have become too high for our pocketbook or that our pattern of life is no longer beneficial for our long-term well-being. Well-being is the interaction between our drive for a higher standard of living and quality of life. It is the balancing of all life choices by each individual at a precise moment in time that creates the utility of choice. It is the cumulative effect of each individual's choice that determines our global energy consumption.

For instance, over the last two decades, many American automobile purchasers decided that buying a sport utility vehicle (SUV) provided what they wanted: good utility. Liquid gasoline was cheap, less than bottled water, and drivers could load up the kids and their friends and still have plenty of room. Automobile exhaust pollution levels in major cities were bad, but tolerable when compared to the good use and flexibility gained from the SUV. Oil wars had not yet created general hardships for the majority of society. The economy was booming, so no one worried much about economic losses, trade deficits, and a depreciating dollar related to increasing petroleum imports that reached about 65 percent of 2008[4] consumption, up from about 20 percent in 1970,[5] and even the horror of 9/11 did little to convince Americans that its reliance on oil from an unstable region was unhealthy.

Americans went on to drive more and more with little to no attention to the building environmental, economic, and strategic risks that their habits were creating for all society. However, the United States must now face these risks of oil addiction and deal with the stark reality that in order to progress as a nation and be among the century's winners, it must move beyond the age of liquid oil. And, in order to achieve global energy and climate success in the twenty-first century, China must not follow the United States to oil addiction, nor must it continue the development of an electric power system based on the age-old energy technologies of coal, but, rather, lead the rise of Asia toward the Age of Energy Gases (see Chapter 13).

Need for Creative Destruction of Coal and Oil

Acceleration of the GET into the Age of Energy Gases will cause large-scale Schumpeterian creative destruction within the coal and oil industries. Creative destruction in coal and oil is necessary to release the technological invention and innovation needed to create our clean, efficient twenty-first-century energy infrastructure. The continued use of solids and liquids will only delay the day civilization can evolve to a sustainable, nonpolluting energy system for society's continuing economic growth that must always be fueled by vast quantities of energy consumption.

$E = mc^2$ teaches us that *energy is everything.* Therefore, the use of energy is fundamental to the civilization we have created. The energy input to an economy is even more fundamental than money because the expenditure of energy is required for the production of all goods and provision of all services and their consumption. Energy use is part and parcel of all we do each waking and sleeping moment of our lives. For this reason, the energy choices by all society drive the powerful, evolutionary long term waves of energy change within societies, which are more powerful over the long term than government intervention. Our energy past shows us that government actions, mandates, and policies that oppose these waves are eventually overpowered. Policies in opposition to the Grand Energy Transition waste taxpayer money, direct badly needed brainpower in the wrong direction, waste venture capital, and slow progress toward more sustainable economic growth and higher quality of life. By contrast, policies that are organized in conjunction with the GET accelerate the way forward—they jet the GET!

Civilization's continuous imperative for growth and the need for increasing energy consumption power the GET. Because the expenditure of energy is required for every transaction that creates the economy, the long-term growth of the economy cannot run on efficiency alone. Throughout most of their history, coal and oil have been relatively inexpensive, so there has been little motivation to expend capital for efficiency technologies. However, concerns for supply and greater demand have pushed prices of oil and coal higher, and this has been the driving force to a shift in attitudes toward energy conservation and fuel efficiency. Increased efficiency is not enough, though. The economy will always require increasing quantities of energy consumption. The enormous gains to be made in energy consumption efficiency will eventually be used to increase productivity and economic activity and, thereby, grow the economy—which uses up the extra quantities of fuel saved by efficiency gains. Because throughout most of the history of coal and oil, they have been relatively inexpensive, little has been spent for efficiency technologies, so there are very large energy efficiency gains achievable in the near-term.

Our conservation of the environment and conservation of wealth are moral choices, but efficiency is an economic imperative. Without innovation and technological development leading to energy efficiency, economies will stagnate. Only so much volume of carbon-based energy can enter or be input into the economic system before that fuel begins to create its own limits by way of increased costs (both price and external costs), a diminished environment, and intolerable economic and/or strategic risks. At some increased volume, each carbon, nonhydrogen fuel begins to lose its utility. The combination of the price of coal-generated electricity, plus understanding of the health and quality-of-life issues related to coal, and considerations for the future, will at some point lead a person, family, neighborhood, community, state, or nation to a decision to prohibit future coal plants and go with clean alternatives such as nuclear, wind, solar, and natural gas. It is this awareness of costs versus future benefits that has created the recent public opposition to new coal plants from being built in the United States and other parts of the world. Just a few years ago, 180 coal plants were on the drawing board across the United States; now that number may be down by half.[6]

Energy use is an economic and environmental input that either drives the economy forward (during exponential growth of the particular fuel) or creates economic and environmental constraints that tend to hold back the economy and technological innovation and invention. Each increment of carbon-based energy use diminishes or fouls the environment, creates health problems, lowers economic and agricultural productivity, and drives global climate change faster. At some level of use, the volumes of carbon-based fuels lose their economic utility. It is my contention that early in the twenty-first century, coal and oil have lost most of their utility to increasingly larger sectors of population. That is why, for instance, today more and more petroleum users are ready for alternatives. By contrast, carbon-light natural gas is a large part of today's energy solution and continues to have a large measure of economic utility, so it will displace more and more coal and oil. This is one of the reasons why it is very misleading to lump natgas as a "fossil fuel" along with today's energy problems of coal and oil. In reality, natural gas is a clean energy solution.

My grandfather, who was born nine years after Abraham Lincoln died, watched Neil Armstrong step on the moon. That certainly seems like great change, but change is now accelerating at an incomprehensibly faster rate. And now all of the energy concerns of the global community—the understanding of the potential of human-induced climate constraints, pollution emanating from China and blowing across the Pacific Ocean; the U.S. coal consumption and acid rain that has damaged vast swaths of forests; global society's emotional reaction to huge oil spills such as the *Exxon Valdez* or the giant oil slick earlier this year in the Celtic Sea near Ireland have brought us to a tipping point that will begin to accelerate the next great energy wave, the Age of Energy Gases. This wave began with natgas, wind, and solar, and will transition toward more and more hydrogen-based energy consumption. This will be the last energy transition for civilization as we know it.

The final stage of the GET will create what I call the hydrogen economy before the end of the twenty-first century, based on hydrogen from water, solar, wind, and nuclear fusion. The hydrogen economy will provide civilization a fully sustainable energy system capable of providing economic growth for whatever the world's population may become. The nations that ride this wave and exhibit leadership, as well as create policies and build technologies to accelerate their economies along this wave, will become the winners of the twenty-first century. The grand game of the twenty-first century will be energy.

Summary

In summary, I believe that the history of the Grand Energy Transition has taught us this:

- There is a clear path forward into an era of continuing globalized economic growth that will be sufficient to lift billions more from poverty on an environmentally stable Earth.
- When nations and economies are caught up in the early exponential growth stages of fuel transitions, they become subjected to explosions of innovation and technological invention that grow up around that new fuel and create large, unprecedented economic pulses of growth and prosperity. For instance, the transition from wood to coal produced the Industrial Revolution, and oil carried us to the globalized, connected world. There is every reason to believe that the Age of Energy Gases will again create the next pulse of heretofore unimaginable growth for humanity.
- When the quantity of dirty fuel becomes too costly, and by too costly we include the full-cycle cost to society as a whole, civilization begins to move toward a new source of fuel that enters the market with less full-cycle costs to society. Each cleaner, less-carbon-heavy fuel goes on to drive a new pulse of economic growth energized by the technological innovation surrounding that energy source. In the past, beginning at about each dirty fuel's marketplace peak, the largest component of its full-cycle costs is not the price paid by the consumer, but its hidden external environmental costs, such as the related health costs, economic costs,

and geostrategic costs related to security of supply and strained international relations, often leading to war in the case of oil. We must always remember that as these external costs of old fuels and their technologies are eliminated from the economy by the new, cleaner, better fuel, we are reducing overall costs and increasing efficiencies within the economic system that help to give rise to a new pulse of growth.

- Most comparative analysis of alternate fuels only compare the price the consumer is paying (not including external costs) to the price of the alternative fuel, which does not include either the efficiency gains or the reduction within the economy of the often-macroeconomic external costs, which can be as large or larger than the price being paid by the consumer for the replaced fuel. For instance, in 2008 Americans transferred nearly $500 billion out of our country to foreign producers to pay for oil,[7] a cost that can only increase over the long term without the acceleration of the GET. That economic drain must be included in any analysis of the cost of an alternative to oil.

- When national policies facilitate these energy transitions, they generally work well and accelerate each trend, but when national policies work against energy transitions, at best they flounder without long-term success, and at worst they fail miserably and waste large amounts of taxpayer money, as well as equally large amounts of the time, energy, and creativity of the people they employ. Although each energy transition may be slowed by government policies that work against the trend, the GET has never been reversed.

- That energy transitions are powerful and long-term because they are the cumulative net output of each individual's daily labors and habits of life and are driven by the cumulative effect of each individual's imperative to seek, through innovation and labor, a higher standard of living and higher quality of life. This process was best described in 1776 by Adam Smith, in *The Wealth of Nations*, as the working of society's "invisible hand."

- Each wave of energy transition, when viewed not as an individual fuel but, rather, by that fuel's state of matter—solids, liquids, and gases—combines into a grand transition of elegant simplicity that clearly shows us the path to our sustainable and environmentally stable future.

- The evolution of the energy system can best be described as a series of transitional waves that emanate from the introduction of each new source of fuel and the ensuing invention and innovation of new technologies that grow up around that new source to initially bring large economic pulses but, later, through their very success, because of the volume of the carbon-based fuels consumed, create within civilization the circumstances of limits to growth, and therefore, their own demise.
- Through the process of the GET, civilization has moved away from dirty, carbon-based fuels, and toward clean and sustainable hydrogen-based fuels for 150 years. By the continuation of this process and the elimination of carbon through the use of in-hand and proven technologies, along with creative innovation, civilization can now move into the Age of Energy Gases that will culminate in a hydrogen-based economy to attain sustainable life and growth on Earth before the close of the twenty-first century.
- The GET reveals the energy sources and technologies that will be the most likely winners and losers.

Chapter 4

Rise of the Age of Energy Gases, Decarbonization, and Slowing of the GET

Government intervention and regulation stopped the world for a billion years.

—DON MURRY, ECONOMIST

As can be seen in Exhibit 4.1, the oil wave peaked in 1973, attaining only 48 percent of the global market, and has since declined to about 36 percent.[1] Prior to oil's rise in the global energy mix, coal met the vast majority of humanity's need for energy, and before that, other solid fuels met nearly 100 percent of our energy needs. In the 1900s, coal began its evolutionary decline from nearly 80 percent of the market share to 28 percent today.[2] When nuclear fission is added as a solid, the solid share of the energy mix dropped from nearly 100 percent in 1850 to about 34 percent by 2007.[3] Coal consumption, as a percentage of total world energy market share, peaked in the early 1900s and oil peaked in 1973; however, natural gas has continued its evolutionary rise. From 1950 to 2007, natgas has grown from about 10 percent to almost 24 percent[4] of the global energy mix and is forecast by energy experts,[5] myself included, to continue its rise as the fastest-growing primary energy source.

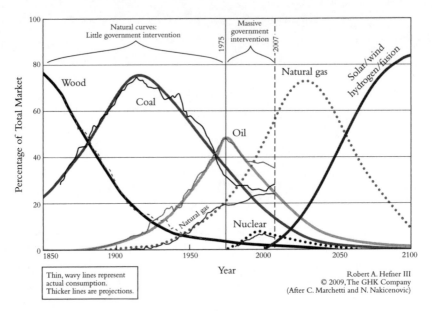

Exhibit 4.1 World Primary Energy Substitution

The final energy wave, the Age of Energy Gases, is now underway, albeit too slowly. By accelerating the GET, we should be living in an environmentally benign, hydrogen-based economy by the middle of the century, or a few decades later. For the first time in civilization's history, hydrogen-based fuels will provide the potential for sustainable economic growth for the 9 or 10 billion[6] human beings who are projected to be living together by then on Spaceship Earth.

What is not generally known about our energy history is that the Grand Energy Transition has continuously moved civilization toward less and less dirty carbon since coal first began to replace wood. Each step reduced the ratio of dirty carbon to clean hydrogen. Wood contains about 10 carbon atoms for each hydrogen atom. Coal reduced that ratio, as coal contains only two carbon atoms for each one hydrogen atom. Oil's rise in the early 1900s once again reduced the carbon-to-hydrogen ratio, as oil contains about two hydrogen atoms per one carbon atom. Natural gas, composed of one carbon and four hydrogen atoms, began its rise in the 1950s and added even more hydrogen to the energy mix.[7] So the process of decarbonization (a better word might be *hydrogenation*) that reduces the ratio of dirty carbon to clean hydrogen has been ongoing for over 200 years.

Amory Lovins, my friend since the 1970s and a great energy thinker, is chairman and chief scientist at the Rocky Mountain Institute. He calculates that about two-thirds of the coal, oil, and natural gas atoms we burn today are actually hydrogen.[8] So the acceleration of the GET will eliminate the last one-third of the carbon within this century to provide us with a fully sustainable hydrogen-based energy system. Another friend and co-energy-worker, Jesse Ausubel, director of the Program for the Human Environment, Rockefeller University, New York City, has correctly pointed out, "The trend toward 'decarbonization' is at the heart of understanding the evolution of the energy system."[9] Roberto F. Aguilera of the International Institute for Applied Systems Analysis, and his father, another of my associate energy workers, Roberto Aguilera, professor at the Schulich School of Engineering at the University of Calgary, charted decarbonization in their 2007 article "Assessing the Past, Present and Near Future of the Global Energy Market," reproduced in Exhibit 4.2.[10] Roberto's chart shows the world hydrogen to carbon ratio from 1850, followed by Exhibit 4.3, which shows global surface temperatures over the same period.

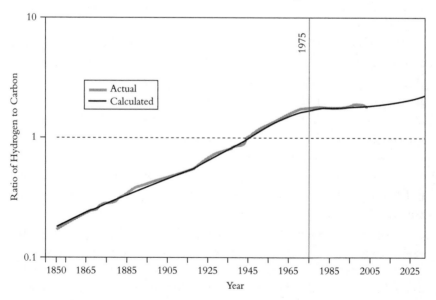

Exhibit 4.2   Hydrogen to Carbon Ratio (A Good Proxy for Environmental Quality)

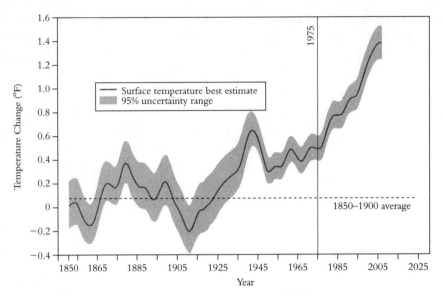

Exhibit 4.3 When World Decarbonization Slowed, Global Temperatures
Accelerated

Data Source: Brohan, P., J.J.Kennedy, I.Haris, S.F.B.Tett, and P.D.Jones 2006. "Uncertainty estimates in
regional and global observed temperature changes: a new dataset from 1850." *Journal of Geophysical
Research* 111:D12106, doi.10.1029/2003JAO09974. © Crown Copyright 2006. Published by the
MET Office Hadley Centre.

Taken together, these two charts make a powerful case that for 120
years before the 1970s, the GET progressed naturally during a period
of little government intervention. The GET was continuously driving
decarbonization of the global energy system, and global temperatures
were simply varying in a normal range.

During the 1970s, everything changed. Decarbonization stalled,
CO_2 emissions accelerated, and global temperatures took off toward the
stratosphere. The 1970s was the period during which the United States
and other countries implemented energy policies that were a combination of backward, GET-opposing interventions and failures to act in the
case of external subsidies. These actions and nonactions sustained the
use of coal and oil for decades past their otherwise normal life cycle.
Although these policies extended the use of coal and oil, and politically
and economically further entrenched their industries, the relatively
cheap energy powered one of the largest periods of economic growth

in human history. The energy policies that came into existence in the late 1970s, particularly in the United States, the world's energy leader and largest energy market, worked against the progress of the GET.

The United States passed laws that prohibited the use of clean, carbon-light natural gas in two of its largest and fastest-growing markets—power generation and new industrial uses—so the demand for growing quantities of energy was met instead by the increased use of coal and oil. The result was about 10 billion tons of CO_2 emissions that would not otherwise be in our atmosphere today. The rapidly increasing use of these two high-carbon fuels to meet economic growth nearly stopped decarbonization of the energy system, which, in turn, shocked the world's atmosphere with accelerating quantities of human-produced CO_2 emissions. The price we have paid for this wave of economic expansion is the current state of global pollution, energy and economic insecurity, and current atmospheric CO_2 concentrations. By accepting the reality that energy is a fundamental input to the economy, we can see that we not only leveraged our financial system but also our economic growth by not charging the full-cycle costs for the energy we consumed. Those unpaid costs will, like unfunded social security, be borne by future generations.

After more than 120 years of continuous progress, the GET began to slow in the 1970s as a result of the U.S. government's macroeconomic intervention in the energy sector. The principal components of intervention began with the 1954 U.S. Supreme Court decision (*Phillips Petroleum Co. v. Wisconsin*) to regulate the price of natural gas at the wellhead, which, by the early 1970s, brought apparent natural gas "shortages" that then led to the 1978 Fuel Use Act that prohibited the use of natural gas in its fastest-growing markets because of the failure to understand natural gas abundance (see Chapter 7). Other components of the 1970s intervention were large subsidies for the use of coal, particularly for coal-fired electric generation, and the sheltering of the energy consumer from the external pollution, climate change, and national security costs that accompany the use of coal and oil. These real external costs began to rapidly escalate during the 1970s because of the increased volumes of use of coal and oil and the high security costs of assuring the free flow of oil following the Middle East oil shocks. I describe this as the Intervention Period in Exhibits 4.4 and 4.5. These external subsidies are the subject of Chapter 9, "The *Real* Inconvenient Truth."

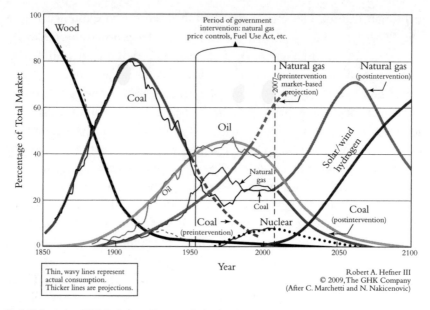

Exhibit 4.4   U.S. Primary Energy Substitution

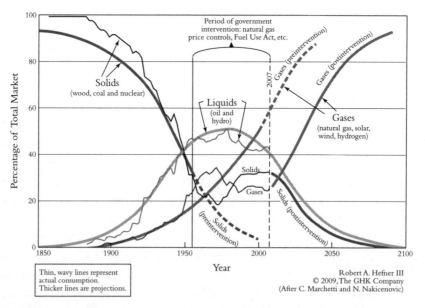

Exhibit 4.5   Effects of Massive U.S. Government Intervention in the Energy Markets

When I think about the GET slowing in the 1970s, I am reminded of a humorous but apropos incident during a trip down the Colorado River through the Grand Canyon, with its thousand-foot walls of the Earth's geologic history on both sides. Knowing most of us were geologists, our guide pulled the raft over to the bank to show us a geological point of interest. He pointed to a four-inch band of rubble rock between vertical beds of rock below and those above that were lying horizontal, like all the formations up to the ridge of the Canyon. He asked us to put our hand over the four-inch band of rock, and we each took our turn. Our guide then said, "The vertical beds below are Pre-Cambrian, about 1.6 billion years old or more. The horizontal rocks above are Cambrian, about 600 million years old. You have just put your hand across the 'great unconformity' that represents a one-billion-year gap in the history of the Earth." My good friend, Don Murry, was the only economist among us. I noticed around that night's campfire that he was contemplatively quiet, but the next moment he jumped to his feet and shouted out, "Eureka! I've got it. I have now seen geological evidence of the first time government intervention and regulation stopped the world for a billion years." This story is relevant because my thesis is that, following the oil shocks of the 1970s, government energy policies and energy policies by default slowed the forward movement of the GET and, by doing so, accelerated global warming, added to global pollution, and created intolerable economic and national security risks. We now face the real, external, largely unpaid costs of the post–1970s economic expansion.

These policies favoring coal and oil remain largely in place today, and the result is that we now find ourselves faced with energy-created intolerable climate, economic, and strategic risks. The slowing of the GET, stalling of decarbonization, and global temperature rise can be largely attributed to the failure of governments to charge energy consumers the real cost of coal and oil. These policies had the unintended consequence of extending the economic lives of coal and oil beyond the period of their natural decline. It is my premise that our misguided energy policies are largely the result of not understanding the historical progress of the GET. As a result, we have probably added about 50 years to what otherwise would have been the natural cycle of decline of coal and oil. Policies that slowed the GET must now be reversed to accelerate the GET and begin to eliminate the three intolerable climate, economic, and national security risks that have come into existence because of our current mix and volume of energy consumption.

Chapter 5 explores why the United States accepted the false belief that natural gas was a scarce energy resource that led to the macromarket intervention of the Fuel Use Act and its prohibition of natural gas use, which created the macro-distortion of today's energy mix.

Chapter 5

How the 1970s Misconception of Natural Gas Scarcity Changed America's Energy Mix for Decades

Natural gas has had it.
    —JOHN O'LEARY, ADMINISTRATOR OF THE FEDERAL ENERGY
                                      ADMINISTRATION, 1977

My lifetime of work requires that I respectfully have to disagree with everything Exxon says on the natural gas resource base.
                    —ROBERT A. HEFNER III, APRIL 26, 1984

T wo hundred eighty-seven trillion cubic feet," said the less-than-friendly voice on the phone. It was 1976. Exxon Corporation, one of the largest companies in the world, was stating unequivocally that there were 287 trillion cubic feet (Tcf) of natural gas remaining in the United States. I knew it was blinded by a history of oil thinking and had made a big mistake about natural gas. Indeed, in the years since, the United States has produced nearly twice that amount, with an additional 1,300 to 2,200 Tcf or more widely estimated by experts to be still in the ground.[1]

In 1976, Exxon had completed its new study on U.S. natural gas supplies.[2] Its vice president of exploration, J. D. Langston, repeatedly announced that "more than a hundred of our geologists and geophysicists contributed to this comprehensive study," which concluded that America's "attainable potential is about 287 Tcf of natural gas."[3] Of course, the assertion that a hundred Exxon geologists and geophysicists contributed gave this study great credibility with Exxon's audiences, which often included America's policy makers. Exxon went on to repeat that frighteningly low estimate over and over for the next decade.

The voice on the phone that day in 1976 also belonged to J. D. Langston. I had called him as a colleague in the energy industry to find out how they had reached such mystifying conclusions.[4] He told me in no uncertain terms that thanks to its team of geologists and geophysicists, Exxon knew better than anyone how much natural gas was left in America. But he also let slip what I knew was senior management's oil-focused mind-set when he said that based on "conservative judgment" and Exxon's "unique global experience," the work of the overly optimistic local division explorationists had been adjusted down to form Exxon's conservative and *responsible* [my emphasis] forecast of America's natural gas future. The word *responsible* will pop up again because that is the impression the oil companies wanted to convey to Congress. He made it quite clear that I, a small independent producer, was not in a position to question Exxon, its army of geologists and geophysicists, and its senior management's responsible assessment.

And yet, that is exactly what I did.

Testimony before Congress

In 18 hearings before committees of the U.S. Congress,[5] I challenged the world according to Exxon. Between 1972 and the 1978 omnibus energy legislation of the Carter administration, in hearings before Congress and innumerable meetings with members and their staffs, I repeated over and over that America had "vast, undeveloped, lower 48 natural gas resources,"[6] always asserting that the oil companies only understood "associated" natural gas, the natural gas produced along with oil. I made a point of lobbying everyone I could in Washington, always affirming natural gas abundance and that "the quickest way to increase supplies was to develop the vast onshore natural gas resources awaiting discovery within our traditional supply areas."[7]

My opponents in this grand game, Exxon, Mobil, and their allies, would always stick together with their estimates of natural gas shortages and would reinforce one another to emphasize their *preponderance of the evidence* argument. I knew by then that this oil mind-set had begun to shape the general consensus of Congress and the Carter administration, summed up famously and often repeated by John O'Leary, administrator of the Federal Energy Administration, that "natural gas has had it."[8]

By 1977, the increasing natural gas supply "shortages," caused by over two decades of wellhead price controls at unrealistically low prices and the Middle East oil shocks, had elevated the energy issue to red hot. Because of what I believed to be the enormous importance and long-term macroeconomic effects of my next Congressional hearing, I stayed up all night preparing my statement for the House of Representatives Energy and Power Subcommittee. I knew I was up against the resources, money, power, and influence of these companies, and it was certainly going to be a tough, nearly impossible task for me to break through the developing consensus that "natural gas has had it" and make my case for natural gas abundance.

The next morning, March 24, 1977, I found my way to the third floor of the Rayburn House Office Building hearing room, which was overflowing with lobbyists and press. After all, this was the period of time leading up to the Carter administration's comprehensive energy legislation, and the debate was getting intense. My experience during those years was that Louisiana Senator Bennett Johnston, who later became chairman of the Senate Energy Committee, actually understated the intensity of the energy debate by describing it as the "great energy wars."

In the front of the hearing room, facing the elevated "pulpit" where the members of the House committee sat, was a long table and chairs with name cards that designated where each of us was to sit. I was all the way down at the far end.

Congressman John Dingell of Michigan, who often said that natural gas would only be deregulated "over my dead body," called the room to order.[9] One by one, each of us began to testify. The witnesses before me were Gordon Zareski, chief of resource evaluation and analysis, Bureau of Natural Gas, Federal Power Commission; John O'Leary, administrator of the Federal Energy Administration; and, for the oil companies, John Moody of Mobil.

As I listened to the others testify I knew that my chance of convincing Congress that the United States actually had enormous natural gas supplies for the future was diminishing with every word said. Each testified, in turn, that the natural gas sky was falling, that America's supplies were rapidly running dry, and that the only sensible thing for the United States to do was prepare itself for extreme shortages. In order to give you a good feel of the general mind-set about natural gas at the time, I will repeat a few statements from that hearing:

By Gordon Zareski:

- "Our analysis of historical natural gas reserve additions and prospects for future reserve additions indicates that annual production will continue to decline, even assuming successful exploration and development of the frontier areas."
- "Our policies should be based on the expectation of decreasing gas availability."
- "If we have learned anything at all from our experiences of the past, important elements of our national energy policy must include programs for mandatory natural gas conservation, substitution of alternate fuels for low-priority uses of gas and the allocation of scarce gas supplies by federal, state and local jurisdiction to high-priority end uses."
- "I do not think gas priced at a BTU equivalent of oil would bring forth substantial quantities of new supplies."
- "I do not think deregulation on a national basis would bring forth the quantities of gas we need to hold our production level."
- ". . . at some time in the reasonably near future the deliverability of natural gas is going to begin to decline toward the day when it will no longer be counted among the country's important fuel resources."[10]

By John O'Leary:

- "It must be assumed that domestic natural gas supplies will continue to decline."
- "We must curtail the demand for gas among those who can economically convert to other fuels just as rapidly as we can."[11]

History has proven all of these statements to be totally erroneous.

Next came John Moody, Mobil's witness, who was also president of the American Association of Petroleum Geologists, of which I was also a member. He made a point of looking down the table directly at me as he said, "We have arrived pretty much at a consensus among *responsible* [my emphasis] estimators of some 400 to 600 Tcf as the undiscovered potential for gas in the United States."[12] Now, we can also add this statement to the totally erroneous category.

When it was my turn, I did all I could to make the point that the Exxon and Mobil mind-set was one of oil understanding and that my natural gas experience was outside those limits. I reinforced my long-standing argument that "vast, potential deep natural gas reserves will not be found in association with oil,"[13] and I repeated my earlier argument to Congress to "let the competitive system work to encourage maximum development of one of the most abundant sources of energy we have in the United States."[14] However, I must admit that as hard as I tried, no one really listened to me, but rather, believed in the oil companies' analysis of the future. By then, the accepted thinking in Washington was best summed up by O'Leary's often-repeated statement that "natural gas has had it."

Why I Believed in Natural Gas Abundance

I had learned through direct, personal experience drilling natgas fields that there was far more natural gas than these companies claimed. It was crucial for the nation's future to convince Congress of that. I knew from my early work in the Economic Analysis Division of Phillips Petroleum that Exxon, Mobil, and all the oil majors would be looking at natgas as an unwanted by-product of oil exploration, and their management's judgment would be based on their knowledge of oil exploration.

Their oil mind-set severely limited their understanding of natural gas. Moreover, by then, the domestic budgets of the oil companies were rapidly falling and they were drilling fewer wells in the United States because they all basically agreed that the big oil fields had been found. The now-famous bell curve prediction of peak oil in America, as projected by Shell's renowned geologist M. King Hubbert in 1956, was becoming a reality, so the natural gas they were forecasting was only the small quantities of natgas they expected to find with their diminishing oil exploration and production, as projected by Hubbert's oil curve.[15]

However, I kept working with the science and evidence, developing what I thought to be reasonable, well-grounded, and even larger projections of huge natural gas supplies. At the Aspen Institute's workshop that addressed the gas energy option, in June 1978, at a session directed by Washington energy economist Dr. Herman Franssen, then director, market analysis, Office of International Affairs, Department of Energy, I projected a curve of increasing supply that would "stretch somewhere beyond 1,500 Tcf of recoverable gas resources." My associates called this the *Hefner Curve*. My chart (shown as Exhibit 5.1) projected that future recoverable supplies could be as much as 2,000 Tcf.

The Exxon view was represented by a consultant economist, Dr. Richard Gonzales, who repeated the "natural gas has had it" mantra and predicted general gloom and doom. On the positive side, few of the scientists present at this conference were employed by the oil companies, so the general consensus of the meeting leaned toward my view and was summed up in the final report by the measured statement that America's "resources of conventional natural gas are large."[16]

How America Created Natural Gas Shortages in the Midst of Abundance

It all started in 1954 with a hotly debated 5–4 U.S. Supreme Court decision in *Phillips Petroleum Co. v. State of Wisconsin*, which extended the federal government's authority to regulate natural gas prices at the wellhead when it was sold in interstate commerce. The decision led to the Federal Power Commission's system of setting area rates or

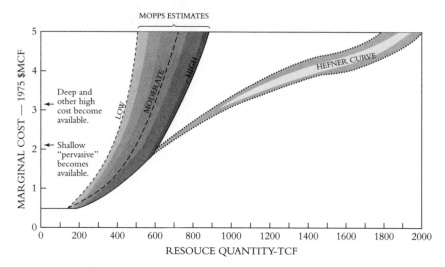

Exhibit 5.1   Gas: Onshore and Offshore Cost vs. Resource Quantity

Source: From Robert A. Hefner III presentation "The Future for Conventional U.S. Natural Gas Supply," at the Aspen Institute Workshop on R&D Priorities and the Gas Energy Option, June 25–29, 1978, Aspen, Colorado.

wellhead prices for all natural gas produced that was sold across state lines. The rates were based on studies of such things as the cost of drilling gas wells, the quantities of gas found, and other such factors within defined producing areas. With this information, prices were set to reflect conservative rates of return for the average natural gas well. The Commission's statistics looked backward, and the rates always favored the consumer's short-term interest rather than the producer's economic interest. The predictable outcome was that producers either did not drill or, when they drilled, it was within states where natural gas was produced and consumed, because they could sell nonregulated *intrastate* natural gas at prices often several times the regulated interstate price.

By the early 1970s, states that did not have natural gas production began to be hit with shortages and rationing, particularly in the industrial Midwest and along the East Coast. In the winters of 1977 and 1978, several schools and industries were closed as a result of natural gas shortages. The Carter administration was faced with the urgent problem of doing something about these highly publicized natural gas shortages. As is often the case, this took place at the very same time

Hubbert's prediction of declining American oil supplies was coming true. The oil and gas industry came to the unfortunate and inaccurate consensus that like the future of oil in America, natural gas has had it.

Natural Gas Deregulation and the Prohibition of Its Use

At the end of the day, with little evidence to counter Big Oil companies' view of continuing natural gas shortages, the general consensus that natural gas had run its course pervaded the Carter energy legislation. There were two principal pieces of legislation. The Emergency Natural Gas Act was a highly complex bill full of years of congressional compromise that partially deregulated natural gas prices at the wellhead, as well as all deep natural gas, or all gas produced below 15,000 feet. In spite of its complexity, this act began the needed process of deregulation and solved the rapidly worsening problem of natural gas shortages by creating one national market. The second was the Fuel Use Act, which prohibited the use of natural gas for all future power generation and effectively stopped its use in new industrial plants, then the two fastest-growing markets for natural gas. Together, these two pieces of legislation had a powerful impact on America's future fuel mix, resulting in a significant slowing of the GET's progress in America and, because America led the world in energy, other nations followed and the global progress of the GET was also slowed. The result was the decades-long extension of the use of coal and oil beyond what otherwise would have been their natural decline.

These two pieces of legislation, combined with the fact that natural gas in America was actually abundant, were the principal causes of the subsequent natural gas boom and bust. There was a short-lived natural gas drilling boom between 1979 and 1982. It rapidly brought on America's natural gas supply *bubble* that triggered the subsequent bust, which lasted for most of the next 20 years. Why so long? Several factors were at work:

- Deregulation of natural gas prices released the free market juices of innovation and new investment necessary to find abundant, new natural gas supplies.

- The natural gas industry had lost it two fastest growing markets— new power generation and industrial plants—and the 80,000 mega- watts of new coal-fired generation capacity added in the decade following the Fuel Use Act are still in operation today.
- National natural gas decline rates were minimal.

This long and deep bust led to the loss of about 500,000 jobs[17] in the natural gas exploration and production sector, and many of these people never returned to the industry. Additionally, there was a sub- sequent widespread contraction of most industry-related education in our universities due to a lack of students, and much of America's natu- ral gas service industry, such as drilling rigs, were salvaged or sold to foreign companies. Because of these factors, we are still witnessing the negative effects of the bust in the form of shortages of up-to-date field equipment and trained industry people.

These two pieces of legislation pretty much destined natural gas to be thought of by most energy experts as a scarce and rapidly declining resource, a mind-set that generally remains today. American homebuilders went to all-electric homes, with tens of thousands of new homes featur- ing electric ranges and heating, one of electricity's most inefficient uses. New industrial plants were fueled with oil instead of natgas. The fledgling natural gas vehicle (NGV) industry disappeared. America was witnessing a two-decade period of strict regulatory limits on natural gas, and worse, the continuation of a mind-set that natural gas was not a long-term option, even though natural gas markets remained in oversupply through- out the period. It was during this period that the United States turned to coal for its growth in electric generation and forgot all about natural gas vehicles. About 80,000 megawatts of new coal-fired electric generation was built over the next decade, and we are still living with the pollution and CO_2 emissions that would not have existed except for the Fuel Use Act and the misconception that "natural gas has had it."

Confronting the Oil Mind-Set Once Again

In spite of all the new natural gas that was being found, my battles with the oil companies did not end. On April 25, 1984, I spent another entire night working on a presentation, knowing I was once again up against the largest companies in the world, challenging every aspect of what they said about natgas. The next day, Exxon's senior vice president, Charles B. Wheeler, testified to the Senate Committee on Energy Regulation, "We estimate the volume of as-yet-undiscovered gas from conventional sources in the United States to be about 300 Tcf. . . . There are many changes in detail in our new gas-resource estimate versus our last published assessment which came out in 1976 . . . [287 Tcf]. However, the bottom line of both estimates is the volume of resources potentially available to the economy, which we call the attainable resource; on this basis the two assessments are very close." He then made the obvious Exxon conclusion that the nation should "conserve our scarce gas resources."[18]

It was hard to believe that Exxon was still talking about shortages when new supplies had already grown larger than demand and the domestic natural gas industry was in an oversupply economic bust. By then, I was really frustrated with Exxon's refusal to look at new natural gas facts. So, I took a deep breath, looked up at the senators, and then turned directly to Mr. Wheeler and said, "My lifetime of work requires that I respectfully have to disagree with everything Exxon says on the natural gas resource base." I deeply believed that, at this time in our nation's energy history, the mind-set of natural gas shortages was destructive to the nation and that it would lead to negative, long-term macroeconomic consequences, along with lots of unnecessary pollution, CO_2 emissions,[19] and foreign oil imports. So, I concluded with a statement about the nation's energy future, that I must admit I then thought might be a little excessive, but I was trying to emphasize this important point: "Mr. Chairman, it is my deep belief that United States history will eventually record the misconception of limited natural gas resources to be so far-reaching and economically fundamental as to be among one of the most economically, geopolitically, and geostrategically costly of the post–World War II era."[20]

Nevertheless, and for the life of me I am not certain why, the oil companies continued to give the public false impressions about natural gas and deny its abundance for another decade. As late as 2005,[21] ExxonMobil publically forecast that "North American gas production has peaked." So all I could do is repeat my 1984 congressional hearing response: "My lifetime of work requires that I respectfully have to disagree with everything Exxon says on the natural gas resource base." However, this bias is finally changing, and I must admit, to its great credit, even within ExxonMobil.

ConocoPhillips was the first big oil company to recognize the importance of natural gas in America, and that led to its acquisition of a large natural gas producer in 2006. At the time, CEO Jim Mulva was ahead of his peers when he publicly announced, "We'll be a major player with respect to gas in North America for decades to come."[22] Subsequently, ConocoPhillips began a national advertising campaign to signal its own bright future in the development of America's natural gas.

Today, we know just how far off ExxonMobil and the oil companies were on natural gas resources. As of the close of 2008, America had produced more than 600 Tcf of natural gas since 1976.[23] Today—and here I use the word from Mobil's 1977 testimony—most "responsible" estimators agree that America has about 1,500 to 2,000 Tcf or more of remaining natural gas resources. The most recent independent review of the nation's natural gas supply, released in July 2008 by Navigant Consulting Inc., forecast 2,247 Tcf.[24] I continue to stand with my assessment of about 3,000 Tcf.

We can further confirm these resource estimates by the success stories of those independent U.S. companies that have been developing large new natural gas resources that have led to a new surge of domestic natural gas production. Oklahoma-based Chesapeake Energy, the number-one natgas driller in America, recently superseded BP and Anadarko Petroleum to become the number-one U.S. natural gas producer.

Chesapeake announced in mid-2008 that the company entered into a joint venture on the Haynesville Shale, likely to become America's largest-ever natural gas field and possibly the fourth largest field in the world.[25] Even some big oil companies are beginning to believe that maybe a large part of their production future will include coming back to the United States to find natgas. However, I doubt that any of them yet buy into my assessment today of about 3,000 Tcf of natural gas remaining to be developed in America.[26] As another signal of the turnabout by big oil, in its outlook for natural gas in America, BP recently entered into two deals (US$1.7 billion and US$1.9 billion) with Chesapeake to develop unconventional natural gas resources.[27]

Intolerable Economic, National Security, and Climate Risks Rise to the Forefront

Thirty years later the stakes are even higher than they were in 1977. As we enter the twenty-first century, I believe the looming energy-related economic, national security, and climate problems will impact the future of America throughout the century in ways that far exceed either the War on Terror or the Rise of Asia. The U.S. energy system is deeply embedded with two principal fuel sources, coal and oil, that simply won't work if the United States is to excel in the twenty-first century. With oil, we are often caught in a supply squeeze and price spiral and depend on relatively insecure and geostrategically disadvantageous sources of supplies. The use of coal continues to bring devastating environmental and health effects, along with their related costs, as well as a contribution to CO_2 emissions so large that the United States will not be able to meet reasonable obligations under international climate agreements as long as coal is used in the quantities of today. Yet, natgas is a clean, abundant American resource that continues to be underutilized. Natural gas is so versatile and abundant that it can be rapidly scaled up to displace both coal and oil.

We are in trouble. Many of the economic, environmental, security, and even social and political challenges we face relate to our current volumes of coal and oil use, so we have been presented one of the greatest challenges that civilization has ever faced. The challenge is to create an energy system that can fuel economic growth for all the Earth's population without building uncontrollable macroeconomic and geostrategic problems, without polluting and degrading our lands and oceans, and without driving global warming to the possibility of ending civilization as we know it.

We Can't Afford the Same Mistakes about Natural Gas

It has been the perception of inadequate supplies of natural gas, along with the heavily fluctuating boom and bust history and artificial barriers to natural gas, that over most of its past have barred the way for it to be recognized in its future role as the principal bridge fuel to a sustainable energy future. One important purpose of this book is to change that perception.

Today, as I contemplate the rapidly increasing magnitude of America's three intolerable energy-driven economic, national security, and climate risks, I have changed my mind about the excessive nature of my warning to the members of the Senate Energy Committee in 1984. Today, let me address all of America's energy policymakers by repeating, "It is my deep belief that United States history will eventually record the 1978 energy legislation based on the misconception of limited natural gas resources to be so far-reaching and economically fundamental as to be among one of the most economically, geopolitically, and geostrategically costly of the post–World War II era."

Whatever we do, we must not make that same natural gas mistake again, because this time the stakes are orders of magnitude higher. However, I am extremely optimistic that we will get it right this time. Having been deeply immersed in natural gas history for about 50 years, I feel a confidence in my bones that natural gas has finally arrived to take its proper place in the United States as the principal bridge fuel to our sustainable energy and climate future, the Age of Energy Gases. All nations must come together to accelerate the GET, and for natural gas to become the go-to acceleration fuel, it must be globally abundant. The next two chapters describe my case for the global abundance of natural gas.

Chapter 6

Natural Gas—The Bridge Fuel to Our Sustainable Future

What gets us into trouble is not what we don't know. It's what we know for sure that just ain't so.

—WILL ROGERS

Everything has changed but our way of thinking.

—ALBERT EINSTEIN

Our Earth's abundant natural gas is the only clean fuel that is ready to go and, most importantly, can be scaled up to displace coal and oil in sufficient time to help meet global CO_2 reduction targets and regain our energy and economic security. Unlike carbon-heavy coal and oil that contain much more dirty carbon than clean hydrogen, natural gas is "carbon light," with only one carbon atom and four hydrogen atoms. Natgas is a green fuel. Its use eliminates most all the toxic emissions and carbon particulates that come along with coal and oil use, while significantly reducing CO_2 emissions.

Natural gas, with its well-developed in-hand technology and versatility, can readily displace coal for new electric generation and oil for half of transportation, which together account for almost one-half of the world's pollution and CO_2 emissions. By replacing coal for new power generation, natgas will double the energy efficiency of newly produced electricity; virtually eliminate toxic mercury, arsenic, sulfur and particulate emissions; and reduce CO_2 emissions by 50 percent.[1] Enhanced turbine efficiencies in process will lower natural gas use per megawatt hour of electricity produced and thereby lower CO_2 output even farther.

When carbon capture and sequestration (CCS), the pumping of CO_2 emissions into underground reservoirs, becomes technologically and commercially feasible, natgas-fired power plants will only need to sequester one-half the amount of CO_2 produced by an equivalent coal-fired plant. Further, natgas-fired power plants with CCS will not only be zero CO_2 emission plants, they will also be virtually pollution free and about as green as wind and solar. President Obama's economic stimulus plan must include funds for natgas CCS technology.

Natural gas power plants use less space, do not require a railroad, and cost about half as much to build per megawatt, so they can be sited, financed, and built in less than half the time it takes for coal-fired power generation. Natgas is by far the best way to go to significantly reduce pollution and cut CO_2 emissions in half while meeting the world's rapidly increasing demand for electricity in a timely way.

When natural gas replaces oil for use in half the transportation sector (about 50 percent of the world's oil consumption is for transportation[2]), it eliminates over 90 percent of most automobile, truck, and bus pollutants, extends the life of internal combustion engines, and cuts CO_2 emissions by nearly 30 percent.[3] Natgas today fuels about 8 million automobiles, trucks, and buses worldwide, a number that is growing and can be accelerated rapidly the world over. Unfortunately, in the United States there are only about 150,000.[4] Honda's Civic GX natural gas car, with an at-home filling appliance, is one of the world's hottest new cars, and its sales are growing rapidly. In the United States and other developed countries, the natgas pipeline grid is extensive and can be used to overcome the "chicken and egg" problem of building new energy infrastructure from scratch. If a home, office, or industrial facility is on the natural gas pipeline grid, all that is needed is a simple compressor and vehicles can be filled up while not in use. In the United

States, 63 million households are on the grid,[5] so about 130 million cars return each night to a place where they can easily be refilled. This is America's largest fleet. Americans have invested about $4 trillion[6] in SUVs, light trucks, and gas guzzlers, so rather than only recouping a tiny fraction of this investment on a trade-in and stepping up to the costs of a new hybrid or fuel-efficient car, why not retrofit them to natural gas for less than half the cost of a new vehicle so they can run on clean natural gas and for less than the price of gasoline?

In the United States, the oil demand for all vehicles is about 11.5 million barrels per day, so replacing half the U.S. vehicle fleet with natural gas–fueled CNG would cut about 50 percent of vehicle transportation oil use and total oil use by over 25 percent. If, by 2015, 130 million vehicles were converted to natural gas at a cost of roughly $1 trillion, U.S. consumers would save about $700 billion[7] in oil import costs over the period and many trillions in the years to follow.

Natural gas is the only scalable alternative to the use of coal and oil and will become the principal bridge fuel to humanity's sustainable energy future. Policies targeted toward encouraging the use of natgas will accelerate the Grand Energy Transition, the GET, and be the most powerful near- and medium-term force to reduce global CO_2 emissions, help jump-start our economy, and regain our energy security.

Natural Gas Is *Not* Oil

The most important concept necessary for a full understanding of the global abundance of natgas and its potential for solving a major portion of the world's energy and climate problems is to realize, simply, that it is *not oil*. The fact that natgas is most often referred to as "oil and *gas*" is at the heart of the misunderstanding of natural gas and its value as a primary energy source.

Natural gas is different from oil in every way. Natgas is physically, chemically, geologically, geographically, technologically, environmentally, economically, and politically different from oil. The mind-set around the term "oil and gas" has become the principal culprit in hiding natural gas abundance, an abundance that I believe far exceeds that of Earth's oil as an energy source. It is just about as accurate to say "coal and gas" as it is to say "oil and gas" because natgas seems always to occur where coal is found, just as it always occurs where oil is found.

Most countries with large coal deposits, such as the United States, Australia, and Indonesia, also have large natgas deposits. I believe we will soon learn that China and India belong in that category. But I'm getting ahead of myself. First, it is essential to understand the differences between natural gas and oil.

Differences between Natural Gas and Oil

In order to understand the abundance of natural gas and make intelligent, long-term policy decisions, we must break out of the oil and gas mind-set by thoroughly understanding the great differences between natural gas and oil.

The Physical Difference

Natural gas is a gas and oil is a liquid. Natgas cannot be seen or smelled. What you see on a gas stove in your kitchen is the flame, and what you smell if it leaks is a chemical odor that has been added for safety. Oil is a smelly liquid and is easy to see. Natgas is lighter than air, so instead of spilling on the ground as oil does, it floats up into the atmosphere. Natgas, like all gases, is compressible, and liquid oil is not. A natgas reservoir found at 20,000 feet below the surface will contain three to five times more natural gas than the same reservoir found at 3,000 feet. However, a barrel of oil at either depth is still a barrel of oil. Oil is a viscous fluid and more difficult to remove from its reservoir deep in the Earth than natgas, which, because it is lighter than air, naturally seeks its way to the surface. Anyone who has ever sucked through a straw knows it takes energy to pull out your liquid drink, but when a cap is removed from a soda pop, the gas in the bottle flows out of its own accord. This is exactly how liquid oil works compared to natgas. Oil has a harder time getting to the surface and for most of the life of an oil field, has to be pumped to the surface. Of course, energy is required to run these pumps. Because natgas flows naturally to the surface, it also naturally voids its reservoir more easily than heavier, viscous oil.

So when a natural gas accumulation is tapped, a larger percentage of the natgas originally in place when the field was found is recovered than is the case with an oil field.

Oil reservoirs naturally produce only 10 percent, and infrequently, up to 30 percent of the in-place oil found before additional secondary and tertiary recovery techniques must be used to increase that percentage to 40 percent or sometimes even 60 percent, but these methods are expensive and do not always work. Also, these methods require more energy use. Natural gas reservoirs generally produce 70 percent to 80 percent of the original natgas in place. So, because a much larger percentage of natural gas is naturally recovered from a given reservoir than oil, and because natgas is compressible, more can be stored in and recovered from a reservoir as pressures increase with increasing depth in the Earth. Therefore, more Btus of energy will nearly always be produced from a reservoir below 8,000 feet if it is full of natgas than if it is full of oil.

Another physical difference is that natgas is created from and exists within vastly more diverse environments. Natural gas is created in our stomachs and the stomachs of most animals, rice paddies, termite mounds, refuge dumps, and environments below the Earth's surface we have not begun to understand, where microbes produce natgas by their very metabolism. Natural gas is always created in the same environments that create oil, coal, and peat, as well as the extreme conditions of depth, heat, and pressure where diamonds are formed. Natgas remains chemically stable in vastly varying domains of temperature and pressure beyond the limits of oil's chemical stability. Natgas has been detected across the universe. It has been detected on Mars, Jupiter, Saturn, Neptune, Uranus, and Pluto, and may well be ubiquitous in our solar system. Pluto is believed to have frozen natural gas on its surface[8] as well as a natgas atmosphere.[9] Natural gas composes a significant quantity of the atmosphere of Saturn's moon, Titan. On Titan, it literally rains methane in the form of frozen crystals, and Titan has lakes of liquid methane that have been detected around the poles.[10]

It is this extreme physical variability in how natgas is created, and the conditions in which it can exist—far beyond the much narrower limits of heat and depth of burial where oil can exist or the comparatively narrow limits of heat and pressure and long period of time required to create oil—that is one of the principal factors in understanding why natural gas is more abundant on Earth than is oil. When thinking about natural gas abundance, we should always consider that unlike oil, significant quantities of non–biologically formed natural gas exist in the universe and throughout the solar system and, therefore most likely, also on Earth. Also, large and possibly commercial quantities of renewable natural gas are continuously being created deep in the Earth by microbes. Unlike oil, where the conditions of origin and accumulation are well understood, there is still much to learn about the origin, accumulation, and abundance of natgas on Earth.

Natural gas is not a viscous liquid like oil, but, rather, a highly mobile gas. Its ability to move through the Earth's rocks is far superior to that of oil. Natgas moves through the Earth's rocks at much higher rates of flow and reaches and accumulates in many places that oil cannot ever reach from its far more limited places and conditions of origin. These physical characteristics, particularly the seemingly ubiquitous conditions of natural gas origin, are why natural gas, not oil, forms on the continental shelves of most of the world's oceans in the form of natgas hydrates that some experts estimate contain more Btus of energy than all the world's coal and oil put together. I will discuss hydrates in the discussion on natural gas's geological difference from oil.

The Chemical Difference

Natural gas is a simple molecule, with four clean hydrogen atoms and only one dirty carbon atom. The chemical symbol is CH_4. This simple chemistry, along with its formidable stability in so many heat and pressure extremes, make it the most versatile of hydrocarbons. One could say the simpler the molecule, the better and more efficient the fuel.

In contrast, oil is a highly complex hydrocarbon with more dirty carbon as compared to clean hydrogen. Oil's chemistry varies widely, but it can generally be represented by the chemical symbol C_5H_{12} to $C_{36}H_{74}$. Oil's chemical complexity and variability require equally complex and variable refining technologies to produce useful fuels.

Because natgas has a higher ratio of clean hydrogen to dirty carbon, its use is much less polluting than oil and coal, which contains even more carbon. Natural gas use also emits much less CO_2 than coal or oil, so its increased substitution for coal and oil becomes a significant step forward in reducing both CO_2 emissions and global pollution.

The Geological Difference

Oil is trapped in very specifically defined geological structures, and so is natural gas. However, natgas is also virtually ubiquitous in most geological basins. Its accumulations extend well beyond the narrow limits of oil fields. It has been my experience that virtually all wells drilled in America's sedimentary basins can produce at least some small quantity of natural gas, whereas most wells drilled outside the narrow limits of oil fields encounter no oil.

The size of a commercial natgas field often depends as much on the price of natural gas and the technology to release it from the particular rocks in which it is contained than the limits of a specific geologic structure. So, the limits of many natgas fields, particularly those producing from coal seams and shales, are defined as much by price and technology as by the character and structure of the rocks themselves. In the United States, an excellent example is the Barnett Shale field in north Texas that has been the country's fastest-growing natgas field. One of America's great independent producers, George Mitchell, struggled to get the field started in a limited area or "sweet spot" covering no more than a few thousand acres when the price was about $2 or less per Mcf. Later, one of our local Oklahoma companies, Devon, bought out Mitchell and carried on the field's development. As the price rose to the $6 to $8 per Mcf level, Devon and others worked to further the technological innovation specifically necessary to liberate more natural gas more quickly from the shale rocks. The Barnett has now grown to over 5 million acres, covering at least 17 counties.[11] The Barnett is rapidly becoming one of America's largest fields.

During the summer of 2008, with natural gas at a price of about $8 to $12 per Mcf, the field was growing as fast as drilling rigs were available to be put to work. Profits bring along the necessary technological innovation to unlock the natgas from the shales of the Barnett, other shales, coals, and tight sands—all rocks that are domains of natural gas and not oil. The Barnett Shale began its growth about a decade ago,[12] and in 2007 produced about 5 percent of America's daily natural gas production.[13] In the last 10 years, over 9,000 wells have been drilled.[14] In mid–2008, it was reported that Chesapeake Energy and Devon Energy, the two largest Barnett producers, were continuously running about 75 drilling rigs.[15] If natgas prices in the United States increase to a general parity with oil prices, as they have in some Asian lique-fied natural gas (LNG) markets, then the Barnett will continue to grow. With shale and coal fields, we know the gas is there, and over the last decade in the United States, we have developed the technology for its extraction, so the only question remaining about commercial produc-tion is the price of natgas versus its cost to develop and produce. All across America, many other "shale fields" are in the early development stage. Their enormous potential area of production is shown in Exhibit 6.1. Remember that throughout most of the history of the "oil and gas" industry, the term *shale gas* on a drilling log meant a natural gas show of *no consequence*.

Much of the world's future natgas supplies will not be developed from the rocks that oil geologists call "conventional" for oil production or where oil geologists expect to find oil. Future natgas resources will

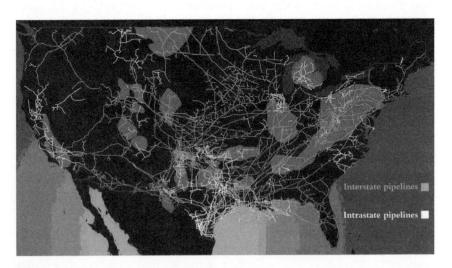

Exhibit 6.1   U.S. Natural Gas Shale Basins with Pipeline Grid
Source: EIA, U.S. Natural Gas Pipeline Network, from American Clean Skies Foundation, Power Point presentation, "The Future Is Natural Gas," received July 28, 2008.

not be found by past conventional techniques used in the search for oil. To be successful, a natural gas explorationist must have a different mind-set than an oil explorationist and must expand the mind and the search beyond the limited thinking of the geological conditions that are likely for oil and how oil accumulates. A successful natgas explorationist thinks outside of "oil and gas." In the future, most of the world's largest natural gas fields will produce little if any oil.

North America is becoming the microcosm for the future of the world's natgas exploration and production. Large natgas accumulations occur in many places where oil production is either mature and declining or within large areas where little oil can be expected. Today, the world's best example is the United States, where oil development matured in the 1970s and oil production has since declined, yet natgas has begun a renaissance. Good examples are the growing Barnett Shale field and the vast swaths of early natural gas shale development from Oklahoma and Arkansas, through Appalachia, across Pennsylvania, Ohio, and New York, and into eastern Canada.

Chesapeake Energy predicts the Haynesville Field of east Texas and west Louisiana will become America's largest natgas field and the fourth largest gas field in the world.[16] It has already been estimated to contain natural gas supplies of Middle East- and Siberian-size, in the range of 700 Tcf in play,[17] with estimated recoverable reserves today in the range of 250+ Tcf.[18] The deep geological basins across North America hold little opportunity for oil but will likely develop to supply many times the natgas supplies that have heretofore been estimated to exist in North America. I believe these limited-oil areas contain vast supplies of nonconventional natgas and will ensure North America has much more than a 100-year supply at the significantly increased rates of consumption necessary to displace importantly large amounts of coal and oil use.

For the world's leaders and policy makers, an important and little appreciated geological difference between natural gas and oil is unfolding. Natgas development in our country is proving that even though there may not be much oil left to be found, that fact is not stopping the United States, by far the world's largest natural gas consumer, from increasing supplies to meet growing needs. "Peak oil" will not lead to a similar "peak natural gas" in America or the world, as many experts suggested.

At prices approaching the equivalent of oil, the world can become awash in natural gas.

These physical and chemical characteristics of natgas are the reason it can be produced commercially from vast volumes of rocks that generally do not contain oil or where oil cannot be commercially produced. Shale, coal, "tight" or relatively dense sandstones—and most of the world's deep basins—contain large, undeveloped commercial supplies of natgas, but little commercial oil. The deep oil production of the U.S. Gulf of Mexico is a rare exception. The fact that there are many times the volumes of rocks that produce natgas than oil is another of the many reasons that lead to the understanding that the Earth contains many times the Btus of energy in the form of natgas than it does oil and, with the exception of the United States, the so-called unconventional reservoirs are largely unexplored the world over.

Another potential target for abundant natural gas can be found in the shallow rocks immediately below the ocean floor of most all of the Earth's continental shelves. This is another enormous volume of rocks that contains what certainly must be the world's largest accumulation of natgas, but little, if any, oil. These vast accumulations of natural gas "hydrates" exist in the form of sort of a mushy, yellowish, icy substance that is created by the cool temperatures and high pressures found just below the ocean floor. The U.S. Geological Survey states that estimates of global resources of natgas hydrates "range from 100,000 to almost 300,000,000 trillion cubic feet of natural gas."[19] To put these vast resources in perspective, they equal from about 4 times to over 10,000 times the world's coal reserves that are estimated to be about 24,000 trillion cubic feet equivalent and about 15 to 40,000 times the world's remaining oil reserves, estimated to be about 6,800 Tcf equivalent.[20] So the natgas hydrates offer the potential of many times more Btus of energy than the entire world's coal and oil reserves put together. None of this natural gas is yet commercially available, but many experiments to produce hydrates are going on around the world, particularly in Asia, and many experts are highly optimistic. If only a small fraction of the world's hydrates become commercial to produce, they will become new, important natgas supplies for most of the world's population who live within the coastal regions of all continents.

The Geographical Difference

Because of natural gas's geological differences from oil, particularly the fact that it accumulates in such large volumes of rocks that often contain little, if any, oil, natgas can be found in volumes sufficient to support large regional economies, located all around the world, where there is comparably little oil remaining to be found. Natgas is much more widely distributed around the world. Because of this fact, unlike oil, it is unlikely for natural gas that there will ever be such a concentration of political and economic power in a few hands: 62 percent of the world's oil is located in no more than 5 percent of the Earth's surface area that covers the Middle East. The equivalent geographical concentration of natural gas need not exist for the long term as it does today, where over one-half of the proven natgas reserves are in Russia, Iran, and Qatar because there are sufficient supplies to meet regional demand within each region of the world's markets. Sufficient natgas reserves are available for the long-term future in North America, South America, Africa, Asia, Europe, and Australia. This geographic distribution's positive political and economic implications will be discussed further later in this chapter.

The Technological Difference

Because oil is both chemically variable and a complex liquid, it requires a lot of complex technology. Natural gas most always flows naturally to the surface at pressures higher than atmospheric pressures. Generally, all that is required for its use is a tank that separates any liquids that may come to the surface with natgas, along with a series of pipelines and compressors to move the natural gas across country to consumers. Some natural gas, particularly if it is "sour" and contains sulphur, requires a relatively small plant with some sophisticated technology to separate the sulphur from the natgas and make it "pipeline quality" and usable for the consumer.

By contrast, being a viscous liquid, oil requires pumps to get it out of the ground. That is why most people correctly envision oil fields with lots of "nodding donkeys," or pump jacks, to bring it to the surface where it is stored in tanks. The photos shown in Exhibits 6.2 and 6.3

Exhibit 6.2   Oil Pump Jacks
Source: Marli Bryant Miller, University of Oregon.

Exhibit 6.3   Two Natural Gas Wells at a Typical Site in Southeastern
Oklahoma

are typical of an oil field with its highly recognizable pump jacks and a similar photo of a developed natural gas field.

Oil's chemical complexities and variability also mean that it must go through large refineries that break it down to its various components before its products are useful to the consumer in the form of liquid gasoline, diesel, jet fuel, or home heating oil. Because oil meets such a large segment of global energy use (about 90 percent of transportation's demand for fuel), the quantities needed each day are enormous and require capital-intensive, behemoth industrial complexes called oil refineries to process crude oil into its usable commercial products. Because refineries are large, dirty, and dangerous, they are difficult to permit and site, so it has been over 30 years since the United States had its last new oil refinery.

Natural gas fields are not generally known or envisioned by the public. They are generally much cleaner because natgas cannot be spilled and the wellhead is only a series of valves extending about 5 or 10 feet above the ground. For the most part, natgas comes out of the ground basically ready to go to the user, so its technology is simple, more efficient, and does not need the economies of scale required by both oil and coal. As natural gas is not a viscous, high-carbon liquid like oil, it is more efficient and much less polluting. Engines that use natural gas tend to last longer and emit much less CO_2 and no solid particulates, which are the cause of much urban smog and its related health problems and costs.

Natural gas is distributed by pipeline grid and can easily be accessed virtually anywhere on the grid. America's 2.2-million-mile natgas pipe grid covers most of the country and all major and most small cities and towns. If used in your car, natural gas can come to you rather than you going to a gasoline filling station. As mentioned earlier, the United States has 63 million households already connected to the natgas grid; so more than 130 million cars return to a place where, with a natural gas tank in your trunk and a small compressor home-filling appliance, you could fill up while you sleep. For the world's drivers who have natural gas at home, it offers the potential to save tens of billions of hours per year that they would otherwise spend driving to and from a petrol station and filling up. This gift of time would add to quality of life and each individual's general productivity.

Another important aspect of this grid is that it provides homeowners the possibility of generating their own electricity with increasingly efficient microgenerators, a big step forward for distributed generation and the certainty of electric supply. As a result of decades of underinvestment in both power generation necessary to keep up with recent and forecast economic growth and the electric distribution grid itself, much of America's electric supply system is in woeful need of repair, renewal, and new generation capacity, so more and more electric users will experience power shortages with increasing frequency over the coming decades. This fact is a serious limitation for the widespread use of electric cars. The certainty of continuous, uninterrupted electricity that comes with distributed generation will continue to gain economic utility and become more valuable to more of the world's businesses because of the growing demand by the globally connected economy to run computers continuously 24 hours a day, 365 days a year.

Natgas by pipe to either large or small electric generators is many times more reliable than large, often neglected power plants and electric grids, as can be seen by the increasing rate of electric power outages, cutoffs, and shortages both in the United States and around the world. Distributed generation along the natgas pipe grid will become an increasingly important solution to the growing and widespread global problem of reliable electric supplies.

Because home heating oil is a liquid, trucks are required to deliver the oil to the storage tank that feeds into the home's heating system. And the home that uses oil for heating is almost never connected to the natgas pipeline grid, so the result is that more energy is consumed to deliver the fuel oil and to heat the home than if natgas were available by pipe. Natural gas is more efficient than fuel oil for home heating. Electricity for cooking is highly inefficient, and as any chef will tell you, it is harder to control when compared to natural gas. The fact is that natgas technology adds to both energy efficiency and, when it comes to cooking, quality of life.

The technology of natural gas is by far simpler, less capital intensive, and more efficient than the technology of oil. The exception is when natgas is delivered across oceans. Because natural gas *is* a gas, it must be cooled, liquefied, and compressed (liquefied natural gas, LNG) in order to fill an oceangoing tanker with sufficient quantities of Btus of energy to make its transport by sea commercial. So LNG requires special liq-uefication facilities on the supply end, cryogenic or super-cooled and pressurized tankers for transport across the seas, and regasification facil-ities at the delivery point. Therefore, natgas delivered by sea as LNG may be as technologically complex as oil that must be refined and delivered to the user, but it is an entirely different technological supply system than that used for oil. Also, an LNG tanker could be blown up, but it could not create the environmental damage of an accident like the *Exxon Valdez* oil spill. From production to consumption, natgas is far less environmentally damaging.

In the big picture, when compared to oil, the technological sys-tem that surrounds natgas from production to consumption is superior in almost every way. Oil and the technology that makes up its system of use is more complex, less efficient, and requires much larger, cen-trally located, more capital-intensive facilities to achieve the necessary *economies of scale* than does natural gas. Last, but not least, the use of oil by consumers often requires the expenditure of important amounts of their precious time that is not required by the use of natgas, a fact that is never factored into any of the efficiency models I have ever seen.

The Environmental Difference

The physical and chemical characteristics of natural gas make it envi-ronmentally superior to oil. Natural gas, CH_4, has far less dirty carbon and more clean hydrogen than oil. As Aubrey McClendon, CEO of Chesapeake Energy, America's largest and fastest-growing natural gas exploration and production company, correctly says, "Natural gas is carbon light." As a result, when natgas is burned to generate electricity or used to fuel your car, the general non-CO_2 pollution from emis-sions are largely eliminated. I have held a white handkerchief over the exhaust pipe of a natgas-fueled bus for several minutes while it was running and it remained just as white as before. Natural gas does not emit the dangerous, health-damaging particulates that are emitted by gasoline and diesel.

The use of natural gas would eliminate most of the foul air in the world's major cities. When natgas is substituted for gasoline and diesel, CO_2 emissions are reduced by 20 to 30 percent; so if CNG vehicles replace a large percentage of the world's automobile, truck, and bus fleet, we will have taken a very large step forward in reducing global CO_2 emissions. If natgas was used to fuel 50 percent of the world's vehicle fleet, global CO_2 emissions from oil would be reduced by about 2 billion metric tons annually from today's levels, lessening CO_2 emissions worldwide by 6 percent.[21] Electric plug-ins still use electricity, and in countries like the United States and China, CO_2-emitting coal generates about 50 percent and 80 percent,[22] respectively, of the electricity used. The highly touted Chevy Volt electric car would run on gasoline for trips beyond about 40 miles, so until coal is no longer used for electric generation, vehicles like Honda's natural gas Civic GX will always be much greener until our electric generation no longer comes from coal. And because of the rundown condition of much of America's electric grid, there is a question whether the current electric grid could handle the conversion to plug-in vehicles without huge, new investments. In America, we must remember that about 130 million cars come home each night to a house that is already on the natural gas grid. So with a natgas tank in your trunk or a CNG vehicle like Honda's and a natural gas home fill station, you can fill up at home. Also, a majority of the gasoline filling stations in metropolitan areas are also on the grid, so they can be ready to fill your CNG vehicle very soon.

Natgas is also much more environmentally friendly when accidents happen. Yes, if natural gas leaks, explosions do happen, both along pipelines and in homes, and people can be killed. But natgas explosions and fires tend to be more contained and not as long-lasting as oil fires that burn from the liquid spilled on the ground. Natural gas accidents have much less environmental consequence than similar accidents involving oil. Oil accidents create larger disasters and more lasting environmental degradation because oil and its products are liquid, and when spilled they spread out on the ground or the seas. Petroleum fires spread out to wherever the liquid runs if spilled from a tank and put lots of toxins in the air. Oil spills soak into the ground or beaches, are absorbed into the ecosystem, and create pollution that lasts for a generation or more.

In the 1990s, I worked in and visited the old 1950s Soviet oil fields in the Samara region of the Volga River Basin and saw oil's enormous environmental degradation that will last for at least another generation. Even today, 20 years later, we can see damage to the ecosystem in

Alaska's Prince William Sound where the *Exxon Valdez* tanker ran into a reef and spilled approximately 11 million gallons of oil. Natgas accidents may cause explosions and fires, but being lighter than air, natgas is disbursed into the atmosphere and does not soil the Earth's land and beaches and seas for generations to come. It is not absorbed into the ecosystem, nor is it long-lasting in the atmosphere. Also, accidents in CNG vehicles are less likely to cause fires than petroleum-powered cars because if gasoline/petrol spills on the ground, it can easily ignite and engulf the car in flames and anyone trapped inside will be severely burned. Because natgas is lighter than air, it will escape upward in a severe accident that pierces the natural gas tank and is much less likely to ignite than gasoline because it requires just the right amount of oxygen to burn. So a CNG vehicle is actually safer than one powered by gasoline.[23] I have seen films of natgas tank testing where a tank filled with natural gas at 3,500 psi of pressure is bathed in flames and shot through with an armor-piercing bullet without an explosion or increased quantities of fire. Yes, natural gas is a greenhouse gas more intense than CO_2, so when it leaks it does add to global warming, but its life in the atmosphere is only about 9 to 15 years,[24] less than the lasting effect of environmental oil disasters. CO_2 lasts about a century in the atmosphere before it is fully absorbed.[25] Because natgas is considerably cleaner and more efficient than oil, its use as an alternative for oil is a big environmental step forward for humanity, not to mention its equally large economic, political and security benefits.

The Economic Difference

Throughout much of the history of natural gas use it has been priced to stay in the ground. Unless, that is, it was found and produced along with oil. I learned early in my career, during my training courses in economic analysis at Philips Petroleum in the 1950s, that natgas was considered to have little to no value. Only in the last decade, particularly when it has been contracted for the long term to be transported as LNG, has natural gas begun to be priced near the equivalent of oil on a Btu basis. During much of the history of natgas, even as it grew to become one of the world's primary fuels, its average price at the wellhead in the United States has usually been in the range of 50 to

60 percent of oil,[26] even though natgas has far superior environmental qualities and adds to our energy security. With the exception of LNG, these large discounts to oil generally prevail today, although the future looks as though natural gas may soon begin to command prices that reflect its superior environmental and security value to society.

Historically, natgas has been thought of and treated as a by-product of oil to be sold off as an added bonus or simply flared away in order to produce the oil. For decades, NASA's night photos showed some of the brightest spots on Earth to be natgas flaring from the Siberian, West African, and Saudi oil fields. Luckily, and to the benefit of the world's gas-consuming economies over the last half century, demand was met by natgas produced in association with oil, so-called "associated" natural gas, or produced from non–oil–associated fields found during the oil industry's search for oil that happened to be commercial to develop at prices of the times that were often government regulated. Low, regulated natgas prices in many areas of the world, including the United States, Middle East, and China, have kept vast quantities of nonassociated natgas in the ground. Because the modern world developed on oil, and oil was the focus of most energy demand growth, particularly in the transportation sector after World War II, oil was king and the thought, exploration, capital, and technological progress was focused on oil. Natural gas, particularly associated natural gas, simply came along for the ride, without comparative focus, understanding, technological innovation, or capital expenditures, both within the oil industry itself and its sister industry, transportation.

For instance, although natgas has been used for vehicles for more than 60 years,[27] by far the most R&D expenditures in the auto industry were for the development of innovation for the gasoline engine and vehicles powered by liquid oil products. The fact is, until the beginning of the twenty-first century, natural gas was a stepchild of the oil industry and, in reality, there was never, nor is there today, an efficient, vertically integrated natgas industry in the United States or, for that matter, most nations of the world. For most of the history of natural gas, both the oil producers and the few companies that focused on natgas exploration and production have been price takers as a result of supplies that have usually exceeded demand over many decades.

In late summer 2008, large economic differences remained between natural gas and oil, often related to political issues discussed in that section of this chapter. Natural gas is generally a regional market even for oceangoing LNG, and so far, even though China, Japan, South Korea, and Singapore have all recently signed LNG import contracts principally tied to the price of oil, in the United States, natgas continues to sell into the pipeline grid at 50 to 60 percent of the equivalent price of oil.

As long as the United States can meet its demand for natgas at a discount to the price of oil without the need for marginal supplies of LNG, as I believe will be the case because of America's domestic natgas abundance, it will be a long time before many LNG tankers begin arriving continuously in the United States. Indeed, that is largely why the stock of the LNG importer Cheniere fell nearly 90 percent from July 2007 to May 2008. Cheniere and a couple of oil companies, including ExxonMobil, repeated the mistake El Paso Natural Gas made in 1978 by not believing the United States had ample, affordable natural gas supplies.

As surprising as it may be, in the late 1970s one of America's largest natural gas companies believed the United States was running out of natural gas. Although it is too long a story, suffice it to say that because of the previous decades of abundance, El Paso Natural Gas, a risk-adverse, regulated pipeline company, did not venture very far into the exploration and production business. Rather, El Paso, like most others not having their own data, relied on the oil companies and was influenced by the oil-related forecasts of declining natural gas production. El Paso went on to build a white elephant LNG system and LNG tankers to bring LNG from Algeria just before America's 20-year natgas surplus. Much of the project was financed by El Paso's general ratepayers, and it became a financial disaster. Most of the tankers for which El Paso was able to get significant subsidies paid by U.S. taxpayers went into mothballs.

For decades to come, the United States will meet its increasing demand for natural gas with its vast shale and other so-called unconventional domestic resources. LNG imports will not be required except possibly to meet an occasional spot need, unless more than half of America's vehicle fleet is converted to natural gas, as I recommend in

Chapter 12, and then LNG will only be a relatively small percentage of America's total natural gas consumption.

Unfortunately, over most of the history of natgas, the global *oil* industry has been the dominant force and focus of ambition, attention, and capital budgets. Because the story simply wasn't there, no one has ever written *The Prize: The Epic Quest for Oil, Money and Power*, Daniel Yergin's classic book on the oil industry, about natural gas.[28] This oil mind-set has been so predominant that in the early 1980s, the Atlantic Richfield Company's contract to explore off the coast of south China for oil did not even address the price mechanism for natgas if it were discovered.

When large supplies of natgas were found off Hainan Island, they were not considered important enough or sufficiently valuable to develop or bring to shore to power south China's new, rapidly growing demand for electricity. Instead, in about 1989, China proposed a nuclear plant to be built on the mainland near Hong Kong. When Hong Kong protested against the risk of the nearby nuclear plant, I proposed to my longtime friend Tang Ke, then China's minister of petroleum, that a deal be made with Arco to pipe the natgas onshore to the same location as proposed for the nuclear plant, so the new demand for electricity could be met by natural gas much sooner and cheaper than with the nuclear plant. A natural gas pipeline would also create the beginning of a natural gas pipe grid for south China's rapid development. Unfortunately, just like the "natural gas has had it" mind-set of the U.S. government in the late 1970s, neither Arco nor China considered these natgas supplies important enough to work out the problems and develop the field. It was more than a decade before the Hainan natural gas field was put into production.

Unlike oil, natural gas is much more widely distributed around the world and can be developed within most consuming regions. It is my bet that despite what Russia and Iran may be saying today, there will be no "natural gas OPEC." The wide distribution of commercial quantities of natgas for local and regional use by nations will keep the economic and political concentration of natural gas sufficiently distributed around the world to prevent a natgas OPEC for two reasons. The first is because of the regional nature of natural gas markets that stem from its method of transportation and distribution. The second is because there are very large remaining supplies to be developed on all the world's continents, even those that have mature oil production, such as North America, that can be available to most population centers by pipeline or regional ocean transport.

Theoretically, these factors should prevent the kind of market concentration that is necessary for an effective OPEC, as has occurred in oil. "Theoretically," because if most of the world's potential natural gas–producing countries continue to keep natgas prices so low that it will not be developed, then sufficient supply concentrations could occur, as is the case today with Russia, Iran, and Qatar. So the possibility of an effective natgas OPEC is really in the hands of the world's natural gas consuming governments.

Until this century, oil's overshadowing role in the development of the world's energy needs has kept natural gas in the background, both economically and politically. That is beginning to change and natgas is stepping up to meet its turn to fuel much of the world's future growth.

The Political Difference

Although oil has always been in the midst of politics, for most of its history, producers of oil have usually collected a market price, whereas natgas prices have been controlled by governments. In the United States, where the use of natgas first became a large part of an energy market, there were two related factors that played a large role in the politics of cheap natural gas. One was the private ownership of mineral rights, which over the past 100 years motivated thousands of individuals and companies to seek their fortune by taking risks to find oil. And lots of oil and gas was found. Private rather than government ownership of most of America's oil and gas rights kept drilling for oil active until most of the United States became a mature oil province in the late 1950s and early 1960s, when the large oil companies began to seek their fortunes elsewhere. In the United States, there have been about 3,600,000 wells drilled, mostly targeted to find oil until recently, when more are now targeted toward natural gas, as compared to a total of about 1,500,000 for the rest of the entire world.[29] The second reason for cheap natural gas in the United States was because it always came along with oil. For decades, sufficient quantities of natgas were produced along with oil to meet its fledgling growth in demand, despite its low price. In the United States, these circumstances lasted until the 1970s, when natural gas shortages began to show up in non–natural gas producing states. These shortages were not because there was not enough natgas for the country, but because oil production and its associated natural gas had began to decline and the politically motivated, low government-regulated price at the wellhead was not encouraging new natgas drilling.

In 1954, the U.S. Supreme Court had decided that natgas sales traveling between states in interstate commerce should be regulated by the federal government at the wellhead. In the ensuing years, non-regulated natgas prices within producing states rose and new supplies were able to meet the growing demand within the producing states. However, by the mid-1970s, low prices for natural gas traveling across state lines to nonproducing states kept the rest of the natural gas in the ground. Growing shortages began to occur in these large consuming states that required natgas to be transported in interstate commerce.

Throughout the years before the inevitable shortages occurred, both governments and the people enjoyed the benefits of natural gas price controls. During such periods, everyone seems to win because no one complains. Supplies are adequate and low, controlled prices create increased use and economic growth. Everyone is happy—until the available supplies run down, as they inevitably did in the late 1970s when schools and industries in the markets relying on interstate natural gas transportation suddenly closed due to shortages of supplies. These shortages occurred in the United States during the oil shocks of the 1970s, and together they created America's first real energy crisis that led to the Carter administration's 1978 omnibus energy legislation. One part of that legislation began the process to deregulate natural gas prices and the other, fearing shortages and consumer price shocks, prohibited the use of natgas in its fastest-growing markets, power generation and new industrial facilities. Although it took about 20 years to unravel these macroeconomic natural gas market distortions, they are now largely behind us. That is, except for the 80,000 megawatts of coal-fired electric power generation that otherwise would have never been built in the decade following the 1978 legislation and will be with us for another decade or two.

Today, the same general politically and economically motivated natural gas price controls exist in many other countries around the world, and just like the 1970s in the United States, price controls around the world are beginning to create natgas shortages in the midst of abundance.

Probably the most striking recent example of shortages in the midst of plenty is taking place in the Gulf Cooperation Countries (GCC) of the Middle East, composed of Bahrain, Kuwait, Oman, Qatar, Saudi Arabia, and the UAE. In these countries, natgas, like oil, is heavily subsidized and prices are kept low for consumers. There are only a few non–government-owned producers and they, along with the government-owned producers, are only allowed to sell their natural gas within their own country for a fraction of a freely traded global price. In mid-2008 in the GCC countries, that price varied from about 20 cents to $1.50 per Mcf,[30] compared to the $8 to $12 market price in the United States and the $12 to $15 price range for most global LNG transactions.[31]

In 2008, high oil prices led to enormous accumulations of new wealth in the GCC, and the entire region embarked on massive infrastructure developments, including the building of many entirely new cities. Demand for natural gas soared to meet the need for equally soaring growth in electric power generation, water desalination, and other industrial uses. Although the development of Dubai has been the most visible to the world, the same explosive infrastructure growth was going on across the Gulf. It has been said that King Abdullah of Saudi Arabia desires to build five more large cities from scratch, in addition to the King Abdullah Economic City that is already in progress.[32] New cities and industrial growth exponentially accelerate the need for electric power. So just as in the United States in the 1970s, the GCC countries that once had more associated natgas than needed as a by-product of increasing oil production, much flared away, are now facing forecasts of natural gas shortages because oil production has at best plateaued and internal natgas demand is growing exponentially while nonassociated natural gas remains priced to stay in the ground.

These circumstances may have blindsided many intelligent Arab leaders, just as they did in the United States in the 1970s. With the exception of Qatar, most GCC countries have focused on the development of oil—refineries, infrastructure, and chemical industries—while the internal price controls left what I believe to be their vast domestic, nonassociated natgas supplies locked in the ground. Now, several Gulf states have begun to study the feasibility of building coal-fired power generation[33] and nuclear facilities.[34] I believe recognition of this frightening trend a few years ago led Saudi Arabia to invite Western oil giants back to the country again to explore for natural gas in the "empty quarter." Unfortunately, after three unsuccessful test wells, one of the group, TOTAL of France, pulled out.[35] The prospects for more natural gas in Saudi Arabia in the near term have diminished.

My advice to the Saudi royal family and, for that matter, all governments of the world, is to forget about the international oil giants if you want more natgas, because it is the independent American-based companies that are developing unconventional natural gas in the United States today that possess the technology and experience of innovation needed to find and produce unconventional natgas. It is within these companies that the special natural gas–oriented talents and mind-sets reside.

Middle East experts have estimated that as early as 2015, the GCC countries cumulative supply shortfall could exceed 7 Tcf.[36] So, because oil drilling is even more vital for their economies than natgas drilling and there are only a limited number of drilling rigs and people available for exploration and new drilling and natural gas prices are so low, it is unlikely that this forecast shortage will be met by increased domestic natgas supplies, but rather by imports, energy shortages, or reduced infrastructure building. Although an attempt will be made to meet this shortage with coal and nuclear, the fact that it takes a least a decade to build and put a nuclear plant on line, and at least half that for a sizable coal plant, leads to the conclusion that it looks as if the GCC countries will not be exporting additional supplies of natural gas anytime soon, even though the entire region is well endowed with supplies far in excess of that needed for its population and all the new cities and industry these countries desire to build. Although I am not an expert on the potential for natural gas supplies in the GCC region, my friend Sadad Al-Husseini, the former executive vice president of exploration and production for Saudi Aramco, shares my view that the GCC has large, undeveloped natural gas resources.

This is a perfect example of politics and politically related prices keeping natgas locked in the ground when it is not associated with oil production. The early decades of increasing oil production gave governments the false comfort that there was always going to be sufficient amounts of natural gas to be had at low, controlled prices.

It is my contention that a similar natural gas tragedy is taking place in China. In the mid-1980s, I investigated natgas potential in China at the request of the Ministry of Petroleum. I came away with my own "expert" opinion on China's natgas abundance. I reported to the Ministry of Petroleum, Ministry of Geology, and groups of scientists that China probably has about as much natural gas as the United States.[37] I based this estimate on my studies of China's sedimentary basins, mostly focused on the Sichuan Basin and the Ordos Basin, the study of regional seismic lines, China's general geology, the age and thickness of the sediments, a general understanding of natural gas exploration and supplies, as well as China's abundance of coal. I estimated that natgas in China had the potential to approximate the quantities of natural gas supplies in America. There is potentially many trillions of cubic feet in Sichuan province's overthrust belt, a small part of which has come to fruition with the recent discovery of the Longgang natural gas field.[38]

Today, China remains largely unexplored for natural gas. Most of China has hardly been scratched, as we say in the industry, and many opportunities for large accumulations of domestic natgas remain unexplored. Neither Sichuan nor the Ordos Basin or the far west's Tarim Basin are fully explored, and although it looks like Husky's recent natural gas discovery in the South China Sea may be very large, that area still has lots of room for exploration. Then there are the deeper zones below the famous Daqing oil field, as well as the potential for large supplies in Inner Mongolia. But like the United States, China's potentially huge onshore natural gas abundance will occur within unconventional reservoirs that are not associated with oil.

If one believes China has natural gas reserves that could equal those of the United States, as I do, the sad fact is that these natgas resources remain locked in the ground by price controls on onshore natural gas and state ownership of all subsurface resources. Worse, even though China would like to displace much of its coal-generated electricity with natural gas and fuel even more of its vehicles with natgas (buses in Sichuan have been running on natural gas since the 1950s; see Exhibit 6.4), last year the nation began to import foreign-produced LNG at prices near to the equivalent of oil. This is particularly unfortunate for China, since most of the onshore natural gas exploration and production activities and the jobs and economic impact these activities create when vigorously pursued would take place in the countryside, where economic development and jobs are vitally needed. Like the GCC countries, as long as China keeps a cap on domestically produced natgas prices, it will also be keeping a cap on its domestic natural gas production while it exports capital to import higher-priced LNG. I urge China's leaders not to repeat America's energy mistakes of the 1970s.

In the end, if natural gas is there, a free market price for natural gas and access to fair and balanced contracts for its exploration will bring the world's vast resources to the surface for use by the world's consumers. But the continuing political reality is that producer price controls in much of the world, particularly in many countries and regions with abundant natgas, such as South America, the Middle East, Russia, and

Exhibit 6.4   CNG Bus, Shawan District, Zigong City, China, 1984
Source: Paul Noll, www.paulnoll.com

its former Soviet satellites, and I believe China and India will continue to create distorted markets by creating incentives for more use through subsidies, while large supplies remain locked in the ground. To have the best chance to solve our energy, environmental, and atmospheric CO_2 concentration problems, over the next 30 years the world's leaders must solve these special natgas-related political problems so that natural gas can be released from its regulatory chains. Could the World Trade Organization's (WTO) role be expanded to include global natgas trade and deal with the problems of subsidies within national markets?

Such issues will be discussed in Chapter 12, "Policies to Accelerate the GET." As natural gas awareness and understanding continues to grow around the world, natgas will break through the many historic barriers of its association with oil and become known as a clean alternative to coal and oil that has the potential to scale up and become a principal solution to current energy and related climate, economic, and security problems.

Natural gas is ready to fuel your car, generate your electricity, and may well become NASA's twenty-first-century fuel for interplanetary travel. Natgas is beginning to accelerate the GET even without help from governments.

Chapter 7

Natural Gas Abundance

Even a little certainty is a very dangerous thing.
—Sir Hermann Bondi, master, Churchill
College, 1983–1990

The mind-set of *oil and gas* has hidden the importance and understanding of natural gas within the perception of oil and the understanding of liquids. My college degree is in petroleum geology, and today most students continue to study petroleum geology and petroleum engineering. Petroleum is defined in Webster's dictionary as "an oily flammable bituminous liquid," and it has been my lifelong experience in the "oil and gas" industry that the mind-set of this industry that searches for and produces an oily, flammable, bituminous liquid is difficult to change. One of the early oil industry's most successful and highly regarded geologists, Wallace Pratt, once famously said, "Where oil fields are really found . . . is in the minds of men . . . "[1]

This statement has been widely quoted and accepted by explorationists as a mantra, so if one's mind-set developed beginning with education in the technical fields of petroleum and continued through the daily vernacular of the industry with such statements as "I am an oil field hand," or "We are headed out to the oil patch," when in fact, they are going out to a natural gas field to work on natgas wells, it becomes easier to understand how the mind-set bias is toward oil and how oil accumulates and is trapped. We must never underestimate the lasting and controlling power of words.

It has been this oil mind-set that has led to an underappreciation of natgas abundance even within the oil and gas industry itself. Unfortunately, it will be a while before the thinking of the largest international oil companies (IOCs) really begins to change, although the process has indeed begun. It is very difficult to break out of the blinders that are generally created by what we learned during our college educations, particularly in the scientific disciplines. Because a majority of senior staff and management of the IOCs are over 50—most approaching retirement—they are deeply steeped in the ways and thinking of oil. After all, this has been the basis of an oil-focused education and of decades of enormous successes.

A true story illustrates the point. In October 2007, I spoke at London's globally renowned "Oil and Money" Conference. I delivered a speech about my belief that the world's energy future is what I call "The Age of Energy Gases," Chapter 13 of this book. Included were the topics of natural gas abundance and the many characteristic differences between natgas and oil, as described in Chapter 6. After the speech, a young man who appeared to be in his mid-40s came up to me and introduced himself as a graduate of the University of Oklahoma with a degree in petroleum engineering. He was employed by one of Houston's most successful energy investment banking firms. He went on to tell me, "I feel a little embarrassed about this, but I must admit that I have never thought about all those differences between oil and natural gas."

After decades in the industry, I know this is no isolated incident, but rather that his way of thinking is the mainstream. No one can really understand and grasp the significance of natural gas and its capacity as a major solution to our energy and climate problems until these differences are thought about. As a broad generality, the senior technical staff and management of the IOCs, the state-owned oil companies (SOCs), as well as many of the smaller exploration and production companies of the world operate within the same controlling mind-set as that young man from Houston. It is no surprise that the general public and most politicians also lack a depth of natural gas understanding. Even in 2008, Red Cavaney, then president and CEO of the American Petroleum Institute, was being interviewed by CNBC's Maria Bartiromo. She asked, "The most viable alternative to oil when it comes to transportation—what is it?" Cavaney instantly responded, "There really isn't a viable alternative . . ."[2] Thus, natural gas, which already runs more than eight million vehicles in the world, wasn't even a possibility in his mind.

The United States during the past few years has been the best example of how this oil mind-set has determined the successful players in the ongoing development of new so-called "unconventional" natural gas supplies. The IOCs and other oil companies—with their legacy U.S. natural gas production (most of which was found decades ago in their search for oil)—all have declining natural gas production today. For decades, they have viewed the United States as a mature, highly developed oil and gas province with little remaining potential. The accurate oil forecast that has now become quite famous, made by Shell Oil's renowned geologist M. King Hubbert—that oil *and gas* production would peak in the United States in the 1970s[3]—became reality. The potential for large fields of oil and gas was largely eliminated from the minds of exploration geologists in the oil companies that were charged with finding new and ever-growing giant oil accumulations. This oil and gas mind-set translated into the mistaken thinking that if there is little potential for oil in the United States, there is also little potential for natural gas. Although natgas may be on the verge of breaking out of this—even within the oil companies—it is still difficult because senior management and technical staff will continue to struggle to think beyond the limits of oil.

It is no surprise that the most successful natgas producer in the United States, Chesapeake Energy—which has recently surpassed all the oil companies to become the number one producer of American natural gas—is led by a former *history* major from Duke University with no technical petroleum education. Aubrey McClendon, Chesapeake's chairman and CEO, co-founded the company only 20 years ago. Then, it was just another tiny Oklahoma-based independent energy company in the midst of America's oil-mature, natural-gas-abundant Mid-Continent region. But Aubrey the historian had a sense that natgas, as he often likes to say, is "on the right side of history." He believes in natural gas abundance, and he has a lot of entrepreneurial determination, drive, and luck. Moreover, he has no real competition from older, well-established, and financially more capable oil companies, such as ExxonMobil, BP, Chevron, and Conoco Phillips, all with enormous legacy assets in the United States. With all this going for him, he was able to surpass all the oil companies in spite of their hundred-year history and legacy oil and gas production in America.

There is no question that this outstanding accomplishment by Chesapeake belongs in the list of good examples of the "could only happen in America" success stories, but it is an equally important story of the profound value of going beyond the mental limits placed on us all by decades of conventional wisdom. Without the technical bias of petroleum, Aubrey easily grasped the understanding that natural gas supplies in the United States were abundant and not connected to the mature stage of development and limits of oil. As Aubrey said to me during a discussion about geology, "the shales are something I can understand," and it certainly did not hurt that he knew the history of natural gas production in the United States—that natgas was first produced near Fredonia, New York, from a reservoir that was not conventional in oil parlance, but rather from unconventional shale. During the last decade, as prices rose and natural gas became profitable to produce, Chesapeake and other like-minded independent gas-not-oil producers began to drill in these areas.

As a matter of fact, during this same period of phenomenal growth by the natgas-oriented group of American independent contenders, many of the oil companies—because of their own perception of limited opportunities within the oil and gas industry—were liquidating themselves through large stock buybacks and increased dividends. Today, the oil companies will not be participants unless they catch up by buying out natural gas independents, just as Conoco Phillips did when it acquired Burlington Resources in 2006, an offshoot of El Paso

Natural Gas Company with excellent American natgas reserves and potential. Jim Mulva, the CEO of Conoco Phillips, seems well ahead of his peers. Upon the acquisition of Burlington Resources, he said, "We'll be a major player with respect to gas in North America for decades to come."[4] Natgas is truly the one alternative to both coal and oil that can be scaled up around the world to solve our looming energy and climate challenges. Of course, to have the capacity to scale up to the quantities of production necessary to become an effective alternative to coal and oil requires natural gas *abundance*.

Mother Nature: Cookin' with Gas

As noted, natural gas is physically and chemically different from oil. We know that natural gas has both biological and nonbiological origins, can be created biologically within hours in our stomachs and refuse dumps, and was also part of the primordial molecular cloud at the creation of the universe. In our solar system, recent decades of space exploration have shown conclusively that natgas is abundant throughout our solar system. This gas is thought to be nonbiological. Natgas has now been detected on so many planets in significant quantities that NASA is studying the possibility of using natural gas for interplanetary travel.[5] The only possibility for biological origin of these vast quantities of natural gas in our solar system would be natgas generated by microbes below the surface of all of these planetary bodies. This would also mean that there is abundant, primitive life throughout our solar system and probably much of the universe, ratifying the Pan-Spermia or Pan-Galactic theory of life put forth by Cambridge's renowned cosmologist Fred Hoyle. Indeed, if this was reality, then because we know that the same process of microbe-generated natural gas takes place below the Earth's surface, it would be realistic to assume this microbial biological process may account for the creation of larger quantities of natgas on Earth than previously thought to be the case. "Unconventional" indeed.

The conventional wisdom that flows from the thinking surrounding the idea of oil and gas is that virtually all the commercial quantities of natgas on Earth come from the exact same geologically limited origin of oil that requires source rocks containing large quantities of microbiological material that are subsequently buried to exactly the right depth necessary to create the conditions of pressure and temperature over a sufficiently long geologic period—at least hundreds of thousands if not millions of years—*to create liquid oil*. This has often been called by oil geologists the *kitchen* that is required to *cook* the oil, or the *physical window* for the conditions of oil's origin.

Natural gas is, of course, *also* created in large amounts right along with oil's process of origin. However, the natgas kitchen is vastly larger. That kitchen begins with the nearly ambient pressures and temperatures on Earth's surface, such as our stomachs and refuse dumps—right through and beyond the oil window—to the extreme and widely variable conditions of our solar system to the even-larger extreme of 900 degrees Celsius detected in the atmosphere of a planet in the constellation Vulpecula about 63 light years from Earth.[6] On Earth, natural gas exists and most likely also originates from the extreme conditions of great depths and extremely high pressures and temperatures where diamonds are formed of the purest carbon. We know natgas is present during the creation of diamonds because diamonds often have natural gas inclusions within them.

To further affirm the presence of natural gas deep within our Earth at levels where oil is almost nonexistent, natural gas has been found in the deepest wells ever drilled, including two test wells that were drilled entirely in granite rocks where most oil geologists don't believe oil and gas exist. Two of the granite test wells were drilled within the Siljan meteorite crater of Sweden. I was a consultant on that project because of my company's extensive deep natural gas drilling experience. The two wells were drilled to about 22,000 feet and 21,300 feet (6.7 and 6.5 kilometers, respectively), and I can personally attest to the fact that the natural gas measuring devices confirmed the presence of natural gas all the way to total depth. Although the two wells were never adequately tested for production potential, it is doubtful that commercial quantities of natural gas were found. Still, the fact that natural gas was present within granite rocks at great depths that have no biological accumulations or source rocks that the oil industry believes are *required* for the creation of oil and gas, and the fact that natural gas shows seemed to increase with depth, are certainly good indications of the wide occurrence of natural gas and its possible nonbiological origin on Earth.

Deepest Wells in the World

In 1972, our company and Lone Star Natural Gas began drilling the deepest vertical well in the Western World to a depth of 31,441 feet in western Oklahoma. At that depth, the well encountered a strong, positive flow off bottom that began to lift the drill string, which weighed about a million pounds. The well's driller correctly lifted the drill pipe up in the derrick and closed the blowout preventers. The surface pressure gauge instantly indicated over 4,000 psi and built up to over 8,000 psi in about 10 minutes. The indicated pressure was over 31,000 psi at the well's total depth. This indicated the highest pressure ever encountered in the Earth at the time and probably remains a world record today. I won't go into all the exciting details of trying to deal with these never-before-encountered pressures, but suffice it to say that the technology of the time was not up to handling these conditions, and after about a day of watching the well circulate up natural gas and about a pickup-truck load of pure sulphur, we capped and cemented the well.

To this day, we have no understanding as to whether commercial quantities of natural gas were actually encountered, but we do know that significant amounts of natural gas exist at the total depth of the wellbore. While we were drilling the well, we entertained a group of Soviet scientists at the rig, a tour organized by the U.S. State Department. A few months later, when I delivered a paper about our experience drilling that well and other deep, high-pressure wells to the World Gas Conference in Nice, France, a group of Soviet scientists filled the entire first two rows of the auditorium and furiously took notes during my entire presentation. We would learn many years later that the reason for their great attention and the visit to the wellsite was that the Soviets were drilling the world's deepest test well in the Kola Peninsula. After more than a decade of drilling through solid granite rocks, this well reached 40,233 feet.[7] Much later, when scientific reports of the well reached the West, we learned that just as in the Sweden's Siljan crater, shows of natural gas were encountered throughout most of the borehole down to total depth. The logic that flows from the fact that natural gas is present in deep boreholes in granite rocks that do not contain the biological debris found in sedimentary rocks necessary for biological origin—combined with the presence of so much natural gas on most of our solar system's planets—led to reasonable beliefs that natural gas is continually flowing from the Earth's interior mantle, just as it must be on planets throughout our solar system.

Ubiquitous Natural Gas

So because natural gas exists in the universe at extremely high temperatures—throughout our solar system at extremes of both hot and cold—and is found deep within Earth at the depths, pressures, and temperatures where diamonds are formed, is encountered in measurable quantities in most of the world's boreholes, and found in the stomachs of animals and refuse dumps, I believe it is reasonable to believe its existence must be nearly pervasive in all the Earth's rocks.

Because of the pervasive nature of natural gas, the chance for commercial accumulations to be found are much better than those for oil, a liquid, viscous substance that cannot move through rocks easily and is encountered far less frequently within the world's boreholes. Oil's physical and chemical characteristics have created a comparatively limited window of existence compared to that of natural gas. These facts are a good indication that not only does more natural gas exist on Earth than oil, but also, unlike coal and oil, large quantities of natural gas may actually be renewable.

Additionally, natural gas can always be found in quantities varying from commercial production to only traces in coal deposits that are thought to have a somewhat similar origin as oil, but in contrast to the microbiology of oil's origin, coal is formed from macrobiology of the Earth's flora. It is logical to assume that significant quantities of natgas were also formed during the geological process of coal's origin. There is also lots of natural gas found with the world's peat bogs, but peat is created on or near the Earth's surface, and in a relatively short time period of thousands of years rather than over the geological eons of time required for the creation of coal and oil.

To sum up, we know much about natgas that does not apply to oil:

- Natural gas exists in the widest range of physical conditions of pressure and temperature.

- Natural gas was an abundant substance in the primordial molecular cloud following the Big Bang.
- Natural gas is created continuously by microbes within the Earth—we just don't know in what quantities.
- Natural gas was either around in large quantities from nonbio-logical creation beginning at the origin of the solar system or it is being created continuously at rates sufficient to create vast accumu-lations of natgas on planetary bodies throughout our solar system. Possibly, both are occurring.

Therefore, we can conclude that, in addition to the natural gas that was created during the creation of oil, and the natural gas that was also created in the same biological manner outside the physical conditions of the oil window, it is highly likely that Earth may also be blessed with an abundance of either nonbiologically created natural gas that has existed from the origin of our solar system, or that the Earth's nat-gas-producing microbes are creating natural gas in larger quantities than previously thought. The fact that all this natgas is *in addition* to the natural gas created along with coal and oil, coupled with the fact that natgas can be commercially produced from so many times the volumes of Earth's rocks than can oil, leads me to the conclusion that natgas should be considered the world's most abundant hydrocarbon. This conclusion is given further credence by the fact that gases are by far the most abundant state of matter in the universe, followed by the much smaller quantities of solids. Liquids are a transitional state of matter and only exist in relatively very small quantities on Earth, within our solar system, and across the universe. The evidence on Earth tends to con-firm this same pattern of relative quantities. Exhibit 7.1, from Dave Gallo at Woods Hole Oceanographic Institution, shows Earth with all the water removed. The small sphere on the right represents all the oceans' waters and to its right, the tiny sphere, all the fresh water.

Another strong confirmation of the magnitude of natural gas abun-dance on Earth is provided by the ocean's vast natgas hydrate accumu-lations, estimated to hold at least several times more energy than all the world's coal and oil put together.[8]

So because the wide conditions of origin and places of existence, accumulation, and production of natural gas extend far beyond the

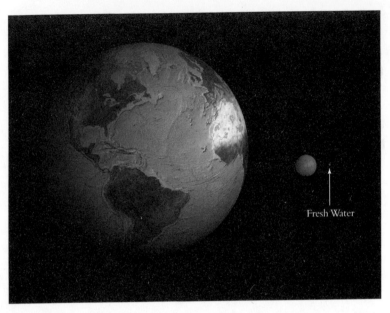

Exhibit 7.1   Water Planet? We frequently hear that more than 70 percent of the world is covered by water. But how much is there really? On the left is an image of the Earth with all water removed. On the right is a sphere representing all the water on Earth (oceans, icecaps, glaciers, lakes, rivers, groundwater, etc.). To the far right (tiny sphere) is the FRESH water that is readily available to humanity to sustain life.
Courtesy of Dave Gallo, Woods Hole Oceanographic Institution.

relatively narrow limits of coal and oil, we can better understand that natgas must be considered the most abundant hydrocarbon unless we can establish hard evidence to the contrary. Certainly, all the accumulated evidence over recent decades from natgas exploration and production, space exploration, and deep ocean exploration tends to confirm natgas abundance. This is why I believe natural gas resources are not only far larger than oil and most likely larger than coal, but possibly larger than both together.

No Peak Natural Gas

The next important point in understanding natural gas abundance is the fact that natgas is not connected to peak oil. This is because of its geologic difference from oil. Natural gas is always produced along with oil within limited and specifically defined geological containers we call structures or traps. But it also accumulates and can be commercially produced from so-called unconventional reservoir rocks, coal seams, shales, and tight sands not favorable for oil accumulations that may underlie an entire geologic basin. This means that the Earth's areas and volumes of rocks favorable for commercial natural gas production far exceed the volume of rocks favorable for the conditions of oil and gas accumulation. In fact, the Earth's volumes of unconventional reservoir rocks capable of commercial natgas production are many times, if not an order of magnitude, greater than the volumes of rocks capable of commercial oil production. Natural gas always exists and is produced along with oil, often equaling 20 percent to 40 percent of the total accumulation within an oil field. So because natural gas can be produced from so many times the volumes of rocks as can oil, it is easy to understand why the world's supplies of commercially accessible natgas are many times larger than those of oil. The only relationship natural gas has to peak oil is the natural gas that is produced along with oil from oil and gas fields from conventional reservoirs. It is only this oil-associated natgas production that will peak and decline along with oil production.

Because natural gas is also produced from unconventional reservoirs that likely hold much more natgas than conventional reservoirs, *peak oil* does not mean *peak natural gas*. This same mistaken fear of natgas shortages in the United States in the 1970s, coinciding with the beginning of peak oil in the United States, translated into many bad policy decisions, particularly, as we have seen, banning of natural gas's use in power generation and new industrial facilities. That one policy act has macroeconomically distorted the quantities of use of coal, oil, and natural gas in the United States until this very day. The large quantities of coal and oil consumption in the United States today—and their highly negative pollution, climate, economic, and security impacts on American society—are continuing remnants of these misguided policies, the result of failing to understanding that peak oil does not mean peak natural gas and missing the fact that U.S. domestic natural gas was then, and is now, abundant.

Unconventional Is Conventional

We must not make such mistakes again. The success of what the oil industry has called unconventional natural gas development proves that, although these rocks were called unconventional given the mind-set of the oil industry, they are likely to become the largest natgas-producing rocks for the world and should henceforth be considered *conventional* for natural gas production. I mention this because of the power of words and the concepts they convey. The fact is that the word *unconventional* conveys a large measure of limits and uncertainty that will tend to inhibit the world's policy makers from relying on natural gas.

Policy makers need the comfort of certainty to create policy that will impact populations for decades. So let me appeal to the world's policy makers. Today, we have more certainty about the abundance of natural gas supplies than oil. From the beginning of the natural gas industry in Fredonia, New York, natural gas has been produced from shales, so this really is not new. It is time to abandon the oil industry's concept that shales are unconventional and add them to the long list of *conventional* natural gas reservoirs.

The reality of this conventional-versus-unconventional paradigm shift in America's energy evolution can now be seen in the official U.S. statistics. The Energy Information Administration, in its *Energy in Brief* (June 2008), announced that "Natural gas production in the lower 48 states has seen a large upward shift." Further, the brief stated, "Recent growth in natural gas production in the lower 48 states breaks with historical trends." Exhibit 7.2 shows the dramatic change that is largely the result of new production in unconventional reservoirs. These official announcements were all *before* Chesapeake Energy announced that it had entered into a joint venture in the Haynesville Shale in northwest Louisiana and east Texas that it said will likely become America's largest natural gas field. The company announced the Haynesville Shale may contain 250 Tcf of recoverable natural gas, which would make it about the fourth largest in the world.[9] If natgas prices within most of the world's countries were uncapped, the global natural gas production chart could soon look exactly the same.

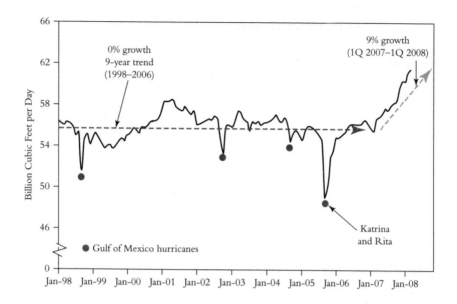

Exhibit 7.2   Recent Growth in Natural Gas Production in the Lower 48 States Breaks with Historical Trends

Source: Energy Information Administration, *Energy in Brief* (June 11, 2008).

More Natural Gas than the Market Can Use

As I write in early 2009, natural gas producers have been so successful in their efforts that once again there is a natural gas supply bubble— more natural gas than the market can possibly use. Cash prices last fall in the Rocky Mountains and Mid-Continent United States collapsed below $2 per Mcf, or about $12 per barrel of oil equivalent, even with significant Gulf of Mexico production still shut in from Hurricane Ike.

Because the price is dropping below the cost of finding, and gas flows are more than the market wants, American natural gas produc- ers are once again cutting drilling budgets by billions for the coming years. Drilling rigs are being laid down, and once again we are going through another boom and bust. Although we are importing nearly $500 billion in foreign oil each year and sending those payments to foreign producers, the United States is awash in natural gas, which is clean, secure, and creates domestic jobs, but which is not being used for the benefit of the U.S. economy. It is a travesty, particularly during this time of great economic weakness, that we have policies that foster the continuing use of oil and keep domestic natural gas in the ground to the detriment of economic growth. By early spring 2009, as the price of natural gas crashed to below replacement cost, tens of billions of dollars of capital expenditures for future natural gas development had been canceled, revenue to U.S. farmers and landowners plummeted by tens of billions of dollars, and tens of thousands of jobs in the U.S. natural gas industry were lost.

In the Search for Oil We Find More Natural Gas

Another good indication that natgas is far more abundant than oil is the fact that in the global search for oil and gas, a search that is principally funded by the big international and state-owned oil companies and focused on finding new oil reserves to replace declining oil production, more natural gas is being found than oil.

The AAPG, the world's most prestigious association of petroleum geologists, keeps records on the giant oil and gas fields found in the world each decade. During the last decade available, 1990 to 1999, 37 giant oil fields were found that contained 36,800 million "barrels of oil equivalent" (BOE). (The fact that the oil and gas industry normally keeps its statistics in BOE is another reminder of the oil mind-set and bias.) However, during the same decade, 40 giant natgas fields were found that contained 119,387 million BOE.[10] So, in a search directed largely by oil geologists seeking new oil supplies, *three times as much natgas was found than oil!* Digging a bit deeper, we find that about 30 percent of the BOE in the oil fields was actually natural gas. So in that decade, in spite of the fact that petroleum geologists and capital budgets were largely directed toward replacing oil supplies, *three to five times more natural gas was found than oil.*

Nigeria is a recent example of vast quantities of natural gas found in the search for oil. Nigerians have a saying that the country is a drop of oil in a bucket of natural gas.

Today, even with the continuing mind-set and bias of oil, nat-gas is revealed to be an abundant resource of primary energy world-wide in the estimates made by the world's experts. One of the most respected keepers of global energy statistics is the oil giant BP, formerly British Petroleum, whose former CEO, Lord John Browne, presciently launched a marketing campaign based on the letters BP, standing for "Beyond Petroleum." In 2007, BP estimated that the world's proven[11] natural gas reserves stood at 6,405 Tcf compared with 6,778 Tcf equivalent for oil and 23,727 Tcf equivalent for coal.[12] That would equal about a 64-year supply of proven natural gas at the world's present rate of consumption of about 100 Tcf per year.

More Proven Natural Gas than Is Estimated

There is a very important point that must be made about proven natural gas reserves as compared with *estimates* of proven oil reserves that are generally in the ballpark or even sometimes overestimated, as we learned from Shell Oil's rather famous writedown of oil reserves. In 50 years of experience, the estimates I have received for the proven reserves of our company's natural gas wells and other natgas wells that I have studied in the early years of production equal only about 25 percent to 50 percent of the ultimate amount of natural gas that will actually be produced from those wells. It is only after about a decade of natural gas produc-tion, when well over half of the ultimate quantity of natgas has already been produced, that petroleum engineers begin to estimate ultimate proven reserves of natural gas wells near reality. Even then, estimates often only equal 70 percent to 80 percent of what wells will actually produce. These statistics do not apply to oil wells, but I won't go fur-ther into natgas reservoir engineering here. For those interested, check out my article "New Thinking about Natural Gas."[13] Before leaving this issue of underestimated natgas supplies, which I am quite certain is cap-tured within all the natural gas statistics we see, let me make it clear that most of my natgas reserve understanding and experience comes from the onshore Mid-Continent region of the United States.

No doubt, my thinking is biased toward onshore natural gas production and its geologically older rocks that are generally not found offshore in the oceans, where most reservoir rocks tend to be conventional, younger, and conform better to the understanding of petroleum engineering. Offshore reservoirs are usually classic sandstone reservoirs of high porosity and permeability, and therefore produce at very high rates and decline rapidly, so that the life of offshore wells is relatively short compared to onshore natural gas wells, with production lives that most always extend many decades longer. Therefore, reserve estimates for offshore natural gas wells are generally much more accurate. However, these younger offshore conventional reservoirs are also subject to the conventional natural gas bias of underestimation of ultimate recovery.

A good example of such underestimation that proves how mistaken these estimates of natural gas recoveries actually are is the 1977 study requested by the Secretary of the Interior, *The Potential for Increasing Production of Natural Gas from Existing Fields in the Near Term.* The study was conducted by the National Research Council (NRC) on six large offshore natural gas fields thought to be a good representation of all offshore Gulf fields. Three of the fields had been producing almost 20 years, two for about 10 years, and one for only 4 years when the report was published. Since the study, five of the six fields combined have produced 3.2 times the original 1977 estimate of remaining reserves.[14] One produced *only* 1.5 times the NRC's estimate; taken together, all six fields have produced 2.3 times the NRC estimate of remaining reserves. So as a general rule for natural gas reserve estimates, we are safe to assume that most proven natgas estimates of the ultimate quantities to be produced are significantly understated and often *dangerously* understated from the point of view of good policy decisions. Personally, I attribute these sustained underestimations to the physical difference between oil and natural gas that petroleum engineers have yet to grasp, and that is natural gas's ability to flow through rocks at rates so much faster and farther than oil. As pressures decline at the wellbore, natural gas will be drained commercially from much larger volumes of rocks than will oil. However, I am open to other ideas and would like to hear from those in the professions.

In short, the world's estimates of proven natgas reserves—that is, reserves that petroleum engineers give at least a 90 percent certainty of being present—are significantly underestimated. Even BP's proven natural gas estimate for the world of 6,405 Tcf is in all likelihood no more than 50 to 60 percent of what will become the ultimate amount of natgas produced. BP's proven natural gas reserves are more likely to represent at least 80 years of consumption for the world at current rates. Not so bad when we recognize the yet-to-be-drilled natural gas reserves in the world will no doubt equal many times today's proven reserves. There is plenty of natural gas to step up natgas use globally in sufficient quantities to reduce the use of coal and oil and, by doing so, begin to clean up the planet, lower CO_2 emissions, and generally lower national security risks.

For the United States, I have even more confidence that the current EIA estimate of 238 Tcf of proven natgas reserves[15] will actually be about 50 percent of what is ultimately produced from those properties. I hold this view for three reasons:

1. My own historical experience with reserve estimates.
2. The NRC estimates for the six offshore fields turned out to be less than 50 percent of their ultimate production.
3. Nearly 50 percent of all producing wells in the United States are less than five years old, and the reality is that wells in their early years are significantly underestimated, often by at least 50 percent or much more.

So my bottom line is that U.S. proven reserves are much more likely to be over 400 Tcf than the 238 Tcf reported and generally accepted.

A major benefit for the future of natural gas as an energy solution to displace coal and oil is that it is a relative newcomer to the market. Comparatively little natural gas has yet been used or flared away. Unlike coal, mined and used in vast quantities for over 200 years with most of the "easy" coal long gone, and which has likely peaked in many of the world's mining areas, and unlike oil, produced in large quantities for over 100 years and which has also peaked in the majority of the producing regions of the world (and is in the process of peaking globally today), natgas has yet to hit its stride. Compared to the vast volumes of natural gas left for development in the world, only a small fraction has been found or used. With the exception of the United States, where the development of formerly unconventional, but now conventional, shale natural gas resources has only recently begun, the rest of the world is virgin territory for the development of these natgas supplies.

Earth's Vast Supplies of Undeveloped Natural Gas

Now let us look at the world's potential undeveloped natgas supplies. In 2000, the USGS estimated that 15,400 Tcf[16] was still in the ground, or about 150 years' natural gas supply at today's rate of consumption. This also means about 100 years' more natural gas if it successfully grows, as all indications show it will, to 150 percent of its current use, in the very near future, to displace large quantities of coal and oil.

Although this is a very important quantity for the world's natural gas consumers, it is overly conservative, for two reasons. First is the oil mind-set bias discussed previously. The second is that in the year 2000, when these estimates were made, the Middle East/Siberian size supplies of natural gas that can be developed from unconventional reservoirs in America's highly mature, declining oil provinces and several non-oil provinces such as Appalachia was not understood at all. These enormous new indicated supplies will no doubt cause the EIA and other energy-reporting institutions to begin working on new studies that, for the first time, will include the significance of the U.S. unconventional reservoirs. Natgas is just beginning to experience many of the breakthroughs necessary for unlocking the minds of estimators to the global potential for natural gas.

If my hypothesis that the world's largest natural gas supplies (not including ocean hydrates) are actually the unconventional supplies, not the conventional oil-related supplies, then a better estimate for the world's supplies still in the ground would be in the range of 30,000 to 40,000 Tcf, a supply that far exceeds the quantities of natural gas needed for it to become the principal bridge fuel to humanity's sustainable energy and climate future. And if natural gas hydrates become commercial, that estimate will double again. My bottom line is that the world has plenty of natural gas supplies to meet all its future requirements.

My 30,000 to 40,000 Tcf estimate of recoverable natural gas in the ground is partially confirmed by one of the world's largest and most globally knowledgeable oil and gas service companies, Schlumberger. Chris Hopkins, president of Schlumberger's Data and Consulting Services, looking toward the company's future, conducted an analysis of the world's potential for unconventional natural gas. This study concluded that about 30,000 Tcf of these natgas resources[17] remain to be developed. Chris made his presentation during the summer of 2007 at the annual meeting of the Aspen Institute's Program on Energy, which focused on natural gas for the first time since the program began in 1978, the only other year that also focused upon natgas. With the subsequently developed abundance of shale gas in the United States, I wouldn't be surprised if Chris increases his estimate in the near future.

That 1978 Aspen Institute Energy Forum was held during America's last energy crisis and the years of false fears of natural gas shortages. It was at this 1978 conference that I presented my forecast at the time that if natgas prices were deregulated and not priced by the Federal Energy Regulatory Commission at rates that kept it in the ground, U.S. supplies equaled about 1,500 to 2,000 Tcf.[18] As discussed, during those years of the oil industry mind-set, Exxon, Shell's M. King Hubbert, and Mobil Oil[19] all publicly asserted that the United States only had between 200 and 600 Tcf left in the ground. The United States was consuming about 20 Tcf per year, so they all forecast that in about 10 to less than 30 years America's natural gas would run dry. Since that 1978 conference, about 600 Tcf of natural gas has been produced in the United States.[20] According to Exxon, we should have run out of natural gas by now, but after producing this 600 Tcf, most official U.S. estimates are now in my 1978 range of 1,500 to 2,000 Tcf and once again the United States has a natural gas supply surplus.

Luckily for the United States and its natgas understanding, the old boys of the oil era are being left behind by America's new independent natural gas producers. Understanding of the significance of what used to be called unconventional natural gas and the reality of natural gas abundance is growing exponentially with each new discovery.

In the next year or two, most of America's long-standing natgas estimators, including the EIA, the USGS, and Potential Gas Committee, will certainly continue to increase their estimates for U.S. natural gas supplies, just as I have since my early presentations to Congress and the Aspen Institute in the 1970s. My 1993 article "New Thinking about Natural Gas," included in *The Future of Energy Gases,* a volume of papers produced by the U.S. Geological Survey on natgas origin and abundance that I recommend to all as a remarkable bible for the understanding of natural gas, stated my newly increased estimate for the United States of about 3,000 Tcf, as compared to my 1978 estimates of 1,500 to 2,000 Tcf. With the recent shale and other unconventional natural gas field development, I feel even more confident that 3,000 Tcf for the United States is a reasonable estimate.

To the Open Mind

The lead editor of that USGS volume was David Howell, a Ph.D. geologist who served in the USGS for many years. Among the many articles in the volume was also an article by the world-renowned scientist Thomas ("Tommy") Gold, who described his theories of nonbiological origin of natural gas and oil. My article referred to Tommy's nonbiological hypothesis because my own reality, derived from drilling deep onshore natural gas wells (experience I think most experts will agree is considerable), was that Gold's nonbiological theory explained much better many of the conditions we had actually encountered in drilling deep, high-pressure regions of Oklahoma than what I was taught at the university.

I remain open to the possibility that, unlike oil and coal, important quantities of the world's natural gas may not be of biological origin, just as is generally believed to be the case on so many planets in our solar system, where we know abundant natgas supplies also exist.

I tell the story of Howell's volume because the subsequent ramifications confirmed my own deep belief about the rigidity and limits of the oil mind-set. Before it was ever published, three of the original eight members of the editorial board resigned because Dave Howell refused their demands to eliminate from the volume the articles by Tommy Gold and myself, which were perceived by them to be almost blasphemous because of our views about the possibility of natural gas's nonbiological origin. That was only the beginning. After publication, large numbers of petroleum geologists and engineers raised such a fuss that several long-standing members of the AAPG circulated and collected signatures on a petition that was presented to the USGS that demanded the volume be removed from all public libraries and schools.

The old oil mind-set remains strong and limiting. The days of burning books or placing Galileo under house arrest are still around within segments of the oil industry. On the one hand, I know I tell this story at the risk of annoying many peers, and I recognize that this is only an anecdotal incident and certainly doesn't relate to everyone in the broad membership. On the other hand, it is my anecdote, and it dramatically indicates the power of words, thoughts, and education to limit the minds of men and women. In this century, the understanding of natural gas is rapidly changing. Natural gas, to paraphrase Wallace Pratt, is beginning to be found in the minds of men and women.

A Case That Earth's Attainable Natural Gas Supplies Are Equal to or Larger than Minable Coal Supplies

Because of the pervasive nature of natural gas in the universe, in our solar system, and on Earth, it is my hypothesis that commercially attainable natural gas resources on Earth may actually be larger than coal. The question the world's policy makers must ask is how much of the world's coal, oil, and natural gas resources are actually attainable by using in-hand technology at an economically reasonable price projected into the future. The concept of proven reserves takes into consideration technology, minability, and commerciality. By using BP's *Statistical Review of World Energy*, we see that proved coal reserves are 909 billion tons, or about 23,700 Tcf of natural gas equivalent. Proven world natural gas reserves are estimated at 6,400 Tcf.[21] However, the BP statistics are based on public data from the world's coal-producing nations, most of which were gathered more than 30 or 40 years ago, and recent investigations have shown that the "data quality is very unreliable."[22] For example, two recent European studies, "Coal: Resources and Future Production" (2007) by the Energy Watch Group (EWG)[23] and "The Future of Coal" (2007) prepared by the Institute for Energy (IFE) for the European Commission,[24] have called into question these decades-old reserve estimates. The EWG study indicates that Botswana,

Germany, and the U.K. "have downgraded their reserves by more than 90 percent" and that Poland's coal reserves are "50 percent smaller than was the case 20 years ago."[25] In 1990, even China cut its recoverable coal reserves to one sixth of its 1987 estimate.[26] The EWG study goes on to say that "these downgrades cannot be explained by volumes produced during this period. The best explanation is that nations now have better data from more thorough surveys."[27] The IFE study states that "world proven reserves (i.e., the reserves that are economically recoverable at current economic and operating conditions) of coal are decreasing fast" and that "coal might not be so abundant, widely available, and reliable as an energy source in the future." The IFE study concludes that "the world could run out of economically recoverable reserves of coal much earlier than widely anticipated."[28]

So when we take a critical look at the world's coal reserves, we find that they are based on sadly outdated, unreliable information generally collected in the 1970s, or possibly even decades earlier, and they do not reflect current mining safety or environmental regulations nor current economic conditions in many nations. These writedowns are only now beginning to be reported in national statistics and will no doubt continue in the future as more studies are initiated. As retired U.S. Geological Survey coal expert Harold Gluskoter said, "40 percent of the world's coal disappeared in three years"[29] of reporting.

It should trouble policy makers that most coal reserves have been established using methods and data from the 1970s or before, and that recent studies in Europe[30] and the United States[31] are significantly downsizing the reserve estimates of commercially minable coal. Although the BP statistics indicate 23,700 Tcf equivalent of proven coal reserves, over three times larger than the 6,400 Tcf of proven natural gas, a credible case can be made that proven natural gas is probably closer to twice what is reported, or over 12,000 Tcf equivalent (see "More Proven Natural Gas Than Is Estimated" earlier in chapter). When independent and standardized modern estimates of coal are completed, proven coal reserves could be no more than half of what is currently reported, or also about 12,000 Tcf.

When we recognize that the recent shale and other unconventional sources of natural gas supplies are not included in today's world estimates, and that estimated coal reserves are based on highly unreliable, outdated information, there is a reasonable probability that the world's proven natural gas reserves are about equal to proven minable coal reserves.

It is clear that there is an urgent need to update coal reserve estimates, as well as natural gas estimates that include today's unconventional reserves, so that policy makers can base their long-term decisions on reliable, modern data. If it hasn't already, the IEA should immediately commence such a study.

America's Attainable Natural Gas Supplies May Equal or Exceed Minable Coal Supplies

I realize that what I am about to say will create great controversy, but I also believe it is my responsibility—so here goes.

We have all heard the coal industry's oft-repeated boast that the United States is the "Saudi Arabia of coal." The idea that the United States has 250 years of coal supplies has been repeated so often that it has become almost a part of our culture and, unfortunately, gives policy makers what I believe to be excessive comfort. Until I recently began to dig deeper, I, too, was part of a public assuming nearly unlimited coal supplies. However, a 2007 report, "Coal: Research and Development to Support National Energy Policy," by the National Research Council of the National Academies,[32] originated by U.S. Senators Robert C. Byrd and Arlen Specter, reveals that this assertion is based on unreliable and outdated information that was collected in the early 1970s and before today's increasingly stringent mining safety and environmental regulations, which have rendered large amounts of what was formerly thought to be reserves either noncommercial or environmentally out-of-bounds.[33] The Council states, "It is *not possible* [my emphasis] to confirm the often-quoted assertion that there is a sufficient supply of coal for the next 250 years."[34] That 250 years has been based on approximately 267 billion tons of estimated recoverable reserves.

Because of the old age and poor quality of this essential data that the Council called "outdated, fragmentary or inaccurate,"[35] we must not base future policy upon these estimates until they are further confirmed. Indeed, in its attempt to spot-check these outdated estimates, the

Council reviewed "limited areas"[36] and warned that "only a *small fraction* [my emphasis] of previously estimated reserves are economically recoverable."[37] Therefore, it is likely that the ongoing USGS systematic inventory of the U.S. coal reserve base will significantly reduce available supplies. Indeed, in its first recent assessment of America's largest coal field around Gillette, Wyoming, which currently produces 38 percent of U.S. demand, the USGS reduced its estimate of the coal reserves by about 30 percent.[38]

In order to carefully assess the future of coal, we must understand the difference between coal resources and reserves. Resources are the quantities of coal that the mining industry think might be in the ground and are potentially minable. Because there is a lot of coal in the ground, the United States and the world has huge resources, but these quantities have no practical bearing on how much coal can be commercially mined. Rather, these quantities are similar to the enormous amounts of natural gas hydrates around the world that we know are there but are not yet technologically or economically attainable.

To understand the future of coal, we must carefully inspect the coal *reserves* defined as "the part of the coal resource that can be mined economically, at the present time, given existing environmental, legal, and technological constraints."[39] By applying these constraints and taking into consideration the Council's warning that only a "small fraction" of the previously indicated reserves may be commercial, the future of coal looks much less reliable than what is widely assumed.

In answering the question of whether the United States has reserves sufficient to meet the EIA's production estimates until 2030, the National Research Council says "definitely yes,"[40] citing about "19 billion tons of recoverable reserves at active mines,"[41] or about an 18-year supply. The Council goes on to say that this is augmented by another "60 billion tons of reserves held by private companies."[42] However, to assess these reserves in the near- and medium-term future, we must remember that to the extent the additional 60 billion tons are not located within existing mines, it will likely take from "7 to 15 years"[43] to plan, permit, and open a new large mine. Like all large infrastructure projects, costs are skyrocketing and times to completion are increasing dramatically.

The 19 billion tons, or 496 Tcf natural gas equivalent, of coal reserves that can be produced from active coal mines compares to U.S.

proven natural gas reserves of 238 Tcf.[44] However, two facts keep this from being a truly "apples to apples" comparison. First, it is my analysis that the SEC reporting regulations are more stringent for natural gas than coal. The SEC requires the annual natural gas engineer's reports to have at least 90 percent probability, which generally results in overly conservative calculations.[45] However, as a comparison, the "old and out-of-date"[46] coal data that continue to be used have been shown to be too large as a result of the spot checks reported on by the National Research Council and the recent 30 percent writedown by the USGS of the coal reserves around Gillette, Wyoming. Because the Gillette mines have been so important for America, producing about 38 percent of America's coal, my experience leads me to believe that the former estimates that predated the USGS writedown should have been the country's most detailed, up to date, and accurate. This calls into question the rest of the nation's remaining reserves.

The second difference arises from my 50 years of experience that estimates of proven natural gas reserves *in the early years* of production are generally less than 50 percent of ultimate production, as explained earlier in this chapter. Considering that nearly 50 percent of U.S. natural gas production is from wells that are less than five years old, a credible case can be made that a more realistic estimate of America's ultimate production from proven natural gas reserves would be in the range of 400 Tcf. If the USGS's comprehensive, ongoing study of coal reserves from active mines results in an across-the-board 30 percent writedown, proven coal reserves will be the equivalent of about 350 Tcf (19 billion tons of "recoverable reserves at active mines,"[47] or 496 Tcf equivalent times 70 percent, which equals about 350 Tcf), as compared to U.S. proven natural gas reserves that I estimate to be near 400 Tcf. U.S. proven natural gas reserves may well be larger than its proven minable coal reserves.

The coal industry argues that there are an additional 60 billion tons, or 1,566 Tcf equivalent of reserves, "held by private companies"[48] that must be included. I accept the position, but in order to have an apples-to-apples comparison, I believe that much of this 60 billion tons (1,566 Tcf) of coal not attached to "active mines" should be compared to the natgas supplies that are not from producing natgas wells or their immediate offsets and, therefore, are generally comparable to an important portion of the estimates of undeveloped natgas supplies as estimated by the Potential Gas Committee, USGS, EIA, and Navigant. These supplies, which are beyond the limited area of producing natgas fields, are estimated to be from about 1,300 to 2,000 Tcf. Based on the premise that coal reserves that are not assigned to active mines, sometimes called "unassigned," are not further reduced by the forthcoming USGS work, then their 60 billion tons, 1,566 Tcf equivalent, may be generally compared to the recent natgas estimates of about from about 1,500 Tcf to over 2,200 Tcf[49] by independent estimators and about 2,800 Tcf by my own work. The difficulty here is attempting to achieve a realistic comparison. I recommend that the USGS try to do this as soon as its new coal assessment is completed.

Once again, when we look beyond the coal industry's rhetoric of abundance, there is a good case to be made that for the mid- and long-term future, natural gas and coal may be about equal. Although they may be about equal now, there is no question that the trend for coal reserves estimates in the United States and around the world is down and that natural gas reserve estimates are being increased rapidly.

When the Council looked further into coal's future, the situation became much less clear. The Council states that "there is *probably* [my emphasis] sufficient coal to meet the nation's need for more than 100 years at current rates of consumption."[50] In the big picture, this may be the most realistic comparison between coal and natural gas supplies. If we do the math, this forecast approximately equates the Council's coal projections of a 100-year supply with the 2008 Navigant, Inc. estimate that also indicates a 100-year supply of natural gas. So 100 years of coal consumption is about 110 billion tons, or about 2,870 Tcf equivalent of natural gas. This 2,870 Tcf coal equivalent compares to Navigant's 2,247 Tcf and my personal estimate of 3,000 Tcf.[51]

Once again, based on the most recent information and evidence, there is an equal or slightly larger quantity of attainable natural gas than there is coal.

The point of this exercise is to initiate an important debate about America's energy future by calling attention to the reality of natural gas abundance in the United States, and by calling into question the widely held assumption, thought to be a fact by many policy makers, that coal is so abundant that we don't have to worry about basing long-term policy on this presumption.

The reality is that enormous quantities of coal have been mined in the United States, especially over the past 100 years, and most of the best and easiest coal is gone. Many recent safety and environmental regulations have eliminated lots of coal from the possibility of ever being mined. For the last 30 years, national policy has been based on the understanding that we don't have to worry about coal supplies because America is the "Saudi Arabia of coal" and, therefore, it has almost been presumed that it is our *obligation* to figure out how to use coal for America's future. As a result, large quantities of the U.S. taxpayer's money has gone for development programs for the use of coal (\$538 million in 2005[52]) and tragically little has been expended to understand natural gas and its technology and future.

Based on the information I have just recited, it seems logical to me that our research for carbon capture and sequestration (CCS) should also be undertaken in conjunction with natural gas generation that produces 50 percent of the CO_2 as the same-size coal-generation facility. And because natural gas contains little of coal's other non-CO_2 emissions and virtually none of its toxic wastes, a natural gas power plant with CCS will be just about as green as wind and solar.

Natgas Ascends; Coal Declines

Looking to the future, we recognize that because most of the nation's highest-quality coal has already been mined, our future coal reserves will be of lower quality. Indeed, in terms of energy content, one analyst says U.S. coal production peaked in 1998[53] and may continue down. This reduction in energy content has been more than compensated for by Wyoming's lower-grade subbituminous coal; so to maintain the energy produced by coal today we will need to continue to increase the volumes of coal used. Larger volumes of lower-quality coal will increase the CO_2 that will be produced from coal electric generation, resulting in the need for ever-increasing carbon capture and still larger quantities of CO_2 sequestration.

To drive this point home, I will quote the National Research Council:

> Almost certainly, coals mined in the future will be lower quality because current mining practices result in higher-quality coal being mined first, leaving behind lower-quality material (e.g., with higher ash yield, higher sulfur, and/or higher concentrations of potentially harmful elements). The consequences of relying on poorer-quality coal for the future include (1) higher mining costs (e.g., the need for increased tonnage to generate an equivalent amount of energy, greater abrasion of mining equipment); (2) transportation challenges (e.g., the need to transport increased tonnage for an equivalent amount of energy); (3) beneficiation challenges (e.g., the need to reduce ash yield to acceptable levels, the creation of more waste); (4) pollution control challenges (e.g., capturing higher concentrations of particulates, sulfur, and trace elements; dealing with increased waste disposal); and (5) environmental and health challenges.[54]

None of this is true for natural gas. Indeed, because of the ongoing increases in turbine efficiency, we can confidently project increased efficiencies for natgas-generated electricity that will lower CO_2 emissions per megawatt produced.

In conclusion, to have a bit of fun during the deadly serious debate over America's future energy and climate policy, let me say that when I presented my natural gas estimates at a prestigious energy and climate roundtable held during the Democratic National Convention, Fred Palmer, senior vice president of Peabody Energy and a member of the executive committee of the National Coal Council, called my natural gas estimates "wildly optimistic." In view of the most recent assessment of coal reserves that I have laid out here, I believe Fred's "wildly optimistic" remark might better be applied to the coal industry's boast that America is the "Saudi Arabia of coal." What is obvious is that it is extremely urgent that studies be conducted to validate both coal and natural gas reserve and resource estimates in time to formulate and pass long-term energy policies for America's energy future.

A Call for More Natural Gas Education

To sum up, oil is either at or fast approaching its peak ability to meet future demand, and there are indications that coal may also be on the way to its own limits. Yet, development of the world's vastly abundant natgas supplies has only recently begun to accelerate. This acceleration is principally due to the overdue recognition of the abundance of natural gas and the fact that in many countries, the price of natgas, for the first time in the history of its use, had recently began to rise to levels sufficient to bring forth new private-sector capital budgets focused on natural gas exploration and production. As a result, the days of the mistaken perception of peak natural gas are rapidly fading away and will continue to be replaced by a new natgas mind-set of abundance. We will see evidence of this change of mind-set as forthcoming publications are presented by the various institutes charged with presenting natgas supply estimates. Most important, after nine years of generally flat production, the recent breakout of growth in the United States is a positive indicator of a new natural gas paradigm.

From now on, natural gas will continue to come to the forefront and break through the many historical barriers of its association with oil, becoming known as the number one clean alternative fuel to help solve the world's energy and climate problems in the near and medium term. Natural gas is truly the bridge fuel to civilization's sustainable future.

I believe that in order for civilization to meet its natural need for growth, continually increasing quantities of energy will be required and that natural gas abundance will provide the bridge to meet that growth, along with the rest of the sustainable, virtually unlimited fuels of the Age of Energy Gases.

Much of the evidence for natural gas abundance I have expressed is based on a large accumulation of personal experiences within the natural gas exploration and production industry, as well as anecdotal evidence, yet, as sound as I believe the experiential evidence to be, I recognize that it is not the equivalent of hard academic and scientific evidence.

Vastly more academic studies and field reality checks are needed to produce more scientific evidence. So I recommend that the world's governments immediately allocate more funds for natgas research and development, which has always been a low priority. In 2000, my alma mater, the University of Oklahoma, took a stride forward and developed its first program for a master's degree in natural gas engineering. I encourage universities around the world to originate in-depth programs focused on natural gas, and I encourage all students interested in science, energy, and changing the world for the better to enroll.

As a lifelong worker in the natural gas field, one whose estimates have proven more accurate than most of the world's natural gas forecasters over the last 30 years, I respectfully submit that the entire field of natgas science and studies stands about where we were in the 1980s with climate science. Then, evidence clearly pointed toward the belief that human CO_2 emissions were driving global temperatures upward, but we needed hard scientific evidence. It is equally important that we advance natural gas studies—just as we did climate studies that are now more grounded in scientific evidence—so natural gas resources can gain the widespread scientific credibility necessary to serve as the basis of policy decisions for the resolution of civilization's energy problems.

A Plea to the World's Journalists

This chapter closes with a plea to the world's journalists. As you know better than anyone, words are powerful and leave lasting impressions. In this critical period that demands enlightened action on energy and climate policy, there is great confusion in contemporary energy vernacular, as sketched in this presentation on natural gas abundance. One of the most dangerous terms used is *fossil fuels* as a catchall for coal and "oil and gas."

This presents a real problem. "Fossil fuels" lump natural gas—one of our twenty-first-century energy solutions—with the two largest energy problems, coal and oil. By repeatedly reading and hearing those words, the public and policy makers are bombarded by a highly negative connotation that rings true for coal and oil, but that could not be further from the truth for natural gas.

First, there is a reasonable probability that significant quantities of natural gas may not be biological but rather an outgassing from the mantle and, therefore, not "fossil" at all. Certainly all the natural gas from garbage and refuse dumps is not fossil in origin. If the Earth's deep hot biosphere turns out to contain more microbes that produce natgas than we know, then these quantities of natgas should actually be considered *renewable*.

There is little question that coal and oil are fossil, nonrenewable, and represent the majority of the world's energy problem. But, there remains an open question about how much natural gas is of fossil origin and how much may not be. No matter the origin of natural gas, there is no question that it is globally abundant and will become an increasingly important part of the world's energy solution. We must not mix *problems* with *solutions*.

Journalists of the world: Please stop using the term *fossil fuels*. Rather, call each fuel by its name: coal, oil, or natural gas. By doing so you will serve your audience well and help the world sort through its civilization-threatening energy and climate problems. Coal and oil must rapidly become our energy past, but natural gas is truly a critical part of our energy future. This book's Glossary is recommended reading for journalists, policy makers, and the public.

Chapter 8

My Historical Grounds for Natural Gas Abundance

My high school experience with Dr. Ray Alf was formative, but my involvement in the energy industry was perhaps foreordained. I grew up around oil wells operated by my grandfather's and father's company. My predominant childhood memory of a typical oil field was of grimy surface facilities, old tanks, cracked and barren ground laid waste by oil and saltwater spills, and old oil pumps that were continually breaking down and being repaired. Oil was smelly and dirty. The industry was volatile, with a boom–and–bust rhythm that was often difficult to withstand.

Studying petroleum geology at the University of Oklahoma (OU) in the 1950s, it is perhaps not surprising that I gravitated away from oil and toward natural gas. It seemed better in every way—a powerful, clean, and even more versatile fuel, but without oil's drawbacks. It does not carry a strong smell like crude oil does (the aroma consumers detect today is added for safety, like a perfume). It does not have to be pumped from the Earth, resisting all the way, as oil does. Indeed, if natgas is "spilled," it just floats up into the air rather than staining the Earth.

The entire Earth and all the oceans have leaked enormous quantities of natural gas continuously over millions of years of geologic time. Even though it is a greenhouse gas, it only lingers in the atmosphere for about 9 to 15 years,[1] as compared to CO_2 emissions that stay in the atmosphere for a century.[2] At the time of my schooling, natgas was not a distinct field of study. Following the economic reality of the day, academia focused mainly on oil. Prevailing wisdom was that natgas had little value and was a mere by-product. Still, I learned a great deal of basic geology, physics, and chemistry that later enabled me to challenge a lot of accepted truths.

After college, I worked briefly at Phillips Petroleum. The company had put together a superb training program in which we worked at actual jobs in all phases of the industry by day and went to school at night. Our training manuals covered each sector of the business. I worked on regional geology and seismic studies within the Mid-Continent. Later, I learned to be a scout. In those days, scouts were supposed to keep up with what everybody else was doing and get hold of information behind the scenes, so that nothing went on that our company did not know about.

In northwest Kansas, I spent a hot summer among vast fields of sunflowers working on a Phillips-owned seismic crew. In Denver, I worked in the geological research department for Dr. Orlo Childs, a brilliant geologist with Ph.D.'s in both geology and English and who went on to become the president of the prestigious Colorado School of Mines. My last post was in Bartlesville, Phillips Petroleum's corporate headquarters, in the economic analysis section, where we looked at the economics of each and every project. It was there that I learned a lasting and fundamental lesson: Natural gas had little or no economic importance to the oil industry and was often considered a nuisance.

Phillips was a great learning experience that gave me a broad knowledge of the oil industry and, particularly, how little regard it had for natgas. Next, I went to work for The Hefner Company—my father's and grandfather's oil business. But I found I was fascinated with natural gas, and they were not. So in 1959, I started out on my own to pursue my natural gas dream.

How the "#1 Green" Became a Historic Landmark in the Natural Gas Industry

I cofounded the GHK Company, an independent Oklahoma City–based natural gas exploration and production company, in 1959, with partners Laurence Glover, a financier, and David Kennedy, a New York floor tile manufacturer. Natgas prices were regulated at the time, which seriously restricted the industry. Even though the resource base was ample, supplies were declining in the United States because no one could make money producing it at such low prices. Ironically, demand was skyrocketing because natural gas was government-controlled at unrealistically low prices, in addition to being clean and efficient, so its use was growing rapidly. I was a young man without much drilling experience, but deep down, based on my education as a geologist and on my gut instincts that there was more to the world than what we knew, our company persisted in deep natgas exploration, where I believed reserves from individual wells might be large enough that a profit could be made at the low, controlled prices of the day. We drilled many deep world-record wildcat wells while always struggling to make the company's payroll.

Oklahoma and neighboring states had vast sedimentary geological basins. One that fascinated me was the Anadarko, which contained sedimentary rocks as deep as 40,000 to 60,000 feet. Around the shallow flanks of the basin, giant natural gas deposits and some oil accumulations had been found. I had been taught in college that the depth of those basins really did not make much difference for oil exploration, because below about 15,000 feet the weight of the overlying rocks would be so heavy as to crush or compact the rocks to the point there would be no remaining pore space. Therefore, the accepted thinking was that there could not be any "reservoir" rocks that held oil or gas deposits in commercial quantities below such a depth. Yet my gut instinct said that large natgas accumulations could actually exist in the deep regions of the world's geological basins, particularly in the Anadarko Basin.

After years of struggle to find partners to put up the money, I finally convinced Northern Illinois Gas, Amerada Petroleum Company, and Sun Oil Company to join us in a venture to drill a structure in the deepest regions of the Anadarko Basin, searching for natural gas at depths below 20,000 feet. Our efforts began to pay off in the spring of 1969, when we completed drilling a deep well in the Anadarko near Elk City, Oklahoma, where GHK had around 200,000 acres of leased mineral rights. We called it the "#1 Green." Although a prescient name today, the well was actually named after the man who owned the farm where we drilled.

After about a year of drilling, overcoming many problems and once redrilling several thousand feet of hole, we reached a total depth of 24,453 feet. From logging devices and measurements of gas in the drilling mud, and pressures encountered while drilling, we correctly felt we were going to have a large natural gas well. Indeed, we believed it was one of the country's great energy discoveries, proving that contrary to what I had learned in school, there was commercial natgas and the potential for large supplies at great depths.

Discovering the well was only half the battle. Next, we had to run a very long string of pipe all the way to the bottom of this deep hole in the ground. This was a significant technical challenge: There was a lack of high-quality tubular steel that could withstand the high-pressure temperature and depth.

For the #1 Green we had decided on the German company Mannesmann Tube, which then had a steel mill at Sault St. Marie in Canada. It rolled the entire 25,000 feet of 5 and 1/2 inch diameter pipe in one special, continuous two-day rolling, promising that it would have the highest quality control in the world because it knew we wanted to run the pipe to the deepest levels in history. After the run, the pipe was thoroughly tested and loaded onto a special ship that was able to make it through the St. Lawrence Seaway, all the way around Florida into the Gulf, up the Mississippi into what was the then-new Port of Catoosa, which Oklahoma's U.S. Senator Robert Kerr had worked with the federal government to create on the Arkansas River, connected by locks to the Mississippi. Our shipment of tubular steel pipes preceded the official opening and was the first commercial business at the new port. There we offloaded the 550-plus joints of pipe onto 14 or 15 trucks.

The pipe was then transported 235 miles to western Oklahoma, just south of the town of Elk City, where the #1 Green was located.

I was there to watch the process, which I knew would go on for about 36 hours. After about half the pipe had been run in the hole, I went up on the derrick floor to watch. I knew that because of the great weight of the pipe, the situation would get very tricky, and if we had a failure it would probably be from that point on. I was also afraid that something would happen in the deep hole and we wouldn't even be able to get the pipe to total depth. If that had occurred, all would have been lost, because it would be unlikely that we could get back to 21,600 and below, where we knew the zones existed that we wanted to produce. We kept going, joint by joint by joint.

Mannesmann's lead engineer, in typical precise German manner, stood on the derrick floor among all the roughnecks who were covered in mud and drilling fluid, swinging the chains around the pipe and connecting the automatic tongs or huge wrenches that are used to make up each joint. As the final turns on each joint of pipe were made, the German engineer would put his fingers on the joint, holding it like a musical instrument so he could feel that it had *just the right amount of tension*. When we hit 24,147 feet, we had all the plumbing in place for a producing natgas well—indeed, it is still producing today, and that string of pipe still holds the world record.

The #1 Green broke virtually every technological record of its time. It was by far the highest-pressure well ever drilled in the world and the second deepest. Cameron Iron Works specially built the largest and highest-pressured gas wellhead ever constructed to contain the highest pressured gas well in the world (15,130 pounds per square inch at the surface). Because we had encountered such a high world-record pressure, there was no pressure gauge in the world to measure it. Luckily, one of our partner companies, Amerada, had a research and development facility in Tulsa that worked with high-pressure natural gas. It constructed the first-ever 20,000-psi gauge. I will never forget installing that gauge and watching the dial climb to 5,000, then 10,000, and finally to just over 15,000 psi, wondering if it would indeed hold such pressure. I watched, knowing that any small leak would rapidly break up the gauge and could easily cause many times the damage of firing off a large-caliber armor-piercing weapon.

We prevailed, but our discovery brought other problems. "Oil and gas experts" called the accomplishment a freak of nature and claimed that the new well was of "high pressure, low volume." The maximum amount of reserves engineers would assign was an exceedingly small 2.3 billion cubic feet (Bcf). Typical of the very large underestimates of natural gas reserves that continue to prevail even today, the well has subsequently produced about 21 Bcf and continues to produce, so it will eventually produce ten times the original estimate. From the start, I had an uphill battle convincing people of the potential energy supplies of this deep well and others like it—and at the time, without the evidence of actual production, that eventually bore out over the years.

To make matters worse, the regulated price of natural gas was about 17 cents per thousand cubic feet around that time, as set by the Federal Power Commission (FPC).[3] To get around the low wellhead price, we tried to bring in a gas turbine engine to generate electricity on the spot and sell it to the local electric grid, but electricity regulations did not permit "independent generators" to sell to the grid—a continuing problem across America.

Although the well was a geological and technological success, the regulated low price guaranteed it would be an economic failure. In that business environment, we could not afford to drill more wells to develop the field, so I tried to persuade regulators to make an exception for deep natgas production.

Working to Overcome America's Regulatory Pricing System That Kept Natural Gas in the Ground

On August 13, 1970, I went to Denver, Colorado, to testify at a Federal Power Commission (FPC) hearing about area prices for natural gas. A few years later, out of frustration with continuing low prices, I traveled to Washington, D.C., to meet with FPC Commissioner Lawrence J. O'Connor Jr., who listened politely and then told me in no uncertain terms that the Federal Power Commission wasn't going to make exceptions for deep wells. I thanked him for his time and got up to leave, when he added, "All you can do about your problem is convince Congress to deregulate natural gas." Later, I set out to do just that.

Deep drilling was expensive, and such regulation severely limited the extent to which exploring for and producing deep natural gas could pay off. The average depth of a natgas well in the area at that time was less than 3,000 feet and cost about $100,000 to drill. However, as I later testified to Congress, the "costs of developing gas are high in the Deep Anadarko Basin, as evidenced by the GHK #1 Green, which cost $4.5 million for drilling and completion alone." I requested that the FPC raise the price ceiling for natural gas, advising them that to bring this natgas to the market "demands initial prices in the Deep Anadarko Basin of 30 to 35 cents per thousand cubic feet (Mcf) at the wellhead [which equals $1.60 to $1.87 per Mcf, adjusted for inflation in 2007]. Initial prices in this range will bring forth the multibillion-dollar expenditures necessary to bring to the marketplace from 3 to 4 billion cubic feet of new flowing gas per day."[4]

Although we were certainly out to make a profit, we deeply believed that higher natural gas prices sufficient to bring our deep gas to market would be important for America. Deep natgas held great potential for the U.S. economy. I knew the United States could meet rising demand with innovations like ours and new reserves, but only if prices would rise to levels that allowed a profit for these high-risk and high-cost deep wells. Tapping new domestic natural gas resources could decrease our dependence on the foreign oil that was already hurting the economy, as became evident in the oil shocks of 1973. Furthermore, the search for profits drives innovation and plays a key role in economic growth—and it certainly played a key role in what we did in the Anadarko Basin. We worked with research departments of the industry's best service companies, researchers, technicians, and engineers to develop new technology to create what we needed to drill successfully to deep levels and bring to market these undeveloped resources. Much of the technology we developed then was the foundation for today's deep natural gas exploration.

The 1973 Arab oil embargo drove oil prices up and, for the first time, shook America's complacent reliance on Middle East oil. The federal government response was to further distort the market with price controls, which had the unintended effect of further reducing the amount of U.S. oil that was being explored and increased our imports. For the first time since World War II, the public worried about gasoline shortages, and so many drivers filled their tanks that shortages became so severe that drivers spent hours in the infamous long lines at gas stations trying to fill up. Those were the good old days when net U.S. foreign oil imports only equaled about 20 percent of U.S petroleum consumption, as compared with about 65 percent today.[5]

Going to Washington to Tell My Natural Gas Story

In 1976, I organized a group called Independent Oil & Gas Producers for Carter, to support Jimmy Carter. Working with then-Governor David Boren of Oklahoma, we were able to get Jimmy Carter's written pledge to "deregulate all newly discovered natural gas." I had realized that the only way I could change the economics for the #1 Green— or for any other deep wells, or for the future—would be to convince Congress to pass legislation to deregulate natural gas.

Because of the low federally regulated interstate price controls, flows of natgas across state lines were rapidly declining. And because the natgas prices within producing states had been rapidly rising, supplies could easily meet the *intrastate* demand while companies didn't have a market incentive to sell *interstate* because that price was capped. These market distortions created the perception that natural gas supplies in the United States were low—a misconception reinforced by many oil and coal companies. The most widely repeated saying of the day by the Carter administration was John O'Leary's famous quote, "Natural gas has had it."

By 1977, I had had enough. I moved to Washington, D.C., to be in the midst of the fight and lobby for the deregulation of natural gas. President Carter resolved that his new energy plan would be a cornerstone of his first 100 days in office and declared that solving the nation's energy problems was "the moral equivalent of war." My colleagues and I from GHK felt like David up against the Goliath oil companies, because oil companies produced much of the nation's natural gas, and there was no group before we arrived really advocating for the sake of natural gas's future in America. To tell the truth, when we first began to lobby, there were only two of us: myself and Robert Belfer, whose family company owned and operated one of the larger natural gas fields in Wyoming.

Taking on the American Gas Association

At the time, most people thought the American Gas Association (AGA) lobbied for the natural gas industry, but in reality the AGA was the lobbying group for the natural gas *distribution* industry, which was controlled by the distribution utilities and therefore lobbied for the interests of the natural gas utilities, including many gas and electric companies—not producers. I asked the president of the organization, Bud Lawrence, who later became a great friend, how we could work together. The problem was that the AGA did not have the interests of people like me—an independent natgas producer—at heart, particularly when natural gas went head to head with coal companies because so many AGA-member gas and electric utilities also relied on coal-generated electricity.

One day, the AGA released a widely publicized report on the future of the nation's natural gas supplies, which included optimistic, moderate, and conservative scenarios. I immediately looked at the "optimistic" scenario, and it seemed totally pessimistic to me. I called Bud and asked if I could come by and see the economists who had done the studies. I will never forget meeting with the two economists. I asked for the basis of the study, and they laid out what at first blush seemed to be a sensible methodology. They had looked at the history of the industry and gone back to the period in the United States during which the largest quantities of natural gas had ever been discovered. They then divided the total amount of gas discovered by the number of gas wells actually drilled that year to compute the natural gas discovered per well drilled. The economists then used the highest amount of natgas per well and multiplied by their most optimistic prediction for the number of wells that might be drilled by industry after deregulation.

Although on the face of it this may sound reasonable, I felt compelled to ask what years the most natgas had been discovered in the United States. They said that was in the 1950s, about the time I had been at Phillips working on economic analyses. I knew that oil companies in those years placed very little, if any, value on natural gas. So I asked the economists if they had considered the fact that in those years oil companies placed no value on natural gas and were drilling exclusively in areas and at depths where they thought oil would be found. This relationship meant that their study was only predicting how much natural gas might be found when oil people drilled for oil, and it had absolutely nothing to do with America's potential natgas supplies. The economists' thinking was representative of the shallow understanding of natural gas at the time that, unfortunately, too often persists today. The focus was about oil and oil statistics, not relative for forecasting America's future natgas supplies.

Political Infighting over Natural Gas

Because the oil companies had sold Congress and the Carter administration their oil-related beliefs that we were running out of natural gas, those opposed to natgas deregulation argued that if it were deregulated, supplies would not increase as necessary to keep up with demand, and the only real change would be that consumer prices would explode. All of the official government natural gas price estimates for the future pointed to the sky. As Gordon Zareski said during our 1977 appearance before the House Subcommittee on Energy & Power, ". . . we cannot expect price increases to provide the solution to declining gas production." He stated, "I do not think gas priced at a BTU equivalent of oil would bring forth substantial quantities of new supplies."[6] Today, the reality shows us that all of this was as wrong as the idea that "natural gas has had it." To this day, on a BTU equivalent to oil, natgas costs only about half as much as oil, and new natural gas supplies continue to surge ahead to meet demand. Only during brief periods, such as Hurricane Katrina, has natural gas attained the BTU equivalent of oil. In early spring 2009, natural gas was trading in the range of 50 percent of the equivalent of oil.

Battles in Washington were not just educating legislators on natural gas. We also had to adapt and maneuver with political reality. My first official policy recommendation was that only "new" natural gas be deregulated. Although the oil industry reacted to this idea with great animosity (a press conference was actually called to denounce me and the idea that only new natural gas should be deregulated), the idea was embraced by Senator Gary Hart and Congressman Tim Wirth, both of Colorado. Although they made a heroic effort to pass new gas deregulation legislation, it failed by one vote in the Senate; I then proposed "deep" natgas be deregulated, so that at least some natural gas could earn a fair price and the nation's shortages might be alleviated by the development of America's vast, deep supplies.

Meeting with the First Secretary of Energy, James R. Schlesinger

To make my point about deep gas to one of the most important players in the natural gas deregulation battle, I had requested a personal meeting with President Carter's Secretary of Energy, James Schlesinger. I knew that all the oil guys had made their pitch, and I was eager to tell our natural gas story. One day I learned that the secretary was actually going to give me an audience. The meeting was scheduled and set to be held in the secretary's office, which was then located in the old Executive Office Building. When we walked in, I was reminded of a professor's office at any college. Maybe that was about right, because Secretary Schlesinger had his professorial pipe and fit the part of the academic he was.

I had prepared as carefully as I had for the congressional hearings to make the case for the immediate deregulation of all deep gas and the importance of a process to deregulate all new gas. I told Secretary Schlesinger the entire #1 Green story about how vast quantities of deep natural gas were locked in the ground by price regulations at the very time the nation needed new natural gas supplies. Jim, who has become a good personal friend over the subsequent years, got it right away. He interrupted my story to say, "You independent producers won't take 'yes' for an answer." It took a couple of minutes before I "got it," and understood that he was telling me that the administration could possibly deregulate deep gas by administrative emergency order. However, he was right about not taking yes for an answer, because we worried that an administrative order could be set aside as easily as it could be created.

I went on to make the pitch for legislation that would set in motion the process to deregulate all new gas, adding that one of the compromises could be the immediate price deregulation of deep natural gas, or gas produced below 15,000 feet. Jim countered that argument, probably convinced by big oil that America's natural gas supplies were running out, with his belief that if you only deregulate a small slice of the nation's natural gas, "You will release macroeconomic forces upon a microeconomy that will only create hyperinflation."

Jim was absolutely right. Deep gas was immediately deregulated as part of Carter's omnibus energy legislation, and the macroeconomic forces of unmet national demand for natural gas and enormous flows of capital were unleashed upon the microeconomy of deep drilling within the few states with deep possibilities. The 1979 to 1982 hyperinflationary boom was on. Prices for deep natural gas skyrocketed. The cost of natural gas and oil leases, drilling rigs, services, and labor went straight up. Demand for labor was so high and the wages so good that so many out-of-work laborers flowed into Oklahoma from around the country that a "tent city" went up in Elk City, Oklahoma, the center of our deep drilling activities.

But what Jim didn't anticipate, because of the oil companies' natural gas pessimism, was the size and speed of the natural gas supply response. By 1982, natural gas had met all the pent-up demand, and the bubble burst. Prices plummeted, ushering in the bust that lasted until about a decade ago.

The Great Energy War

The natgas price decontrol issues became the most contentious of Carter's goals, as many in Congress found the administration's projections of skyrocketing natural gas price increases for consumers intolerable. John Dingell of the House Committee on Energy and Commerce flatly stated that natural gas would only be deregulated "over my dead body." The administration and various legislators went through cycles of proposing and rejecting schemes to keep the price ceilings on oil

and natural gas the same, raise them slowly over many years, or eliminate them entirely and immediately. After years of intense lobbying and
one of the most emotional, contentious, and complex policy battles in
America's history and many heroic acts of persuasion, on November 9,
1978, Congress and the Carter administration passed the Natural Gas
Policy Act.

The key Senate confrontation was so intense and controversial
that the leaders called for continuing debate before the final vote. Cots
were brought into the Senate anteroom. It was 2 A.M. when I watched
Senator Barry Goldwater come into the Senate chamber in his pajamas
to cast the deciding vote. The Act provided for an extremely compli-
cated system of natural gas deregulation over several years, as well as
immediate deregulation of natgas produced below 15,000 feet. Separate
inter- and intrastate pricing was eliminated.[7] Today, when I look at the
photograph and official pen given to me by President Carter from his
signing of the legislation, I am reminded of America's greatness. If you
work hard and follow what you believe in, the American system allows
each of us to make a difference. This is precisely what all of us must do
today to resolve America's and the world's great energy and environmental problems.

Also in 1978, the fears created by the oil companies and their allies,
the coal interests, that natural gas was an unreliable fuel for America's
future carried the day, so part of the omnibus energy legislation, the
Fuel Use Act, prohibited natural gas in power generation and new
industrial facilities, its then-fastest growing markets. Natural gas was
no longer America's "fuel of choice." America's home builders went to
all-electric homes. And, instead of natural gas, we could rely on coal
and put up with its pollution and CO_2 emissions because, after all, as
the coal interests always boasted, America was the Saudi Arabia of coal
reserves. As a result, coal usage grew rapidly, and 79,000 megawatts of
new coal generation went on line over the next decade.[8] A terrible,
unintended consequence was that today we are paying the environmental costs that may well continue for decades more. When the bill was
signed, about 90 percent of Oklahoma's electricity was natgas-generated.
Today, 50 percent of Oklahoma's electricity comes from dirty coal.
Oklahomans, like Americans in many other states, will have to live with
those old, polluting plants that are producing so much unnecessary

pollution and CO_2 emissions for another 20 to 30 years. Moreover, the approximate 100,000 megawatts of new coal-fired generation that the United States added after the Fuel Use Act released some 15 billion metric tons of CO_2 to our atmosphere[9] which will remain for a century. Had natural gas been used instead, we would have 7.5 billion metric tons less CO_2 in the atmosphere today.

Although it was too late for the Carter energy legislation, we subsequently began to prove that the oil companies did not understand America's abundance of natural gas. The #1 Green well eventually produced at a rate of over 19 million cubic feet of gas per day and at the initial production rate on an annual basis was capable of producing an amount of energy equivalent to two-thirds the energy produced by a nuclear plant at that time; 300 such superwells could have provided the annual energy requirements, including home heating, electric, and industrial needs for the city of Chicago at that time.[10]

With deep natural gas deregulation in place, more wells like the Green could finally be drilled profitably. GHK and other companies soon discovered more than 20 superwells, each of which produced the energy equivalent of over 1 million barrels of oil per year, or about 2,750 barrels of oil per day. That compares with the average non-U.S. oil well production of 185 barrels of oil per day, U.S. average of 10 barrels of oil per day, and a world average per well of 85 barrels of oil per day.[11]

The deep natgas boom had been unleashed. By 1982, supplies in the United States had become so abundant that the price of deregulated natgas collapsed, which led to over 20 years of supplies in excess of demand, unrealistically low prices, the decommissioning or shipping abroad of drilling rigs and other service equipment, and the loss of 500,000 jobs from 1982 through 2000.[12] The upstream U.S. natgas industry was left in shambles and, with it, much of Mid-Continent America's banking system. Coal had won the first battle, but the war will begin again in 2009 with the Obama administration. This time, we must all work to ensure that the GET will win the war.

Chapter 9

The *Real* Inconvenient Truth

We have met the enemy and he is us.

—Pogo

Al Gore's *An Inconvenient Truth* was a wake-up call to all of us living on Spaceship Earth. His tireless and highly regarded public campaign to inform all of us that we have met the enemy and he is us earned a well-deserved Nobel Prize. The inconvenient truth is that CO_2 emissions have set civilization on a course toward intolerable, multiple catastrophic climate disasters.

The continued use of coal and oil, at their current levels, has created intolerable global economic risks, as well as intolerable distortions and geostrategic and security risks. These rapidly rising risks are what I call the *three intolerables*.

The first is the looming catastrophic risks and enormous future costs of global climate change. The next is the accelerating economic imbalances and their potential of risks for larger and larger global economic contractions. There is little question that the enormous transfer of wealth to oil-producing nations and its recycling through the global banking system helped fuel our 2008 financial and credit disaster. And the last is the continually growing potential for insoluble global geostrategic tensions that may lead to larger oil wars or even the remote

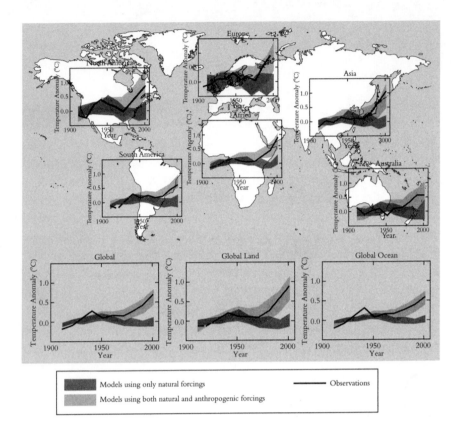

Comparison of observed continental- and global-scale changes in surface temperature with results simulated by climate models using either natural or both natural and anthropogenic forcings. Decadal averages of observations are shown for the period 1906–2005 (black line) plotted against the center of the decade and relative to the corresponding average for the period 1901–1950. Lines are dashed where spatial coverage is less than 50 percent. Thick dark gray bands show the 5 to 95 percent range for 19 simulations from five climate models using only the natural forcings due to solar activity and volcanoes. Thick light gray bands show the 5 to 95 percent range for 58 simulations from 14 climate models using both natural and anthropogenic forcings.

Exhibit 9.1   Global and Continental Temperature Change
Source: "Climate Change 2007: The Physical Science Basis." Working Group I Contribution to the Fourth Assessment Report of the Intergovernmental Panel on Climate Change. Figure SPM.4. Cambridge University Press. For more information on the IPCC copyright policy, please see http://www.ipcc.ch/copyright.htm.

possibility of coal wars. Life on Earth is not sustainable unless humanity embraces great and rapid energy changes to avoid or contain these risks. In the coming decades, energy will either tear us apart or bring us together.

The evidence is overwhelming that the current energy mix is releasing CO_2 emissions into the atmosphere at unsustainable rates, causing the Earth's temperatures to rise rapidly (see Exhibit 9.1). These increases will cause dramatic climate events, catastrophic sea-level disasters, and chaotic social upheaval, if they have not already begun to do so. Add to these various climate-related disasters, intolerable economic contractions, and national security risks that are emanating from the continued use of oil at present or increasing levels. It is clear that if anything goes wrong, civilization as we know it could come to an end.

Simply said, civilization cannot be sustained without changing the mix of the energy used to power our global economy. Lord Nicholas Stern, who authored the "Stern Review on the Economics of Climate Change" for the British government, reported in October 2006[1] that with business and economic growth and energy consumption as usual and with forecast energy consumption levels rising, we could expect the detrimental effects and disasters emanating from climate change to equal both World Wars and the Great Depression combined.

In 2008, Stern went on to say that new data collected since his earlier report had convinced him that he *underestimated* the magnitude of potential weather-related disasters and the urgency to commence major reductions in CO_2 emissions necessary to avoid most of these dire consequences.[2]

Gore and Stern have done excellent work on a global scale to alert humanity of the stark reality that civilization must drastically change its energy use. The problem is that these truths from Gore and Stern only capture the symptoms, not the disease.

The real inconvenient truth is that government policies that generally represent the will of the people have been largely responsible for the disease—or root cause of this stark reality. In one way or another, all the world's governments *subsidize energy consumption*. And the lower the price, the bigger the incentive there is to use more. So the *real* inconvenient truth is that as long as the energy we use today continues to be subsidized—specifically coal and oil, which generates

80 percent of our pollution and CO_2 emissions[3]—humanity will continue down the energy path toward catastrophic climatic, economic, and geostrategic disasters. In that case, the three intolerables will continue to grow until one, or all three, end civilization as we know it.

Each year subsidized energy consumption continues, it will become more difficult for governments to rid themselves of this grave disease. The macroeconomic distortion of energy supply and demand will continue to increase, vested interests will dig in deeper, and the levels of general economic pain required to eliminate price caps and subsidies will continue to increase.

The first half of 2008 saw social unrest and increasing inflation taking place as fuel and food prices rapidly increased and government-regulated gasoline prices were adjusted upward. This was particularly true in the high-growth Asian nations. The public tells its politicians, in no uncertain terms, to do *something* to bring down high energy prices. The politicians' normal reaction, particularly in democracies in election years, is to roll back taxes on fuel.

Early in the 2008 presidential campaign, two candidates, Hillary Clinton and John McCain, advanced this backward thinking. Barack Obama's judgment was sound in refusing to support such energy-policy foolishness. In Germany, public demand was so intense that gasoline tax subsidies that had been abolished the year before *were reinstated*. The Merkel government probably spoke for all the world's politicians by saying, "We will not have the political strength to resist it."[4] Pogo's truism remains: "We have met the enemy and he is us."[5]

Until recently, energy consumption has generally increased society's standard of living and quality of life. But now, because of these enormous external costs and the rapidly growing crises caused by continued consumption of the old and inefficient energy sources (coal and oil) we are, in many ways, beginning to diminish both the standard of living and quality of life for all the world's citizens.

In addition to polluting our planet, coal and oil subsidies—both direct and external—tend to increase their demand, and the external costs are now beginning to reach levels that are actually working against economic growth. However, economic growth will most likely struggle forward, particularly in developing countries, until the magnitude of risks from the three intolerables builds to the point that one or all three severely disrupts or reverses the development of civilization that we have experienced since World War II.

The Disease Is Subsidies

The real inconvenient truth is that *the disease is energy subsidies*, or at least counterproductive energy subsidies that work against the GET. They come in two forms, direct and indirect. Direct subsidies come as government loans, tax breaks, payments to producers, and explicit price controls. Indirect subsidies hide costs that economists call *externalities*. Granted, these external subsidies are a very murky part of economics, but they are indeed real, and the external costs for coal and oil have now grown to macroeconomic proportions. They may be thought of as similar to the negative side effects of taking certain medicines. You may cure one illness, but the side effects create larger and potentially longer-term systemic problems. The costs of these side effects are the costs of energy consumption *not paid by the consumer*, but by society in general.

Direct subsidies are created to shield the consumer from otherwise higher market costs. These subsidies are effective in the near term for stimulating economies but, of course, at the same time they are stimulating the dirty and inefficient (but cheap) energy consumption we wish to rid ourselves of—coal and oil.

Most developing countries and oil-exporting nations maintain stringent price caps on gasoline, diesel, and fuel oil, and a few countries even maintain price caps on some types of coal consumption. For instance, in Venezuela and many Middle Eastern states, gasoline is far less than $1 per gallon.[6] In many developing countries, China included, gasoline costs much less than it costs in the United States.

However, in Europe, gasoline sells for twice or more than twice what it sells for in the United States because of added *green taxes*. As a result, Europeans use petrol (gasoline and diesel) much more efficiently. In summer 2008, gasoline in several European nations, including the United Kingdom, was typically near or above $8 per gallon.[7]

In developed economies, most renewable energy sources are subsidized in order to create incentives for their market entry, or are mandated into the market, or both. These subsidies are only necessary because the fuels they are meant to replace are also heavily subsidized. To make things even worse, governments are notoriously inept at picking winners and are quite good at making policies that turn out, in hindsight, to be disastrous. This is particularly true in the field of energy, with its great complexities and cloudy vernacular, leading to the forgivably, but often destructively, misty understanding of policy makers. Hopefully, by understanding that the GET clearly shows the way forward and reveals the most likely winners and losers, policy makers can correct their past poor record on energy policy.

The best recent example has been the largely emotional reaction of many governments to subsidize and mandate biofuels. This is particularly true of corn ethanol subsidies in the United States, which were legislated with little scientific study or forethought. In December 2007, President George W. Bush signed the Energy Independence and Security Act that included the Renewable Fuels Mandate, which will increase the use of renewable fuels by 300 percent, requiring fuel producers to supply at least 36 billion gallons of subsidized renewable fuel in the year 2022.[8]

The result is that the U.S. government is now committed to ethanol at the same time the world is facing agricultural shortages emanating, in particular, from Asia's economic uplift and partially from the early effects of climate change. Asian typhoons, Australian and Chinese droughts, and American floods have drastically reduced the quantities of food available for the world market. By rushing into corn ethanol, which has no hope of helping humanity evolve into our sustainable future, the United States both slowed the progress of the GET and exacerbated the 2008 global food crisis. As always, when governments create such programs, they are hard to stop and tend to go on distorting markets and making things much worse for the long term. The U.S. corn ethanol program should be abandoned. As the GET tells us, corn ethanol is extending the life of liquids beyond their natural decline to the detriment of viable, sustainable alternatives.

The insidious externalities are a second type of subsidy. They are hidden, indirect subsidies that result from governments not charging the consumer for many of the costs that governments pay to sustain energy use. These costs are either paid by the taxpayer or fall directly on society as a whole. External costs include the expense for the U.S. military to ensure there is a continuing global supply and distribution system for oil. Externalities also include costs that result from allowing unregulated pollution to be discarded into our atmosphere, rivers, oceans, and lands. In China, pollution-driven external costs to the economy—including losses of human and agricultural productivity—are so large today that the World Bank estimates China is losing about 5.8 percent of its GDP, or about $100 billion, per year.[9] Eventually, such costs must be paid in some form by the general population.

To summarize, coal and oil externalities include the following:

- Costs the U.S. government pays for its blue water navy to ensure the free flow of daily oil needs across the open oceans
- The cost of America's Iraq wars, to the extent they were triggered and fought because of the need to protect the global oil system
- The current and future cost to the U.S. economy of sending nearly $500 billion annually to foreign oil producers, and trillions more in future decades—certainly one of the largest transfers of wealth in human history[10]
- The cost of the current financial and credit collapse to the extent it is related to the recycling of petrodollars
- The cost of foreign oil payments—the single-largest component of America's trade deficit—and the effect this has on the value of the dollar
- The cost of the possible end of the U.S. dollar as the world's most important reserve currency
- The cost of the U.S. Strategic Petroleum Reserve and those of other countries
- The wide-ranging costs of pollution in major metropolitan centers of the world, to the extent that they exist because of petroleum-fueled vehicle emissions
- The costs of respiratory disease, cancer, and other illnesses resulting from coal and oil pollution, and the immeasurable costs of shortened lifespans
- Economic losses from diminished agricultural and human productivity
- The cost of America's loss of geostrategic power and national security
- The eventual costs to the world's population from the triggering of one or all three intolerables

Coal's External Costs

To be sure, coal's hidden external costs are intangible and difficult to measure. In the United States, it is hard to assess the impact of a half-mile-long train rolling through a town in northern Oklahoma, bringing commerce to a halt, while vehicles and people wait for the coal cars to pass. In Houston, where I once lived, what is the cost incurred by the economy as drivers on the way to work or home wait for the five minutes it takes for a long line of coal cars to pass on the rail line and before the inevitable traffic jam disappears and we start again? Certainly, that scene, repeated over and over again for decades, has had considerable effect on human productivity and adds substantial demand for oil while automobile engines idle and we wait for coal to be delivered.

In China, what were the external costs of the 2007–2008 winter's extraordinarily heavy snowfall, a possible consequence of global climate change,[11] that disrupted coal delivery by rail? There were factory closures, lost production, and a surge in the use of higher-cost oil use for electric generation to compensate for the coal generation losses, increasing the cost to Chinese society in multiple ways. If those same industries and power plants were on natural gas pipelines, their energy supply would have been available throughout the storms.

So we may finally have at least an intuitive feel for these coal costs: pollution, acid rain, mercury emissions, particulates, shortened life spans, lost personal productivity, diminished agricultural productivity and crop growth, and commerce-debilitating smogs and fogs, all from coal use.

Coal is falsely cheaper—as long as we ignore its pollution, its health costs, diminished life expectations, and contribution to global warming, which is to say nothing of the loss of forests to beetles because of decades of acid rain, diminished agricultural productivity, and, more important, human productivity. When these are included, coal is obviously more costly and has likely been more expensive than natural gas for decades. One study notes that the costs may vary from adding about $13 per megawatt-hour to the price of coal-fired power to possibly as high as adding $33 per megawatt-hour. In comparison, the cost of the externalities on a natural gas plant are estimated at only 40 cents per megawatt-hour.[12]

Now it is time to go to work and bring this important research up to date, because all economic analyses of the cost of alternatives—natural gas, wind, solar, and hydrogen—must include these costs of coal for an accurate and fair comparison. Economic forecasts must include all these costs—costs that will disappear as alternatives displace coal and, by doing so, create real economic benefits.

Oil's External Costs

At the end of World War II, President Roosevelt met with King Ibn Saud of Saudi Arabia and struck a deal for the United States to provide security to Saudi Arabia in return for access to oil supplies. All U.S. presidents since have followed this policy, which has led to enormous military commitments and two Iraq oil wars. I concur with former Federal Reserve Chairman Alan Greenspan, who said, regarding the 2003 Iraq invasion, "I am saddened that it is politically inconvenient to acknowledge what everyone knows, the Iraq War is largely about oil."[13] Over the years, in one way or another, Roosevelt's deal with King Saud has cost taxpayers trillions of dollars, which were not included in the price of gasoline at the pump.

The 1970s brought both the disruption of the energy market and the natural progress of the GET. The Yom Kippur War, the political decision by Saudi Arabia's King Faisal to declare that oil could be used as a weapon, the fall of the Shah of Iran, and the diminished stability of the Middle East caused the United States and other governments to expand military commitments to the region in order to ensure continuous oil supplies. Increasingly, large military costs, to maintain the free flow of oil around the world, and other related external oil costs—such as the Strategic Petroleum Reserve—were not passed on directly to the consumer. Much of these hidden external costs have been passed along to taxpayers, and the balance became government debt or fell, one way or another, upon society. The heaviest cost of all fell on those who lost their lives in oil-related wars. Particularly in the United States, oil's largest consumer, external subsidies continued to accelerate, so oil consumption was increasingly subsidized by the government. For decades, consumers have not paid the full price of oil so there has been no real free market, but rather a failed market macroeconomically distorted by external subsidies that has led to America's current oil addiction. Although the cartoon in Exhibit 9.2 was published in 1990, it is even more true today.

Exhibit 9.2   The Real Cost of Gasoline
Source: Ed Stein. Reprinted with permission.

For the United States, the big picture that results from the enormity of external subsidies for oil includes the building of an exceptionally inefficient energy infrastructure and way of life.

After World War II and for decades thereafter—partially because of subsidized petroleum—the United States rapidly expanded super-highways, suburbs, exurbs, strip malls, and automobile use, accelerating urban and suburban pollution, traffic jams, and road rage, all of which diminished human productivity. These societal costs and related economic losses of traffic jams and inefficient auto and truck use became additional external costs, not paid by either the consumer or the producer but charged to society in general in the form of losses to economic growth. If gasoline consumers had been charged the real cost of gasoline over those decades, I suspect the energy inefficient, suburban, long-commute-to-work, strip-mall way of American life would have looked much different. Without these subsidies, I doubt we would order a pizza to be delivered across town by an automobile. Certainly, larger efficiencies would have been built into our way of life. China has recognized the enormity of the problem and has decided to build mega-cities, each accommodating tens of millions of people, each the population size of a major country. In March 2008, McKinsey Global

Institute recommended 15 "super cities" with average populations of 25 million or 11 "city-clusters" each with combined populations of more than 60 million.[14]

The ultimate result is that America's 4.6 percent of the global population consumes 21.3 percent of the world's daily energy consumption,[15] and produces about 25.4 percent of the global GDP.[16] Cheap, subsidized oil and coal also led to America's highly inefficient energy habits, which rank the United States close to the bottom of both the energy efficiency and the pollution list for developed countries. Imagine how much more powerful the U.S. economy would be today if it were the world's most energy-efficient economy.

It has been these external costs, amounting to trillions of dollars of *incentives to use oil more inefficiently*, that continue to accumulate as debt to be paid by the U.S. taxpayers and society in general. To drive home the point, as the consumption of oil grew substantially over the last decades, external costs skyrocketed. The price paid by the consumer for gasoline since the rise of externalities began in the 1970s was always only a fraction of the real cost. Because these externalities were not reflected in consumer prices, we went right on consuming oil as if there were no tomorrow.

Today, we find ourselves faced with the consequences of being 65 percent dependent on foreign oil producers for the existence of our economy. In many ways, these costs are beyond measure. Certainly, it is almost the same as being 100 percent dependent. We must not let the early 2009 collapse in oil price lull us to sleep because if there were a successful terrorist attack in Saudi Arabia, or the blocking of the Straits of Hormuz or the Bosporus, or uprisings in Africa or a political standoff with Russia, several million barrels of oil per day could easily be lost from the market for a few months. What would the costs and lasting consequences be? Oil at $300 a barrel? Probably! The effect on the global economy is difficult to imagine, but there would certainly be a large disruption and contraction. And what if political or logistical circumstances extend such a loss of oil flows beyond what we have saved up in the strategic reserves of the world, and we face shortages and rationing? Who in the world gets the oil? Will it be to the highest bidder? What if Asian nations outbid the United States? What will this do to international relations for decades to come?

I have attended two of the Oil Shockwave games staged by Robbie Diamond's company, Securing America's Future Energy, where oil-loss scenarios of this sort are played out in near real-life. One game I attended was in Aspen, at the Aspen Strategy Group, and the second was at Harvard's Kennedy School Forum. The setting was "the White House situation room," where the "President's advisors" convened to play out the scenario. At Harvard, two of the players were Robert E. Rubin as national security advisor and Lawrence Summers as secretary of treasury.

We received continuous news updates about terrorist attacks, information on skyrocketing oil prices, and discussion concerning how to advise the president for his public address to the United States and the world. Two main points surfaced after one and a half hours of the simulation. The first point was that, at the end of the day, we had no other real short- or near-term answer but to "call the Saudis." As that startling realization began to set in, and while contemplating the potential loss of America's strategic power, I found myself truly shocked, even after having been part of the oil and gas industry all my working life. I am reminded of former Saudi Arabia Oil Minister Sheik Yamani's comment in his 1988 book about oil supplies, ". . . America will be forced to rely on the Persian Gulf, which is a part of the world, I assure you, that you do not want to allow yourselves to rely upon."[17]

The second realization was that in the participants' search for medium- and long-term answers, and their advice to the president on programs to present to the United States and the world during the emergency, there was never any mention of natural gas until I stood up following the program. Not once was there a reference to America's abundant, clean natural gas supplies, which could fuel half of our automobiles in less than a decade and reduce our oil imports by about five to six million barrels per day, if we really set our minds to it!

Frankly, if I were a member of the president's national defense team, in spite of all our economic, military, and political power, it would be difficult for me to express the helplessness I would feel about what to do with the potential of losing our "lifeblood," oil. But there is no question that I would propose an urgent program even larger than President Kennedy's Challenge to America, to put a man on the moon in a decade, because I believe the stakes for America today are dramatically larger. You will find such a proposal in Chapter 12.

Oil is truly our lifeblood, and it is difficult to contemplate the reper-
cussions of its loss. I don't put these questions to the reader in search
of answers, because these costs are immeasurable, but rather to stimulate thinking and imagination. Suffice it to say that the aftershocks of
the partial loss of oil flows and price spikes are all *intolerable risks* that the
United States, the largest oil consumer, faces each day, and unfortunately,
without urgency or sufficient attention paid to their magnitude. Indeed,
we cannot determine their possible cost or the current political and economic costs of our ongoing attempts to prevent such risks. But again,
they are of a macroeconomic scale, and they are not paid directly by the
American consumer of oil: They represent an enormous subsidy. There
will be no free market for oil in America until we pay the real costs of
using oil. Without revolutionary changes in policy, I see no way we can
rid ourselves of oil's addiction. One thing is for certain, T. Boone Pickens
is absolutely right when he says, "We can't drill our way out" of our oil
problem. This applies to the world, as well as to the United States.

In 2008, Americans paid nearly $500 billion to oil-producing nations,
a cost that will escalate as supplies decline, and without massive reductions in our oil imports, many trillions of dollars over the coming decades. Until recently we saw the results of this massive transfer of wealth
from oil consumers to oil producers by the frenetic building of new
cities, airports, universities, and infrastructure, without precedent in the
long history of the Middle East.

Huge, possibly catastrophic, risks and costs are mounting within our
society and economy that will have to be paid probably sooner rather
than later. Only in 2008 was a fully justified risk premium added to
the price of oil. It was the inevitable approach of peak oil that brought
extremely tight markets and the realization of the oil shock risks that
was responsible for the price in 2008, as well as global investors and
pension funds that were looking for rising investments. How was the
loss to the economy measured? And what about the purchases by the oil
producing nations' Sovereign Wealth Funds of consuming nations' strategic assets, and the loss of millions of jobs in those consuming nations?
And the loss of geostrategic power as the result of oil addiction and the
possible loss of the dollar as a global reserve currency? These intangible
costs flow from subsidies that impede the GET by extending the otherwise dwindling life of coal and oil.

Past energy policy mistakes slowed the progress of the GET, while a few have worked to accelerate it. This understanding must now be used to build policies to propel the GET into a new world energy dynamic. To make the necessary policy changes to accomplish our goals of sustainable energy and climate stability, we must understand that it has been the failed market that has brought us to this point of sustaining the use of vast quantities of coal and oil beyond their natural decline. This failed market due to external subsidies to coal and oil is why alternative, cleaner, and more desirable sources of energy have had such a hard time getting started. Governments have to outsubsidize coal and oil with subsidies to alternatives so that they can compete. In other words, governments are forcing alternatives into a subsidized fuel system.

Macroeconomic Distortion of Subsidies

A fundamental tenet of economics is that *it takes a real price to have a real market*. Without a real market, supply and demand are distorted. Governments are managing the markets through subsidies. As a tool for managing the market, subsidies are no different from mandated allocation of commodities in a socialist system. If we learned anything from the failure of communist economics in the twentieth century, it was that markets are the best allocators of goods and services. So, what we need for coal and oil, the world's largest commodities, is a *real* free market.

Subsidies are the reason the U.S. Congress often criticizes China, saying that competition between China's state-owned companies and U.S. companies is not fair and not based on a free market. To those, particularly in the coal and oil industry, who believe and often say that the "government should get out of the way and let the free market work," I say there has been no real free market for coal and oil since at least the early 1970s. Coal's renaissance in the United States came largely as a result of the institutionalized misperception of natural gas shortages and the prohibition of natural gas in its fastest-growing markets, power generation and new industrial facilities, combined with few pollution controls on coal emissions. Coal's toxic emissions and CO_2

were released on America, and coal's prices did not include these growing post–1970s external costs, so there has been no real free market for
coal. In the years leading up to the 1978 omnibus energy legislation,
the prevailing wisdom was that natural gas was scarce. This thinking
led to the Fuel Use Act, prohibiting the use of natural gas in industrial
markets and power generation. Unfortunately, the natural gas scarcity
misperception still persists in many minds, although change is in the
air. Hopefully, the understanding of natural gas abundance is coming
to the forefront. Exhibit 9.3 demonstrates how this misperception has
extended coal's use in America for decades beyond when it would have
otherwise become an insignificant energy source, in the late 1990s.

As I have said, the overarching reason we are still hooked on highly
polluting, high–carbon coal and oil is that subsidies have distorted supply

Exhibit 9.3   Coal Percentage of Total U.S. Energy Use
Source: Data figured from BP's online historical data, *BP Statistical Review of
World Energy*, www.bp.com; *Oil Economists' Handbook* by Gilbert Jenkins, Applied
Science Publishers Ltd. (London), 1977; and *Coal: Research and Development
to Support National Energy Policy*, National Research Council of the National
Academies, The National Academies Press, (Washington, D.C.), 2007, based on
data in EIA (2005).

and demand and, by so doing, extended their life and slowed the GET's progress (also see Chapter 4). That extended life brought unnecessary pollution, enormous inefficiencies, and economic costs well beyond what would otherwise have occurred by their natural decline. At the same time, this has slowed their displacement by alternatives that are cleaner and less expensive (when the external costs are included). Subsidies are the root cause of America's oil and coal addiction, as well as the impetus for China's growing coal addiction and looming oil addiction.

As long as the real price is masked, consumers of coal-generated electricity and petroleum are unlikely to change daily habits. This long-term government policy failure has distorted the energy market and brought us near the edge of the cliff we stand before today. Lord Nicholas Stern described our current energy and climate dilemma clearly and accurately to the participants at the Davos World Economic Forum as the result of the "biggest market failure the world has ever seen,"[18] and his book *The Global Deal: Climate Change and the Creation of a New Era of Progress and Prosperity* (New York: PublicAffairs, 2009) describes in detail the basis for that important understanding.

Our real inconvenient truth is that our subsidy disease is the enemy of meaningful change. Subsidies for the fuels that are the principal cause of our three intolerables, the fuels we want to use less of, must be confronted and eliminated. Eliminating subsidies and re-creating a real marketplace for coal and oil, including real price signals through green taxes, will cause humanity to begin to accelerate the GET faster than any government mandates. Under such policies, all the clean alternatives will naturally replace coal and oil at rates faster than we can perceive today.

China understands very well that it must not lead the developing world along this same inefficient and polluting path of growth based upon out-of-date and highly subsidized nineteenth- and twentieth-century coal and oil technology. Unfortunately, China and, indeed, the entire developing world today, have arrived at a place where they can see and feel their glorious future of economic development at the exact historical moment the three intolerables are rapidly building energy crises that must be dealt with, in order to sustain the growth of its own and the global economy. Without acceleration of the GET, it is doubtful that the developing world will feel the full fruits of its glorious future during the first half of this century. In China's case, the leadership has recognized the three intolerables. I am optimistic because they have already begun to put in place policies to accelerate the GET in their economy.[19] As one example, in 2008, China's government standards for gasoline efficiency in cars are already better than the standards the United States has set for its next generation of cars in 2015,[20] and solar is a booming industry. However, I am not naive about the enormity of energy changes that China must yet embrace.

The decades following the 1970s saw a stalling and even short-term reversal of coal's natural decline from preeminence that began in about 1850. Indeed, as a result of misguided government policies based on the perception of limited natural gas supplies and the rise of Asia, coal's decline actually reversed as a percentage of world market share.[21] The Carter administration's Fuel Use Act prohibiting the use of natural gas, coal's natural, clean alternative, for the following decades gave rise to a large expansion of coal-generated electricity without significant pollution controls (see Chapter 5). This one policy act gave rise to a coal mind-set that shaped global energy momentum for decades. The Carter energy legislation mandates, coupled with limited pollution regulation that kept natural gas out of the electric generation market, led to the subsequent years seeing many electric utilities build coal-generation plants that will be with us for numerous decades because coal was perceived by most experts to be cheaper. There was no accounting for the external costs. However, we do know that the additional 100,000 megawatts of coal-fired generating plants built since then have added about 15 billion metric tons[22] of CO_2 emissions to the world's atmosphere. Had the Fuel Use Act not prohibited natural gas power, we would have had at least 7.5 billion tons less CO_2 to deal with today. Real full-cycle accounting for coal's external costs is only now being factored into economic comparisons for electric generation and, as a result, coal generation is being reconsidered.

Good Subsidies, Bad Subsidies

Clean and green wind and solar may require subsidies for all our sakes, because instead of naturally gaining market share today in most national economies, they must be *forced* into an already highly subsidized electric generation market. So new subsidies and government mandates are put in place, even though today most wind- and solar-generated electricity probably costs about the same or, more likely, less than the real full-cycle costs of dirty, coal-generated electricity.

The broad public is beginning to understand this. A wonderful example of the 2007 tipping point for growing awareness of these issues by the American population and politicians has been the successful public battle by environmentalists, natural gas advocacy groups, and the general public that stopped some 59 of the 150 or more proposed coal generation plants across the nation.[23] People are taking action and momentum is growing. As has always been the case, citizens are driving the GET forward, and the ascension of the Age of Energy Gases has begun to accelerate.

For oil use, one now out-of-date, and probably low, estimate of the external cost of gasoline is by the National Defense Council Foundation. It estimated the hidden cost of oil to be "equivalent to adding $8.35 to the price of a gallon of gasoline refined from Persian Gulf oil."[24] If the external costs of foreign oil imports averaged only $3 per gallon since the beginning of the 1980s, then the real cost of that oil would have been not only the price we paid at the pump, but an additional $11.7 trillion,[25] all of which was paid by the U.S. taxpayer. Whatever the actual number, that is, indeed, a very large subsidy.

Following 1850, when the Grand Energy Transition began, its evolutionary process functioned naturally and continuously for about 120 years to provide humanity with a natural, evolutionary energy transition to cleaner fuels and more sophisticated energy technologies. From 1955 to 1978, price regulation in the United States functioned to accelerate natgas demand and the GET, but it kept natgas supplies locked in the ground, so beginning in the 1970s shortages began to appear. Oil shocks of the 1970s brought us rapidly increasing external costs, market instability, and various government interventions. The process of natural gas price deregulation began in 1978, but only after natural gas lost most of its growth market as a result of arbitrary policies based on fear of shortages—policies that prohibited or limited its use. Thus, during the 1970s, the GET began to slow.

Of course, there has been a very positive side to these decades of subsidies. An enormous positive effect of this long-term policy of government subsidies to coal and oil has been abundant supplies of cheap coal and oil, which helped us win World War II and the Cold War and fueled the largest economic and technological expansion in human history—creating today's globalized and connected world. This incredible economic pulse uplifted civilization. Billions of people moved out of poverty, but this entire period of phenomenal growth was stimulated by the consumer paying less than the real cost for coal and oil. Society in general has either paid the balance or the costs have been accumulated as debts to be paid by future taxpayers. This is how we leveraged our energy system, similar to how we leveraged our financial system.

The reality we all know is that *there is no free lunch*. We must now begin to pay the debt of our past energy use and economic growth.

Until these real external costs are paid directly by the consumer, the GET will only move forward at a snail's pace, dragged along by the inexorable but slower-than-necessary rise of natural gas, wind, and solar. Society will be further burdened for decades by more newly built, but inefficient and polluting, energy infrastructure, most with only slight updates of centuries-old, inefficient technologies. Atmospheric CO_2 concentrations will continue to increase and the risks of climate, economic, and strategic disasters will continue to escalate unless the GET is accelerated. The ever-growing, larger costs of the three intolerables will become global realities and be paid for by the world's youth and future generations.

Although this bleak future is clearly possible, the larger the crisis, the larger the opportunity. The wise must seize the moment of opportunity and accelerate the GET to avoid or ameliorate these crises and their costs.

To accelerate the GET toward sustainable life and growth on Earth requires the elimination of all subsidies, direct and indirect, for coal and oil. A green, consumption-based tax system will be required in order to phase in the approximate external costs of coal and oil, so that, eventually, we all pay the real price for their use. Only then will we begin to diminish their use and make room for the growth of clean energy gases.

Creative Destruction

Harvard's renowned economist and (I would add) social philosopher Joseph Schumpeter was properly described as the "Prophet of Innovation."[26] He believed that a process of *creative destruction* was always necessary to unlock new waves of entrepreneurship, innovation, and capital formation. He also recognized that money and credit were fundamental to, and acted as a catalyst for, economic growth. Here I must add my own belief that energy use, or the expenditure of energy, which I think explains its role more clearly, is equally, if not more, fundamental in the process of economic growth. It was the availability of coal, a better fuel than wood, that sparked the innovation and invention that led to the mechanization necessary for the Industrial Revolution. This mechanization, driven by an abundant energy source, multiplied human productivity by orders of magnitude.

Indeed, before the Industrial Revolution few people were free. Most were slaves, indentured servants, or vassals. It was the availability of energy, combined with capital and credit, that allowed these rural laborers to devote their newfound time to creativity, innovation, and invention. These forces of unleashed human energy, combined with mechanical energy, money, and credit, unleashed the new force of capitalism that built the Industrial Revolution, then humanity's largest-ever economic pulse. The result of creative destruction within the old world was the release of many to new freedom and active participation in the rise of capitalism. As I described earlier, this same process occurred again during the period of oil's creative destruction, innovation, and invention. Combined with the opening of China and the global fall of communism, that creative destruction lead to two billion more people being brought to freedom and introduced to the innovative juices of global capitalism. Once again, another phenomenal and unprecedented pulse of economic growth was released that brought us to today's global economy, the largest GDP in human history.

Now, with the current economic collapse, we must do it again, by accelerating the GET and bringing forth the rapid growth of the Age of Energy Gases to drive the next great economic uplift that will bring those remaining into the freedom of global capitalism, to participate in a twenty-first-century economic pulse of a scale beyond our imagination.

Given the *real* inconvenient truth, that subsidies are the disease being manifested today in the three intolerables, the straightforward solution is to eliminate them. However, because the external costs must first be paid by government, the only way to eliminate them is to enact a green tax to be levied on the use of the principal energy problems—coal and oil. Of course, we cannot do that without relief to their consumers. Therefore, a green tax system is inexorably connected to our energy and climate problems. I describe a green tax system in the policy chapter (Chapter 12), but, put simply, a green tax system would phase in consumption taxes focused initially on coal and oil that equaled their external costs and phase out all taxes currently levied on the fruits of our daily labor and the growth and use of our capital. We must free labor and capital from the chains of taxation because they are the source of the next wave of creativity, innovation, and invention.

To solve humanity's energy and climate problems by the middle of this century, the creative destruction, which has indeed recently begun, must continue and be accelerated in our coal and oil industries to release not only the creativity, innovation, and invention necessary to drive the energy alternatives of the Age of Energy Gases, but also to release the tens of trillions of dollars of capital that would otherwise be directed toward and consumed to sustain our energy status quo and the energy business as usual.

Creative destruction in the energy industry will bring vast opportunities for investment, will reduce or eliminate enormous and deeply embedded external costs, and will stimulate a new burst of heretofore unimaginable economic growth. Jeff Goodell said it best about coal in his book *Big Coal*: "Old coal plants are more than just relics of an earlier era; they are giant bulwarks against change, mechanical beasts that are holding back a flood of ideas and innovation. When we muster up the courage to knock them down, the revolution will begin."[27]

To sum up a complex economic picture, all 6.8 billion of us make personal daily short- and long-term energy choices based on multitudes of considerations. Energy transitions are powerful, usually slow-moving waves, and difficult for governments to guide. Transitions are most effectively slowed or accelerated by the price each consumer pays for energy use. Keep in mind the basic economic principle that increasing prices tend to decrease demand and increase supply, while

low prices do the opposite by increasing demand and decreasing supply. After the oil shocks of the 1970s, through the end of the 1990s, the
consumer prices of coal, oil, and gasoline generally declined in inflation-adjusted dollars, while external subsidies shielded the consumer
from the increasing, real full-cycle price and pushed demand for those
fuels to unnaturally high consumption levels that contained high levels
of waste and inefficiency. This is the energy fix in which we find
ourselves today.

Governments add to or reduce the speed and strength of energy
transitions through policies of mandates and market intervention, public communication, leadership, and the bully pulpit. At the end of the
day, each individual, family, neighborhood, city, state, or nation will
make energy choices based on the dialectical tensions between the outlook for a better standard of living and a higher quality of life. Just as
the moral philosopher Adam Smith, in his 1776 treatise *The Wealth of
Nations*, described, the decisions of all people working each for their
own interests come together for the betterment of all society, as if
"guided by an invisible hand." This same invisible hand guides the flow
and source of civilization's energy use.

I compare the GET to the evolutionary process of natural selection
that glides along for geologically long periods with only small adaptations to the surrounding environment, until conditions loom up to create great crises that require rapid adaptation for the survival of life on
Earth. The looming evolutionary crises are those three intolerables, and
the species that must rapidly adapt today is us, *Homo sapiens*. The late,
great evolutionary biologist Stephen Jay Gould called this phenomena
punctuated equilibrium, or as I heard him say one day during a lecture
on evolution at Harvard, "punc-eq." My mentor, Ray Alf, called such
events *crises of evolution*. Today, the three intolerables are looming crises
of evolution through which we must pass to achieve sustainable life
and growth on Earth. Thus, we are entering a period of great crises
that will give humanity the opportunity to begin the rapid adaptation,
innovation, and invention required to accelerate the GET, and with it
humanity's next great economic expansion.

The responsibility of each consumer and citizen is to begin to understand that looming energy crises are larger than any of us as persons,
institutions, or nations. Accelerating the GET is a global responsibility

that will require the world's people to come together and to rise above the deeply embedded vested interests that resist change, usually by fear-mongering about economic collapse and forecasting that it will be impossible for humanity to afford our natural destiny of sustainable life and growth on Earth. When enough people rise above these false Malthusian barriers of pessimism and join with their governments to accelerate the GET through its natural evolutionary process, humanity will be on the way to its sustainable destiny.

Understanding these forces will require real analyses and projections of the cost-saving benefits to society that will come from the elimination of the large external costs of oil and coal. The economic analyses I have seen offer only the relative cost of subsidized coal and oil as compared with the current cost of natural gas, wind, and solar, always indicating that these alternatives are too expensive to afford. Never have I seen an analysis that includes the real all-in costs, including all externalities, as compared with alternatives. I believe the real answer is that coal and oil cost much more. For answers, we certainly need new research and analysis from the world's prestigious institutions.

The last two years brought a tipping point for global awareness about climate, economic stability and security risks, and the need for dramatic changes in energy use. This popular momentum should allow enlightened leaders to bring about GET-stimulating policies. They must understand the evolutionary energy forces that have brought us to this point and let the GET be our clear, achievable energy goal for the twenty-first century. Indeed, the GET is our silver path forward. All of us must begin to formulate our own jet the GET policies.

Chapter 10

Our Energy and Climate Challenge—Los Angeles, A Case Study

L os Angeles represents the perfect example of America's massive energy inefficiencies and the monumental challenge we have before us to solve our rapidly escalating energy and climate problems.

While writing this book, I flew to Los Angeles to visit my mother. As the plane was landing, the monumental nature of our energy and climate problems hit me like a ton of bricks. I wrote the following:

We are landing in Los Angeles, the city where I grew up in the 1940s and 1950s with then crystal-clear skies. We are descending through about 6,000 feet into the ground pall of gasoline smog. It's about 5:30 P.M. and all the freeways are jammed with bumper-to-bumper traffic. The freeways headed away from my view are simply long ribbons of red. As far as I can see, the L.A. Basin is chock full of infinite rows of homes, with clusters of taller buildings piercing through the smog that make up downtown L.A. and Century City. The sun is low and the smog seems to be turning an eerie yellow-orange-brown. Now I can smell and taste the smog. I wonder what my weekend visit will do to my lungs. We are lower now, and as far as I can see there are more rows and rows of energy-inefficient homes than I could have imagined. Now we have landed and I am surrounded by hundreds of planes, all either parked at the ramp, or coming in, or going out, or waiting in line for takeoff, all burning up jet fuel.

As I contemplate what I have just seen, all I can think of is just how incredibly addicted to oil L.A. and cities like it around the world have become, and what a monumental challenge it is going to be to change our energy patterns. All these homes and buildings spread over literally thousands of square miles, all air conditioned by electricity and highly inefficient in their use of energy, represent the perfect microcosm of our energy and climate problem. I think, "My God! How can we ever change so much as to clean up what we have done to the Earth and eliminate the awful air pollution and reduce CO_2 emissions to stable levels? How can we ever rid ourselves of our addiction to foreign oil?"

As I think further and look for solutions, I realize we have to start somewhere. The only way to begin to make significant scalable changes in the fuel all these millions of people use is to begin with the existing energy infrastructure. Luckily, virtually all of these homes, offices, and industrial facilities are connected to America's 2.2-million-mile natural gas pipeline grid. The Los Angeles freeway system handles over 12 million cars on a daily basis[1]—one of the world's largest concentrations of cars and trucks—so by converting the lion's share of these vehicles to natural gas we could make great strides forward toward reducing oil imports, eliminating smog, and diminishing CO_2 emissions. All that is needed to convert a vehicle to compressed natural gas (CNG) is the equivalent of a scuba tank in the trunk, and for the convenience of home fueling, a small off-the-shelf compressor appliance. To retrofit your car or truck will cost about $3,000 to $10,000 when retrofits are massed produced[2] and a filling appliance about $2,000 to $4,000,[3] so the total cost of a CNG vehicle and the convenience of home filling will be less than half the cost of a new base-model Toyota Prius. With these two purchases, you are ready to go with a dual-fuel gasoline-natural gas automobile. Don't trade your fuel-guzzling SUV or small truck in for next to nothing. Rather, retrofit it to natural gas and drive it on clean natural gas at less than the price of gasoline for as long as you want.

Once California gears up, we know from past experience that most of the automobile companies would dust off their already developed natural gas cars, and sales of natural gas vehicles would increase rapidly.

You can already buy a production-model natural gas vehicle, the Honda Civic GX, and GM and Ford have several models that are upfitted to run on CNG. In Europe, all the major automakers already produce CNG cars.

By running the majority of Los Angeles vehicles on clean natural gas, there would be a meaningful reduction of foreign oil imports, CO_2 emissions would be reduced by about 30 percent from each vehicle converted, and most of the other toxic emissions would be eliminated. The people of Los Angeles would benefit because the now infamous L.A. smogs could be eliminated. I know firsthand how beautiful the area is, having grown up there in the days that preceded smog and the world's largest collection of automobiles. In 2008, the drivers of vehicles converted to natural gas would have collectively saved the country about $13 billion in foreign oil imports by using natural gas instead of gasoline.

Another great benefit to those on the existing natural gas pipe grid in greater Los Angeles is that it allows for the rapid deployment of natural gas–fired, distributed, electric generation. Unfortunately, L.A. today is also a microcosm of the dismal state of our long-neglected existing electric utility grid. This overburdened and undermaintained electric grid has already brought L.A. brownouts over the last few years during periods of extreme heat. So if the forecasts of increasing frequency of extreme heat events, projected to be at least four times the number of days[4] than previously occurred in the days before global warming in the formerly temperate L.A. climate, are accurate, heatwave conditions may dominate summer months in coming decades. Without massive new investment in the electric grid, heavily air-conditioned Los Angeles may well be facing decades of brownouts and rolling blackouts. The existing natural gas pipeline system will allow those who need continuous, reliable supplies of electricity to add their own natural gas microgeneration facilities sized to meet their individual needs. Within the high-rise areas like downtown L.A. and Century City, combined cycle natural gas generating/heating/cooling systems could be installed off the electric grid. Certainly, reliable electricity for health, commercial, and industrial facilities will rise in value and utility and justify the installation costs of new distributed microgeneration facilities where they do not already exist.

Additionally, for all those who participate in our hyperconnected global economy and need IT communications 24/7, 365 days each year, I suggest that distributed generation fired by reliable, clean natural gas may be the only way to go. Over the long term, California could even become an "energy-independent" state in the power sector by generating electricity with natural gas under long-term contracts with producers. By doing so, California, a state with the eighth largest economy in the world,[5] would no longer need to rely on out-of-state power generation that continues to be dominated by coal. So, California, I call on you once again to take the energy leadership role and replace gasoline with natural gas in most of your vehicles and eliminate all coal-fired power generation from the state.

Chapter 11

What Won't Work;
What Will Work

Listen to the technology; find out what it's telling you.
— DR. CARVER MEAD, CALTECH

B y understanding the GET, we learn what won't work and what will work. The GET shows that the path to humanity's sustainable future is the Age of Energy Gases. So, clearly, what won't work are all attempts to sustain the status quo with solids or liquids, which keep us trapped in an era of consumption of vast quantities of unsustainable fuels. Civilization must now jet the GET forward at an accelerating pace in order to moderate and avoid, to the extent possible, the risks of catastrophic events brought to us by the three intolerables: The risks of global climate catastrophes, severe economic contractions (our current one has been exacerbated by unprecedented flows of petrodollars), and intolerable geostrategic tensions and oil wars, arising from our increasing consumption of solid and liquid fuels, have grown too large to tolerate. So, what won't work today are solid and liquid fuels, principally coal and oil.

Our desperate and highly capital-intensive attempts to sustain liquid oil beyond its ongoing natural decline, and what will become oil's historically limited role as civilization's transitional fuel, will only work to impede human progress and expand the potential severity of the three intolerables. Biofuels of all sorts are simply liquids and will almost always, in some way or another, compete with the world's food and the maintenance of rainforest for biodiversity and carbon sinks. No liquid should be the solution to our transportation fuel dilemma simply because the tanks of automobiles, trucks, and buses hold liquids when a gaseous fuel works better, cleaner, and greener. Instead, simply install a tank for natural gas.

What is interesting, and what I believe reinforces the validity of the GET, is that all attempts at energy solutions that are not aligned with the GET run into more and more barriers and greater unanswered technological and economic problems as they try to enter the energy marketplace. Biofuels are a great example. The controversy over biofuels is well founded, as they are not a long-term solution, but only a short-term diversion that wastes billions of dollars on what, at best, is only a short-term fix, and wastes the time and creativity of too many intelligent people who could otherwise be working on *real* solutions.

What is certain is that our conversion to twenty-first-century energy technologies will cost trillions of dollars. So, with limited capital, we need every single dollar going in the right place if we don't want to slow our progress markedly. As Carver Mead said, we must listen to the technology. The GET is our best listener and is telling us the path forward. What certainly won't work is to "do it all," as many in the energy industry advocate, mostly those vested in coal and oil. Solid-based energy sources originated with civilization itself around the wood fire. Coal then displaced wood, but coal-related energy production technologies are dirty, inefficient technologies of the nineteenth century. Nuclear fission is a twentieth-century solid energy technology, principally based on uranium, so nuclear fission is not a long-term solution for sustainable life on Earth. However, fusion from hydrogen gases is simply the "sun in a box," and properly belongs to the Age of Energy Gases. It remains an important possibility for the hydrogen era in the second half of this century.

The 2008 collapse in the United States of the coal industry's showcase electric generation facility, highly touted to be the first example of the coal industry's future, which included complete CO_2 sequestration, called FutureGen, is another excellent example. I suspect the collapse of the FutureGen program may have at least begun to burst the bubble

of hope surrounding "clean coal," although within the Obama administration, the politics of its revival are powerful.

Coal-to-liquids is nothing more than an attempt to revive past
failures. However, to prove the point that the gas-based fuels are on
the right side of history, all the energy technologies based on gases are
indeed accelerating into the marketplace. Wind and solar are bursting
forth around the world, often with little or no resistance. Wind will
undoubtedly continue its rapid growth into the future. New turbines
and blades are under development that may eliminate much of the current concern over local noise and the size of the farms. Solar innovation and inventions are ongoing and I believe are certain to lead to
better storage of solar energy and much smaller land use.

Natural gas is gaining momentum globally and is projected to
accelerate its long-term growth as the world's fastest growing primary
energy. So by following the GET that is propelled forward by human
creativity, invention, and innovation and is driven by the imperative of
civilization to move forward, we can learn what will work and what
won't work.

Now that about one-half the world's population lives in urban
centers,[1] in order to sustain growth, the world's economies will require
massive investments in transportation, power, water, industrial, and residential infrastructure. Experts have estimated "ultimate investment in
infrastructure could exceed $40 trillion globally over the next two-to-
three decades."[2] Because this newly built infrastructure will be in place
for about 50 years, nothing could be worse for civilization's progress
than to build $40 trillion of new infrastructure aligned with the use
of dirty and inefficient energy technologies of the past. And nothing could propel civilization forward faster toward sustainable life and
growth on Earth than the expenditure of $40 trillion compatible with
clean, efficient, smart, twenty-first-century energy technologies of the
Age of Energy Gases. Today, civilization is at a critical energy and technological turning point, which will determine the human condition
for the balance of this century. So, I urge our leaders and politicians to
study these consequences carefully and move forward by adopting policies that follow the technology of and accelerate the GET.

For the balance of this chapter, I will address most of the specific
energy ideas that governments and industry are now considering or are

developing. I will start with solids, move on to transitional liquids, and conclude with our future of energy gases.

The Myth of Clean Coal

So-called "clean coal" for electric generation is not a long-term solution. Even if coal sequestration technology—the capturing, liquefying, and pumping of CO_2 into the Earth—becomes an economic venture and all CO_2 emissions from coal-generated electricity were successfully pumped into the ground, the adjective *clean* is still a stretch of the imagination, because the next question is what will happen to the toxic wastes composed of ash, mercury, and acid-rain-causing sulphur dioxide. These are the pollutants that produce coal's large externalities of environmental damage, plus health issues and their costs. We were given yet another disastrous example when the TVA's holding ponds broke and flooded the surrounding rivers and lands with more than a billion gallons of toxic coal ash.[3]

Burning coal releases fine particulates that kill 24,000 Americans annually and causes hundreds of thousands of cases of lung and heart problems.[4] According to various numbers in the extensively researched book *Big Coal*, there are indications that the health costs from coal's pollution could total about $200 billion in the U.S. annually.[5] According to the American Lung Association, research has shown that communities in the vicinity of coal-fired power plants have a higher incidence of respiratory illness, including asthma, than areas more removed from these pollution sources.[6]

Coal's CO_2 emissions are only part of its problems, although significant, because coal use accounts for 36 percent of the world's CO_2 emissions.[7] Coal-powered electric generation is the world's largest source of deadly mercury air emissions.[8] So, in order to stabilize global climate change, the parties at the 2009 U.N. Conference in Copenhagen should set a goal of negotiating a global agreement that would place a moratorium on new coal-powered generation plants that do not sequester all of their CO_2 emissions. No other agreement would put sequestration to the test faster—and I believe we would soon learn that coal-fired electricity with full CO_2 sequestration cannot economically compete with natural gas, wind, and solar electric generation.

Let's look at a few facts. Even if coal plants are actually capable of capturing all of coal's sulphur, mercury, and ash emissions, and can successfully bury the waste in toxic waste dump sites, the whole process from mine to electric consumer, with sequestration, is inefficient and cumbersome and, if fully costed, cannot be economically competitive with natural gas, wind, and solar. According to a recent study by the Massachusetts Institute of Technology, to sequester only 60 percent of America's CO_2 emissions from coal-fired power plants would require pumping 20 million barrels of liquid per day into the ground.[9] That equals four times U.S. daily crude oil production.[10] Obviously, to pump into the ground each day CO_2 equaling four times the amount that the U.S oil industry currently pumps out of the ground would be no easy task and would require an entirely new industry that, even if economic, would take decades to put in place. So why not forget about capturing 60 percent of coal's CO_2 emissions and simply switch to natural gas, which reduces CO_2 emissions by at least 50 percent?

Today, the costs of sequestration, which were made abundantly clear by the collapse of FutureGen, are escalating rapidly and cannot yet be even realistically measured. Our federal government was subsidizing 70 percent of the costs,[11] and when it pulled the plug, the other commercial interests apparently ran for cover because they understood it was not commercial.

What I believe to be an almost equally large problem with coal-fired generation, other than its failure to be an economically competitive technology for our clean future, is the generally noncompetitive way that the entire electric industry is structured, so that new distributed natural gas-fired generation and wind and solar generation are often kept out of the electric grid, holding back waves of potential entrepreneurial innovation and invention. As Jeff Goodell described in his classic study of coal *Big Coal: The Dirty Secret Behind America's Future*, America's coal-fired generation plants "are giant bulwarks against change; mechanical beasts that are holding back a flood of ideas and innovation." He went on to assert correctly, "When we muster up the courage to knock them down, the revolution will begin."[12] Since his book was published, the revolution has actually started.

The one number that I believe should get the attention of all of us more than any other is that to replace all the current coal generator electric capacity in America with a combination of clean natural gas–generated electricity and some wind- and solar-generated electricity would only cost about $250 billion,[13] or about a quarter of the accumulated costs of the Iraq war.[14] What this proves to me is that the United States is capable of infrastructure expenditures of this size. If we get serious about climate change and pollution, it is not beyond our economic reach.

Coal to Liquids

Coal-to-liquids technology is an attempt to convert a nineteenth-century solid energy source to a twentieth-century liquid source that has no place in the twenty-first century. Although the Fischer Tropsch technology to convert coal to oil was successfully developed in Germany in the 1920s, it has proven cumbersome, non-commercial, and highly polluting. The U.S. Air Force is offering private developers 700 acres at its Malmstrom Air Force Base in central Montana to build a coal-to-liquids facility in order to have a secure source of fuel produced from a domestic resource.[15] The first such plant is estimated to cost up to $5 billion.[16] In the past, military research and development, particularly during World War II, produced large benefits and wonderful new technologies, such as turbine engines, supercomputers, and the Internet, that have propelled the American energy sector forward. Unfortunately, this time, as a result of the false belief that coal is the only secure, available domestic fuel sufficient to meet its needs, the U.S. Air Force is encouraging technologies that move us backward.

If the Air Force needs a secure, efficient, clean, and domestic source of fuel, the answer is at hand, and it is natural gas-to-liquids. The technology is well developed. Shell has an $18-billion plant[17] to go online in late 2010 in Qatar that will produce 140,000 barrels[18] of clean liquid transport fuel each day from Qatar's natural gas. This twenty-first-century technology is already in commercial use without government subsidies. Therefore, I must assume that the only reason the Air Force is not promoting a U.S. gas-to-liquids plant is because it does not believe America's natural gas resources are sufficient. I hope this book and our U.S. natural gas producers will soon convince the public, politicians, and leaders of America's best-kept secret: that North America has a more than 100-year supply of secure natural gas.

Coal to Gas

Coal-to-gas technology, pushed forward only by the deeply vested interests of the coal-electric industry, is yet another attempt to convert a nineteenth-century fuel, but this time into a twenty-first-century energy source—natural gas. Unfortunately, the technology is cumbersome, highly inefficient, and noncommercial, as exemplified by the $25 billion (2007 dollars) Synfuels fiasco begun during the Carter administration. We must learn from our mistakes and not repeat them. Based on the same false premise of insufficient natural gas supplies, Congress and the Carter administration created in 1980 the U.S. Synthetic Fuels Corp. (Synfuels) to convert coal to natural gas. By 1982, the United States had more natural gas supplies than demand, so the whole idea of coal-to-gas was an utterly unnecessary waste of time and taxpayer money. To repeat that mistake again in the midst of natural gas abundance and at a time when we must focus our resources to accelerate positive energy changes would not only be another waste of time and money, but a travesty.

Oil

Don't listen to the big oil companies on the future of oil. The old days, described brilliantly in Daniel Yergin's history of the oil industry, *The Prize* (New York: Simon & Schuster, 1991), as well as the seven giant oil companies, the Seven Sisters who controlled the world of oil, have lost their power. Two are gone and the five companies still standing are being replaced by national oil companies (NOCs) that arose with the increase in the price of oil and nationalism in the producing nations. Oil companies are running scared and are very worried they will not be able to grow oil production and that their production rates will continue to decline. Well-known market expert Matt Simmons, author of *Twilight in the Desert*, believes that global crude oil production either peaked in 2005 or is not far from peaking.[19] Most world oil experts expect peak oil in the coming decades. Recently, the shortfall necessary to meet the world's total liquid demand of about 86 million barrels of oil per day was made up by the growth of natural gas liquids and biofuels. Since 2005, global liquid oil production has essentially been flat, but 2007 saw total liquid production of the big five oil companies decline by 398,000 barrels per day, or 4 percent.[20] Simmons's book[21] questioned the viability of future oil supplies coming from Saudi Arabia, but could better have been written about the entire oil industry and been titled the *Twilight of Oil*.

Although world oil demand is slowing a bit in 2009, over the history of its use there "has been a relentless and steady growth in global oil consumption,"[22] particularly for transportation, in spite of the global recession. It is a frightening thought, but it could be a stark reality that global oil shortages reappear in the next few years. Many experts, including myself, believe that even with modest world economic growth, the probability is high. Although dampened slightly in the West, global oil demand will probably continue to grow as a result of the rise of Asia and widespread price controls and subsidies.

Sure, there will probably be more large oil fields found and developed in places like offshore Brazil, Siberia, the Arctic, and the Mideast, but because of either internal political and economic reasons, lack of funds allocated to developing new production, or shortages of people and equipment, oil's growth in daily production flows will most likely not increase from 2008's plateau of about 86 million barrels of oil per day, or may possibly even decline as a result of all the capital expenditures either canceled or delayed as a result of the recent oil price collapse. The large consumers of oil, particularly the United States, the European Union, and China, must immediately put in place programs that will drive consumers toward alternatives that can be scaled up within the coming decade. If not, the oil shocks of price and shortages that we endured in the 1970s will seem like child's play. Civilization and its global economy and environment have simply grown to the point that the use of more liquid oil has lost utility.

Oil Shales and Tar Sands

So what about the trillions of barrels of oil we know exist in oil shale and tar sands, mostly located in Venezuela and Canada? Oil shales and tar sands, like coal-to-liquids, are simply a desperate, last attempt to slow the decline of liquids and put brakes on the GET. For starters, oil shales and tar sands create vast swaths of devastation to the Earth's natural surface, require immense quantities of precious and declining supplies of fresh water, and increase the full-cycle quantities of CO_2 emissions. There have been estimates that the carbon intensity of the production of crude oil made from tar sands could be double those of conventional oil.[23]

In the Fort McMurray area of Alberta, the center of Canada's 175 billion barrel tar sands reserves,[24] more than 80,000 acres of forest and wetlands have been damaged[25] to open the mining pits. To produce just one barrel of oil, about two tons of sand are mined and more than two hundred gallons of water are used, along with enough natural gas to run a home for a week.[26] To use carbon light natural gas to produce high CO_2 polluting oil is simply wrongheaded. For me, it is hard to imagine a production cycle more inefficient than the tar sands of Fort McMurray. And even though Canada's Prime Minister Stephen Harper in 2008 described this feat in glowing terms, "as an enterprise of epic proportions, akin to the building of the Pyramids or China's Great Wall,"[27] I would say it is a modern-day environmental disaster and a giant step in the wrong direction for society, wasting precious capital and time.

Colorado's massive oil shales require lots of fresh water that would be better used for drinking and agriculture, and as the price of oil rises, it seems the cost of oil shale production accelerates at about the same rate. In 1980, I asked an economist who was an expert on the cost of producing oil shales what the world price of oil would need to be in order to make oil shale commercial. He turned the question around by replying that oil shale will always cost at least $10 per barrel over the world price of oil (about $26 in 2008 inflation-adjusted dollars). In the 1980s, Exxon tried oil shale in a large project located near Rifle, Colorado, and it was a billion-dollar bust, so I think my friend's insight into oil shale economics was accurate. It will never make a significant contribution to the liquid fuels market. So forget about oil shale and tar sands: They are ancient ideas that require crude, inefficient production technologies and, if pursued further, will only hold back the GET and the flood of twenty-first-century technologies and innovation that will burst forth as the Age of Energy Gases moves forward.

In 1981, Clifton Garvin, then-chairman of Exxon, announced that "by the turn of the century, we think this country [the United States] will get about 4 or 5 million barrels a day of liquids from shale oil and coal."[28] Exxon even predicted, in 1980, that shale would be producing 8 million barrels of oil a day by 2010.[29] The reality is that at the close of 2007, the United States was getting about 1 million barrels of oil per day from Canada's tar sands[30] and even the most advanced oil shale development in the United States, Shell's Mahogany Project, currently remains essentially in the experimental stage. Exxon was just as wrong on the future of oil shale and coal oil in 1980 as it has consistently been on the future of natural gas. So you can see why I put little credibility today in any of Exxon's optimistic projections for oil from any source. Coal and oil have no future, only their glorious past.

Biofuels

Primitive cultures based daily activities around the use of solid energy sources such as wood, wood chips, sticks, grasses, and animal dung. To create a liquid fuel to run a global automobile fleet based on what the Earth grows is to start with historically ancient sources of energy and attempt to bring them into the twenty-first century by creating a liquid. Additionally, it is doubtful society could afford the consumption of fresh water, as it is estimated the biofuels production cycle "can consume 20 or more times as much water for every mile traveled than the production of gasoline."[31] As the GET clearly shows us, liquids are already on the way out—not on the way in. I think the only *raison d'être* for biofuels is that most automobiles, buses, and trucks built in the twentieth century and the first few years of this century have tanks that hold liquids instead of tanks that hold natural gas or other gases. Biofuels have no place in humanity's long-term future. Like all the fuels that attempt to slow the inevitable progress of the GET, many full-cycle costs and environmental problems are now coming to light through the dense fog of massive government subsidies. The recent rush to biofuels has been emotional, political, and profitable for those who receive the subsidies, rather than a real, carefully thought through technological response to our energy problems.

Biofuels will always compete with food in some way and the world's remaining precious rainforests. So, as the GET shows us, there is no need to create a fuel that will compete with civilization's quality of life. Many highly qualified thinkers, energy experts, and entrepreneurs believe that switchgrass or biological processes using microbes will resolve the looming and accelerating crises surrounding biofuels today. Unfortunately, these technologies, even if they work and are economic, are far from being proven and are many decades away from the possibility of scaling up to become a principal liquid fuel. In the meantime, I recommend changing the tanks or even adding a natural gas tank to the trunk/boot of your car to create a dual-fueled car for usually less capital cost than stepping up to a hybrid. Alternatively, consumers can buy a Honda Civic GX, the natural gas-fueled vehicle. Europeans have many natural gas vehicle choices produced by most all of the auto manufacturers.

Remember, in the United States, because of our 2.2-million-mile natural gas pipeline grid, more than 130 million cars, trucks and buses return most every night to a home or industrial facility with access to America's abundant, clean natural gas. All that is needed to run on natural gas is to add a new natural gas tank, and if you want to fill up at home, you can buy a natgas compressor appliance. Once again, solutions are always signaled by following the technology, and indeed, natgas vehicles follow the technologies. Biofuels do not follow the technology or the direction of the GET and will only bring us more problems than solutions. By following the technology, we would not create a new liquid fuel for existing tanks, but simply *change* the tanks.

Hydro and Oceans

Unfortunately, hydroelectric projects large enough to really matter severely damage the environment, often reduce agricultural productivity, and frequently submerge lots of antiquities, as well as displace large numbers of people from their ancestral homes. They are certainly not ideal solutions, and once again, are a vestige of our liquid heritage.

The Aswan Dam, on Egypt's Nile River, submerged vast archeological treasures and stopped the annual flooding that brought natural fertilizers to vast stretches of highly productive crop lands along the river's more than 4,000-mile course. China's Three Gorges Dam has displaced more than one million people[32] from their ancestral homes, and it has disrupted the natural environment of the Yangtze River. Serious silting problems have already arisen, along with many valid questions of its long-term wisdom.

In America, the Glen Canyon Dam was built on the Colorado River at the head of the Grand Canyon to form Lake Powell in the upriver canyon lands. It was touted as an important hydroelectric facility. However, the hydroelectric power gain was so small that it adds less than 1 percent to the western power grid.[33] Yet, the natural environment of the Grand Canyon, one of the Seven Wonders of the World, was altered forever. At the end of the day, it is questionable whether civilization has had much long-term benefit from large-scale hydroelectric energy projects.

During the last few decades, there have been ongoing discussions of several major projects to harness the great tides of the ocean, such as the United Kingdom's Severn Barrage project. But because of high construction costs and major environmental concerns, this project may never materialize. Although large tidal generation may be benign and renewable, our capital and creativity can be better used elsewhere. Liquids are not an answer.

Nuclear

First, let's divide nuclear into two groups—one based on solid fission, which I do not believe will work as a long-term solution, and one based on hydrogen gases, which has the potential to play a large, long-term role in civilization's future epoch of sustainable life and growth on Earth. Unfortunately, nuclear fusion, which is quite accurately described as the "sun in a box," has been just over the horizon for as long as I can remember, and it will not be a near-term solution. However, because nuclear fusion is part of the Age of Energy Gases—in its case, like the sun, created from hydrogen gas—it is my recommendation to significantly step up R&D on fusion technology. A European Commission report said: "Thermonuclear fusion and hydrogen present limitless possibilities for the future . . . ,"[34] and "Thermonuclear . . . could take over the reins from some of the existing energy sources towards the middle of the century."[35] So, let's get on with making it happen, as it is highly recommended by the GET.

Today, solid-based nuclear fission produces about 6 percent of the world's energy[36] and about 16 percent of the world's electricity.[37] Nuclear's uses outside of the production of electricity include power generation for naval vessels and a wide range of medical applications. The GET eliminates nuclear fission power from our long-term way of life because it is derived from solids, principally uranium. Granted, it is clean, to the extent it does not result in a dirty bomb. It is a workable, in-hand technology, and an energy source most governments and even some environmentalists would like to count on as a "clean," secure energy source. However, because of the proliferation issue; the potential for terrorist attacks; the long, unresolved waste storage problems and their unknown costs; and "not in my backyard" (NIMBY) public opinion, nuclear plants must be heavily subsidized by governments, are nearly impossible to finance commercially without government guarantees, and are extremely difficult to license and site. Maybe the people know more than the experts. For instance, on siting and NIMBY, consider Singapore, a small island city-state that would cease to exist if it had a catastrophic accident at a nuclear plant located in Singapore. No wonder the Singaporeans aren't anxious to go nuclear but, rather, have turned to natural gas.

As to proliferation, many of the world's experts are highly concerned, and perhaps secretly terrified, that a dirty nuclear attack is imminent. Harvard's Graham Allison, who wrote the book *Nuclear Terrorism* (New York: Henry Holt, 2004), presented the evidence for the proposition that "on the current trajectory, a successful terrorist nuclear attack devastating one of the great cities of the world is inevitable."[38] Former Defense Secretary William Perry has expressed the concern that the probability of a successful attack as estimated by many experts underestimates the real possibility. It is my fear that if the great powers, particularly the United

Nuclear

States and China, hail nuclear as the best path forward for clean energy and a solution for climate change, that many smaller but scientifically and financially capable countries, such as Iran, will feel even more deeply that they are entitled to a nuclear future. It is hard for me to imagine a nuclear Iran without a nuclear Saudi Arabia, and possibly others, in that relatively unstable region.

The bottom line is that if the West and China and India offer to the world that nuclear is an important solution to civilization's future, our proliferation risks will only escalate from there, along with the dire predictions of nuclear terrorist attacks. If these risks are what the experts say, we must factor in the large external costs of preventing dirty bomb attacks. The costs of possible future nuclear terrorist devastation and the cost of prevention must be added in when we analyze the real cost of nuclear electricity to society. When the costs of these strategic and terrorist risks, and the insurance costs of attempting to prevent dirty bomb attacks, are added to the unknown costs of nuclear waste disposal—sure to far exceed the $20 billion in America's Nuclear Waste Fund[39]—it is difficult for me to believe that nuclear electricity is less expensive than natgas-generated electricity. One 2008 estimate has the cost of waste storage at more than $90 billion.[40] Recent estimates of the cost to produce nuclear-generated electricity range from 2 cents, which I believe is unrealistically low, to 10 cents per kilowatt-hour, without the external dirty bomb costs included, as compared to 4 cents to 6 cents per kilowatt-hour for natural gas.[41]

The next difficult issue for a nuclear solution is the timing required to scale up nuclear's contribution to the production of electricity. It may take at least a decade or even longer to arrange the government subsidies, guarantees, private financing, licensing, siting, and building of a nuclear facility. Therefore, because of the upcoming mandatory decommissioning of many nuclear plants over the coming two decades in the United States and around the world, even with significant decommissioning extensions, it is highly unlikely that a sufficient number of nuclear plants can be built to accomplish any more than simply maintaining nuclear's current 16 percent of the world's electric market. Pragmatically, with the critical world shortages of the type of materials and expert engineers required to build a nuclear facility, my personal bet is that nuclear will not even be able to maintain its current position. So, even with a nuclear renaissance, it is doubtful that 20 years from now nuclear will meet even 6 percent of the world's energy demand, as it does today. Unfortunately, many climate-change scientists believe we need significant solutions coming onstream within the next two decades. Nuclear will not be able to meet that schedule, so why are we spending so much time, money, and talent on a questionable—and certainly costly—energy technology that can't possibly timely meet civilization's urgent needs? Nuclear fission is a costly, unwieldy, and dangerous dinosaur of the age of solids and, although I recognize many governments will probably use nuclear electricity as a hedge against the failure of other alternatives, it will not be a part of our long-term epoch of sustainable life and growth on Earth.

So what remains are the fuels of the Age of Energy Gases—natural gas, wind, solar, hydrogen, and nuclear fusion. Setting aside fusion, which continues to be an over-the-horizon technology in need of much higher levels of R&D expenditures and a breakthrough, natural gas, wind, solar, and hydrogen are all gaining momentum without the dark clouds of necessary technological breakthrough or economic and environmental concerns that surround all other alternatives. The fact that wind and solar are growing at rapid rates without much of the environmental and economic baggage of other alternatives is humanity's confirmation that they are indeed the important energy sources of the future and have increasing economic utility for us all. The growth of natural gas, and recent phenomenal growth of wind and solar, have just begun to accelerate the GET.

Hydrothermal

Hydrothermal energy is derived by pumping water down wells into the Earth's geothermal zones of extremely high temperatures, which generates steam to produce electricity. I suppose one could consider this a transition between liquids and gases, but because the powering source is steam and steam is basically a gas (formally a vapor), let's include hydrothermal in the Age of Energy Gases. It particularly makes sense in Iceland, where the hot regions of the Mid-Atlantic Ridge, a 50,000-mile-long faulted mountain chain below the ocean, come to the surface. Iceland intends to become virtually oil-free by the year 2050; recently, 72 percent of Iceland's domestic heating and energy requirements were being met by geothermal and hydroelectric energy.[42] Additionally, Iceland also intends to go a step further by using its hydrothermally generated electricity to separate the cleanest fuel, hydrogen, from water and use the hydrogen to power its cars, trucks, and buses, as well as to run its important fishing fleet.

In Lhasa, Tibet, geothermal power meets most electric needs, and there is more to develop when needed. California also has several developed geothermal plants, but they only supply a tiny fraction of California's power needs. At the end of the day, I believe geothermal is great when you have it nearby, but it will never become a major, scalable source of power.

Natural Gas

I have discussed natural gas extensively in previous chapters, so I won't go into detail here, but I'll simply reiterate that because natural gas is globally abundant, clean, and scalable, it is the pathfinder or bridge fuel that will drive us forward into a more environmentally benign, sustainable future. I believe we underestimate the exceptional value of America's 2.2-million-mile natural gas pipeline grid that serves most of our industrial sector, commercial buildings, 63 million American homes, and is connected to 450,000 megawatts of natural gas generation capacity (as compared with coal's 336,000 megawatts of capacity). By dispatching natural gas power before the oldest, dirtiest, and most inefficient coal power, we could cut CO_2 emissions right away by about 350 billion tons a year. This in-place pipeline grid can not only facilitate new distributed generation, either by conventional generators or fuel cells most anywhere along the system, but in effect also creates a fleet of about 130 million vehicles that return each day to those homes that can be converted to run on natural gas.

By scaling up clean natgas, we can put climate change in remission and regain our energy independence. As I recommend in Chapter 12, by converting half the U.S. vehicle fleet and the necessary fueling stations to natural gas at a cost about equal to the Iraq war, we can reduce

CO_2 emissions by about 225 million metric tons per year[43] while further reducing urban smog and pollution. This would also reduce oil imports by 5 to 6 million barrels per day, reduce payments to foreign producers by about $700 billion by 2015[44] and trillions of dollars more over the coming decades, and regain our energy independence.

In the case of China and India, the natural gas grid is not nearly so well-developed. But, as explained in the natgas chapters, because I believe natgas is also abundant in these two major energy-consuming countries, they, too, have an underutilized, clean fuel that can be scaled up to the point of meaningful displacements of coal and oil faster than any other alternative. Additionally, natgas is fully compatible with the rapid development of wind and solar because of its flexibility and ability as a standby fuel to meet generation needs in periods of slack wind or solar. Natgas is a natural partner for wind and solar, while large new coal and nuclear plants tend to drive wind and solar away or delay their market entry for decades. Natural gas is ready to go and must become a large part of the energy solution.

Wind

Wind energy is fast becoming the first choice for new electricity generation capacity in the United States. For the United States, 2007 was a banner year, with wind capacity expanding by 5,244 megawatts, or 45 percent, in one year, and in 2008 capacity expanded by 8,500 megawatts, or 50 percent.[45] In fact, so great is the demand for wind turbines that significant bottlenecks have emerged in the global supply chain. However, the global financial crisis has recently stalled many new projects. As these pressures are alleviated and new manufacturing capacity comes online, I believe we will witness a significant drop in the cost of wind energy and continuing but less rapid growth, although in the long-term, wind will become a primary energy source.

T. Boone Pickens, a Texas billionaire and oil geologist trained at Oklahoma State University, made his real fortune by understanding that global oil supplies were declining faster than new reserves were coming on stream. His BP Capital energy funds went long oil and stayed long, so the rise to near $150 per barrel in 2008 was no surprise to Boone. He is now working on a wind project that would cost him about $2 billion of his fortune for a massive project scheduled to cost about $12 billion.[46] Pickens's plan is to put in place a 4,000-megawatt wind generation facility built along the corridor of the right of way, which he has bought to bring soon-to-be-scarce fresh water from the Texas panhandle to Dallas. (Of course, water is another important story, but I'll let Pickens tell America about that.)

In several countries, wind is already becoming a primary source of energy. Having embraced the environmental, as well as the significant local economic, benefits of expanding wind energy, European countries lead the world in wind adaptation. By 2008, Germany had 22,247 megawatts of wind turbines installed, supplying 7 percent of the country's electricity.[47] America is coming on fast, having become the world's leading wind producer in the summer of 2008.[48]

Solar

Solar is an important component of the Age of Energy Gases and, in recent years, has been exploding into the energy market all around the world. *The energy we receive on Earth each day from the sun is more than all the energy we use in the world each year.* So, the use of environmentally benign solar makes abundant sense for a civilization facing the great risks presented by the three intolerables. Solar technology is improving every day, and costs have been and will continue to fall rapidly. In a January 2008 *Scientific American* article, three credible scientists presented a solar-development plan that could end U.S. dependence on foreign oil and significantly reduce greenhouse emissions by 2050.[49] There is certainly plenty of sun, particularly in the U.S. Southwest, China, India, and much of Africa. The technology is in hand, with solar innovation now coming at the speed of information technology development. Even if the *Scientific American* scientists were optimistic, solar growth in many large energy markets will go a long way to displace oil in the transportation sector with plug-in hybrids, and coal in the electric generation sector with both distributed solar on rooftops and large solar arrays in deserts to feed into badly needed electricity grids in most of the developed countries. Travis Bradford, in his excellent book *Solar Revolution*, projects solar growth to average 20 to 30 percent per year for the next 40 years.[50]

So, solar works; the necessary technology is in hand and improving, it is scalable, and its costs are in decline. If governments charged electric consumers a green tax on electricity produced from coal and oil that equaled the real, external costs of using coal and oil, solar would already be competitive with both. Once again, the energy technologies of the Age of Energy Gases are exploding into our sustainable future.

Hydrogen and Fusion

The hydrogen economy will be civilization's energy end goal. It will provide for sustainable life and growth on Earth. By the hydrogen economy, I mean an economy fueled by hydrogen, wind, solar, and, eventually, hydrogen fusion. Hydrogen is our ultimate goal because when hydrogen gas is produced from water and burned as a fuel it turns to heat and water, so the use of hydrogen is an environmentally benign water-to-water energy system. *Hydrogen is nature's simplest and most abundant element.* It is thought to compose about 75 percent of the mass of our universe. As an energy source on Earth, hydrogen is virtually limitless. Therefore, it will not bring with it the economic and geostrategic liability of oil's use, and none of the pollution and CO_2 liabilities of coal.

The full-cycle cost of our current use of coal and oil is very difficult to measure, but one thing is certain: If we eliminated all the existing external costs of their use, including oil's military and economic costs to society, the savings would be enormous. When we think about the hydrogen economy, we must ask these questions: What is an affordable energy cost in the twenty-first century? How does it compare to the elimination of all the costs of the three intolerables? This analysis must be done to understand the real cost comparison to building a hydrogen economy based on virtually limitless domestic supplies of hydrogen, solar, and wind.

Most importantly, the GET has been hydrogenating our energy system for about 150 years (see Exhibit 4.2, examining world hydrogen to carbon ratios). A century and a half ago, our energy was mostly all carbon, but today two-thirds of the atoms we use are hydrogen. So, the GET is clearly pointing civilization toward the hydrogen economy. Most of the technology to use hydrogen is already in hand. Natural gas will be its pathfinder fuel because some of the natgas infrastructure can be used to begin to phase in hydrogen. Hydrogen has already powered cars, trucks, buses, and planes. Hydrogen powered the first internal combustion engine in 1806.[51] The first hydrogen fuel cell was conceived in 1839;[52] in the 1920s, fuel cell research in Germany paved the way to the development of the carbonate cycle and solid oxide fuel cells of today. In 1932, engineer Francis T. Bacon began his research into fuel cells, and in 1959 he perfected his design.[53] In 2007, Ford Motor Company's fuel cell race car broke the land speed record at 207.297 miles per hour.[54] In 1988, the Soviet Union Tupolev commercial jet was flown with liquid hydrogen.[55] Also in 2007, Ford and Boeing successfully tested a hydrogen aircraft engine with a simulated flight that lasted four days. The president of Boeing Advanced Systems said, "This could help convince potential customers that hydrogen-powered aircraft are viable in the near term."[56]

So, without getting further into the details, my point is that hydrogen is on its way, and as it increases in commercial value to society, as always, lots of new creativity, innovation, and invention will accelerate its use to become a new principal fuel.

Many oil companies, notably BP and Shell, are spending large sums of money on the future of hydrogen, as are many automobile companies. Hydrogen energy technologies are usable and safe, clean and workable. So, to bring the hydrogen economy forward, we do not need to wait for scientific breakthroughs, but only breakthroughs in the will of society.

Today, hydrogen is separated from natural gas on a commercial scale, and some experiments envision it being produced for about $11 per million Btu.[57] As of midsummer 2008, oil was at $21.33 per million Btu and natural gas at $9.79 per million Btu[58]; however, in early spring 2009, oil was at $8.20 per million Btu and natural gas at $3.78 per million Btu.[59] Hydrogen is also liberated from water by electrolysis, a process that has been used for 100 years. All that is needed to continually reduce the cost of hydrogen is to scale up so that, like solar and wind, its costs will continue to decline.

Hydrogen-based nuclear fusion offers society limitless possibilities for a sustainable future, but has always been just over the horizon. However, today, there are fusion research reactors operating worldwide—in Japan, Russia, China, the United States, and the United Kingdom. In France, an experimental reactor meant to generate 500 megawatts of power (ten times more than the energy input needed to keep the plasma at the right temperature and therefore the first fusion experiment to produce net power) is being constructed in the south near Cadarache. The cost is expected to be approximately 5 billion euros, and its operational costs are estimated to add another 5 billion euros over its 20-year operational life.[60] If successful, it will become the first fusion plant with an output power higher than the input power. Participating with France are other EU members, along with Japan, China, South Korea, Russia, and the United States.

Hydrogen fusion is among the technologies toward which the GET is taking civilization. So, as one who believes we should follow the technology, it is my recommendation that *research and development of hydrogen fusion be stepped up by all governments* around the world. We must not let the negative connotation of fusion always being a just-over-the-horizon technology slow our commitment to further funding and research for this technology.

Importantly, unlike nuclear fission reactors that can melt down if the reaction reaches an uncontrolled, supercritical state, fusion cannot become an uncontrolled reaction.[61] Although the fusion reactor vessel does become radioactive, fusion produces no waste like the spent uranium that is a product of fission reactors. So fusion avoids the enormous costs of waste storage and should definitely reduce the not-in-my-backyard feeling society has for nuclear fission.

Hydrogen is truly a noble source of energy, and for 150 years the GET has been moving us along the transitional path to the hydrogen economy. As with all alternative fuels, we must begin to overcome political resistance from the established interests, by eliminating the subsidies for coal and oil, so that we can accelerate energy change forward.

As stewards of planet Earth, there cannot be any more fulfilling and gratifying task than for humanity to make the transition to civilization's ultimate energy source for millennia to come. By so doing, from the

point of view of our energy use, we can place an environmentally, economically, and geostrategically stable Earth in the hands of our children
and grandchildren, and all future generations.

For those of you who want a broader background and some challenging philosophy about the hydrogen economy, I highly recommend
Jeremy Rifkin's prescient book *The Hydrogen Economy*.[62]

Chapter 12

Policies to Accelerate the GET

We can't solve problems by using the same kind of thinking we used when we created them.

—Albert Einstein

. . . the only thing we have to fear is fear itself . . .

—Franklin Delano Roosevelt

T he United States is an exceptional *can-do* country, limited only by the enthusiasm of its people. Time and again when Americans come together, we rise up to accomplish great goals. As I write this chapter in the spring of 2009, we are in two wars and what many experts describe as the greatest financial crisis since the Great Depression. Banking institutions and prestigious financial companies have failed, been force-fed to former competitors, or been taken over by the federal government.

President Obama has worked with the new Congress to pass the $787 billion American Recovery and Reinvestment Act, in addition to the $700 billion bailout to banks that will hopefully ease the credit freeze. In the meantime, our costly financial commitments to the Iraq and Afghanistan wars continue, but no matter how successful the conclusion of our wars and the stabilization of our financial system, the majority of these taxpayer dollars are aimed at financial stabilization and national security and are not designed to reenergize America's economic future. What we need now are equally historic policies that Americans can rally around to create a new future for our country. We must mobilize all Americans, particularly our dedicated and capable labor force, to rebuild our industrial base so that we can be successfully competitive in an energy-efficient, sustainable twenty-first-century globalized economy.

Although all the attention is on our massive home mortgage problems and the financial industry and the unraveling of their supposedly magic debt instruments, we have what I believe to be an energy travesty going on. Once again, very few in Washington are paying any attention to America's abundant, clean natural gas. Because we have never had an overarching policy to use our clean natural gas for either power generation or transportation, our natural gas supplies have far outstripped demand. The price has crashed to below replacement cost, tens of billions of dollars of capital expenditures for future natural gas development have been canceled (expenditures that generate a two to three multiplier in local economies), income to state and local governments from natural gas production has declined by billions, and revenues to U.S. farmers and landowners have plummeted by tens of billions. Eight hundred drilling rigs have been idled,[1] with at least 200 to 300 more on the way to losing work,[2] along with tens of thousands of lost jobs in U.S. natural gas industry. Oklahoma City's two largest independent natural gas companies, Chesapeake and Devon Energy, wrote down the carrying value of their natural gas and oil properties by over $13 billion in 2008.[3] America's natural gas industry is in a disastrous bust that is unnecessarily exacerbating our ongoing economic contraction. Once again, this bust may well deliver a long-term, crippling body blow to our domestic natural gas industry.

While our natural gas industry was crashing because we have so much more than we can use, the United States paid out $475 billion to foreign oil producers in 2008. In the first two months of 2009, it paid another approximatly $30 billion,[4] and there will be trillions more in the decades to come that will work to cripple our economic recovery because we don't have policies to use our clean, affordable natural gas to fuel our cars, trucks, and buses. To me, it seems like an economic, national security, and climate travesty when our country is awash in our own natural gas, which is cleaner, runs automobile engines longer, and emits about 30 percent less CO_2 and 90 percent less other pollution than gasoline.

Natural gas is the only clean alternative to gasoline and diesel that is sufficiently scalable to reduce oil imports by 5 to 6 million barrels per day by 2015. All we need to do is come together behind a large-scale plan such as the one proposed in this chapter. As President Obama has said, the nation must free itself "from the dangerous dependence on foreign oil."[5]

Now, before we go further, let me say that I am completely in favor of wind and solar power and electric vehicles, but until we build a new smart interstate electric grid and quit generating half of our power with coal, we won't be able to accomplish our goal of getting off oil while improving our environment and lowering CO_2 emissions, and it will take decades to do that. So, in the meantime, let's take some big American steps forward and get the job done with natural gas as the bridge fuel to our more idealistic future.

Even more imperative than our economic crisis is the effective implementation of energy, industrial, and tax policies to accelerate the GET to rebuild the U.S. industrial base so we can be successfully competitive in an energy-efficient, sustainable twenty-first-century globalized economy. The acceleration of the GET not only will be our silver path toward a sustainable economic recovery and renewed financial health, but it will unleash the forces that will create the next great, unprecedented economic expansion. Our motto for the coming decades should become "jet the GET."

This chapter will outline recommendations that flow from my life's work in the energy field and a lifetime that has experienced great political swings, from Franklin Delano Roosevelt's first inaugural admonition that ". . . the only thing we have to fear is fear itself . . . ," and his New Deal, of embracing bold change organized to resolve equally dire financial problems, to Ronald Reagan's first inaugural getting-government-out-of-the-way stage, "In this present crisis, government is not the solution to our problem; government is the problem,"[6] and the follow-on financial deregulation that today has brought us full circle.

My two overarching policy recommendations call for, on the one hand, more government in the form of a new twenty-first-century energy and industrial initiative similar in scale to, if not more sweeping than, Roosevelt's New Deal or the industrial tooling-up to win World War II. On the other hand, it also calls for somewhat less government in the form of sweeping tax reforms and a green, consumption-based tax system.

Today, as to our intolerable energy-related economic, national security and climate risks, government is no longer the problem, because today the problems are global and of such scale that they require an enlightened bipartisan government to work with the people and the marketplace. Since the 1970s, as a result of decades of cheap, externally subsidized, rapidly increasing coal and oil consumption, we have now arrived to face climate, economic, and national security risks of such magnitude that government must again lead our way forward.

I put forward the proposition that for the United States to lead the world in climate and energy and create the conditions for renewed economic growth and the rebuilding of our industrial base and infrastructure with energy efficient technologies, President Obama must adopt these two clear and bold strategies. But to be successful, he must have full command of the bully pulpit to articulate, motivate, and educate Americans on the great need for and equally large benefits of these goals so that we all come together to enthusiastically embrace them behind his bold leadership, just as we did when Roosevelt rallied us to lead the way out of the Great Depression, and Kennedy did to put an American on the moon in a decade.

President Obama and Congress must restore the faith in a can-do government. I believe that the confidence of the American people in their government will be fundamental for the resolution of these great issues. That confidence can only be regained by putting aside partisan bickering and moving forward with a new, bipartisan spirit of "America first." We are in an era where continued congressional bickering and grandstanding have become irresponsible. The United States needs bipartisan solutions.

The United States is at an historical turning point with an unprecedented opportunity to ride the wave of energy gases to our next era of extraordinary growth. It is time for the United States to leave behind its nineteenth- and twentieth-century energy technologies and the policies that helped shape them and retool itself for the twenty-first century. Economies cannot sustain themselves for the long-term on services alone, so it is now time for new tax, energy, and industrial policies that will restore our energy independence and place the United States in a global leadership position for the creation of sustainable energy technologies and climate stabilization.

By embracing, rather than fearing, change and accelerating the natural evolution of the GET, humanity can achieve sustainable life and growth on Earth in this century. The United States must lead the way. By doing so, it will become the center of the next great economic expansion.

What follows is a group of policies to get us off to a great start. Following those are my overarching macro policies to jet the GET for the long term.

How to Immediately and Significantly Reduce CO_2 Emissions

There are two policy actions that I believe would be simpler, more effective, and less costly to lower CO_2 emissions faster and in larger initial quantities than either a complex cap and trade system or CO_2 emission capture and sequestration (CCS). These actions should proceed independently of all other energy policy.

Policy action number one. America's 2.2-million-mile natural gas pipeline grid[7] is connected to 450,000 megawatts of natural gas–fired electric generating capacity. That compares with 336,000 megawatts of coal-fired capacity.[8] The reason coal generates 50 percent of America's power and natural gas only 22 percent is because coal plants run at 74 percent capacity and natural gas combined cycle at 42 percent capacity,[9] and natural gas simple cycle at only 11 percent, even though most natural gas–generating facilities can be run reliably at 90 percent capacity or above. Because natural gas power emits 50 percent less CO_2,[10] we should immediately implement a policy that requires combined cycle natural gas power be run at the highest capacity possible and be dispatched first.

This one action could replace about a third of all the coal-fired electricity in the United States without building a new plant and, at the same time, lower annual U.S. CO_2 emissions by an astonishing several hundred million tons per year and put us well on our way to the Intergovernmental Panel on Climate Change's (IPCC) goal for the United States. Unfortunately, we cannot completely eliminate all coal power plants because in many localities on a particular electric grid there are not a sufficient number of natural gas power plants, and on many electric grids, all the coal and natural gas power capacity will be required in order to meet peak power demand. Another problem is that utilities own or unduly control the electric grid and dispatch the coal plants first because they produce more regulated profits for the utility shareholders and also because some coal-generated electricity is about 2¢ per kilowatt cheaper.[11] Of course, it is not really cheaper because there are large health and pollution costs related to coal's use that are not charged to the consumer of electricity but are paid instead by society in general.

If Congress passed legislation that mandated clean, low-carbon natural gas power first where possible, I estimate that enough natural gas generation capacity would be located in a sufficient number of critical locations so that about one-third of the coal plants could be closed down and over 300 million tons of annual CO_2 emissions would be eliminated. To generate one-third of the U.S. coal power with existing natural gas plants would require about 4 Tcf of new natural gas consumption annually. America's natural gas producers could meet that new demand rapidly, beginning with our current excess supplies. LNG, Canadian imports, and eventually Alaskan supplies could also fill in when and if needed. To begin with, policy makers might want to start with our dirtiest, most inefficient coal plants that use about one-third of the annual coal consumption and produce the highest levels of CO_2 per megawatt.

I urge readers to write their congressional representatives and tell them that the United States must use its clean natural gas to generate electricity before we use coal-generated electricity. To do so may cost the electric consumer a little more than from coal plants but a lot less than if laws or regulations mandate the cleaning up of coal power, so-called "clean coal," or require new equipment to lower CO_2 emissions and toxic wastes. Of course, if either a carbon tax or cap and trade are passed, carbon light natural gas will be less costly than coal.

Policy action number two. In order to meet our need for additional electric power we should mandate that no new power plant can be built that emits more CO_2 or general pollution than that of a natural gas plant. After all, during the last two years, some 90 coal plants have been taken off the drawing board[12] and several new natural gas plants announced (with some 17,000 megawatts of natural gas powered generation capacity added in 2006 and 2007[13]), the most recent being a 300 megawatt plant by Idaho Power.[14] So, let's simply accelerate that trend by mandating that all new power plants be as clean and green as natural gas.

Although detailed cost studies need to be performed, I am confident that these two actions would cost the economy and consumers much less than "clean coal" technology and sequestration, and would cut CO_2 emissions immensely faster than any other policy action, including cap and trade.

I know this will cause an uproar from the coal industry but we must keep in mind that the entire coal mining industry employs only about 80,000 miners[15] and that the entire industry is economically less than 10 percent the size of Wal-Mart.[16] So, my point is that the coal industry should no longer have such massively disproportionate power over American politics, our environment, and energy use.

The long-term adverse macroeconomic and environmental effects of the coal industry's political control over the politics of energy have been immense. A large part of the U.S. population has suffered multiple coal-related personal health issues and their ever-increasing costs and the American taxpayers have paid an enormous burden for coal's tax subsidies, at least $10 billion over the last decade.[17] These subsidies are not necessary to go forward meeting all our new electric power demand not met by wind and solar with carbon light natural gas. Indeed, we should help retrain the miners who may lose jobs; however, many miners can easily be trained for new work in the energy industry, as there will be plenty of new jobs. A small portion of the stimulus funds already allocated to the coal industry could be used to retrain miners for safer and healthier jobs. The important point is that we should not adversely impact our energy and environmental goals because of the continuing disproportionally powerful political influence of such a relatively tiny sector of the U.S. economy.

Decouple the Electric Grid

Since its beginning, America's electric grid system has been owned and controlled by local and regional electric utilities and regulated by a patchwork of state and regional regulatory authorities. Because most electric power producers are utilities, their returns on capital investment are regulated by the individual state power commissions in such a way that the utility companies' growth depends upon the amount of capital they are able to invest. As a result, high-cost coal and nuclear power plants provide more growth for the utility companies than less capital intensive natural gas, wind, and solar generated power. Over past decades, large, costly coal and nuclear plants have been the growth strategy of most utility companies. As these plants must be paid for by consumers of electricity over 30 years or more, they tend to limit the number of less capital intensive and often more efficient power facilities. Also, because electric utility power companies often own and/or have undue control over the electric distribution grid system, there is little incentive to allow smaller distributed power systems or more efficient natural gas, wind, and solar power facilities owned by third parties into the electric grid. Thus, under our present system, competition and innovation has generally been discouraged. So in order for the United States to be successful in the development of a twenty-first-century energy infrastructure with a modern smart grid and renewable and distributed power, the ownership and control of the electric grid must be decoupled from and independent of all the electric power producers. Any qualified power producer, no matter how small, must be able to compete 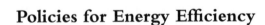 to produce the cleanest and cheapest electricity for America's consumers.

Policies for Energy Efficiency

As I have described in Chapter 9, "The *Real* Inconvenient Truth," because of America's failure to internalize the full costs of coal and oil over the past 30 years, our energy infrastructure and energy habits have been developed without regard for efficiency. Sadly, U.S. energy infrastructure and consumption habits are prolifically wasteful. As a result, enormous, profitable energy efficiency gains with attractive rates of return are possible throughout the entire energy sector.

My friend Amory Lovins, co-founder and chief scientist of the Rocky Mountain Institute (www.rmi.org), has been advocating various policies and technologies to make the United States more efficient for RMI's entire 27-year history. I will not repeat the body of work here, but only highlight one important publication, *Winning the Oil End Game*. One conclusion of this publication is that "fully applying today's best efficiency technologies in a doubled-GDP 2025 economy would save half the projected U.S. oil use at half its forecast cost per barrel."[18] If the enormous external costs of oil are included, Lovins and his team forecast that "it will cost less to displace all of the oil that the United States now uses than it will cost to buy that oil."[19] RMI may be optimistic, but there is no question that there are very large efficiencies to be profitably achieved.

Suffice it to say that in the sectors of oil consumption (particularly transportation) and electric power consumption (industrial, commercial, and residential), there are enormous gains to be made by investment in efficiency. Some experts estimate that efficiencies could be profitably doubled over the long-term. I believe extensive policies focused on making the United States one of the most energy-efficient economies for the twenty-first century are essential to our economic success. McKinsey & Company (www.mckinsey.com) has completed an exceptionally important body of work showing how the United States can profit from energy efficiency solutions. Its July 2008 report says, "One hundred and seventy billion dollars a year invested in efforts to boost energy efficiency from now until 2020 could halve the projected growth in global energy demand."[20] An earlier study concluded that, using high efficiency options, "projected electricity consumption in residential buildings in the United States in 2020 could be reduced by more than a third."[21]

Nuclear Fission Is Not a Long-Term Solution

A brief word about nuclear power: Because nuclear works, it is an excellent hedge, but as described in Chapter 11, "What Won't Work; What Will Work," it is not a long-term solution. Undoubtedly, because it is a good hedge, wise policy makers will include subsidies for the near-term, such as government-guaranteed loans. It will also be necessary to streamline the permit process. Although nuclear power properly fits in the diminishing age of solids and will not be a long-term energy solution, I must join with the pragmatists who say that during the next two or three decades, as we progress further into the Age of Energy Gases, nuclear is a justifiable hedge.

End Subsidies for Coal, Oil, and Biofuels

The next great step forward will be to accelerate the GET by developing policies to transform the fuel mix away from coal and oil and toward energy gases. First, we must eliminate current policies that are working against the GET. Therefore, I recommend the elimination of direct subsidies to the coal and oil industries.

Because of the misperception that the United States has no choice but to rely on coal, there are many special incentives for advanced coal technology, coal gasification, and other coal-related projects, created and funded by the federal government. If you haven't read Chapter 7, "Natural Gas Abundance," I refer you to the section titled "America's Attainable Natural Gas Supplies May Equal or Exceed Minable Coal Supplies" that calls into question the misperception that the United States has no choice but to rely on coal. Sufficient natural gas is available to displace coal in the future.

According to the National Research Council, "more than $538 million was spent by federal government agencies for coal-related research and technology development in 2005."[22] According to Taxpayers for Common Sense,[23] since 1984 the federal government has invested about $2.5 billion in clean coal technology,[24] and the Energy Policy Act of 2005 included more than $9 billion in subsidies for the coal industry.[25] These should all be eliminated, with the exception of government loans, grants, and other payments for development of CO_2 capture and sequestration (CCS). Subsidies for CCS should continue, but be focused only on sequestration technology itself. I will address specific sequestration policies later in the chapter.

No government money should be spent on converting coal to oil, gasoline or diesel, as all that does is spend taxpayers' money to artificially attempt to sustain liquids even further, producing even more CO_2 emissions than with oil use.

Coal-to-natgas is neither commercially viable nor needed, given North America's vast supplies of natural gas. So, today, to create noncommercial natural gas from coal is an utter waste. Let's not make the same $25 billion[26] mistake again that we did in 1980 by creating the Synfuels Corporation to advance coal gasification and oil shale projects.

Government should prohibit all new coal-fired electric generation that is not built with full CCS facilities in operation upon startup.
Legislation could take the form of the 1978 Fuel Use Act, which then
prohibited the use of natgas in new power generation. But, this time,
the prohibited fuel should be coal, for all the reasons given in this book.

Biofuels also work against the GET. Biofuels are merely a misguided attempt to sustain liquids beyond their normal decline, largely
because automobiles, trucks, and buses have fuel tanks that hold a liquid instead of a gas. I address that issue in the transportation section.
As explained in Chapter 11, biofuels are part of the era of liquids and
are not a long-term solution for civilization. One way or another,
scaled-up biofuels production will most always compete with either
food or rainforests. We have too much to accomplish to misdirect time,
brains, and capital toward liquids that are on the way out. All mandates
and subsidies for biofuels should be eliminated.

Use Carbon Capture and Sequestration (CCS)

We should continue CCS programs because sequestration will be
necessary to meet our long-term CO_2 reduction goals. However, it is
doubtful we will use CCS for coal. The first test facility should start
with natural gas rather than coal because natgas is the superior fuel that
produces half the CO_2 of coal and few to none of the other toxic pollutants. Because there is half or less the CO_2 to deal with in the first
place, when natural gas rather than coal is used to generate the equivalent amount of electricity, the volumes of liquid CO_2 to be piped to
locations for sequestration will also be halved, as will the overall costs
to create the infrastructure. In fact, it is my recommendation that the
widely heralded CCS FutureGen project for coal should be resurrected
as NatgasGen. Electricity produced by natural gas with CO_2 sequestration will be completely green. NatgasGen would be just about as environmentally benign as wind and solar.

Begin Opening Restricted Drilling Areas

Important quantities of abundant supplies of natural gas are locked
up by government policies that prohibit drilling. These bans should
be lifted so that environmentally controlled natural gas drilling can
take place in all our offshore basins and in large areas in the Rocky

Mountains, which are now off limits. Because of its physical properties, natural gas is far less of a risk to the environment and our oceans and coastal areas than oil. When natural gas is produced, there is virtually *no* risk of an oil spill. In the lower 48 states, about 85 percent of the Outer Continental Shelf and 67 percent of onshore federal lands are off limits or facing significant restrictions to development.[27] However, in the near term, the natural gas supplies outside of these areas are already exceeding demand and will be more than adequate to meet much greater demand, leaving sufficient time to work out the environmental considerations for drilling in these environmentally more sensitive areas (see Chapter 7).

A Cap and Trade System

Cap and trade, the government-mandated system for establishing declining limits on carbon emissions and simultaneously creating a market for their trade, is a step in the right direction. However, it is not an overall long-term global solution. Cap and trade is flawed from the start, as there will always be enormous vested-interest pressure that will create international competition between governments and incentives for the overallocation of carbon emissions by individual nations. Any international cap and trade system negotiation will be no less rancorous than the arguments over farm subsidies. The system will be gamed by wealthy and poor nations alike at the cost of society in general. National governments will have to set CO_2 emission limits and their rates of decline for individual industries. So the vested interests will be lobbying for their very lives and nations will be competing with other nations for the benefit of their most-favored industries and to protect jobs at home. Therefore, although cap and trade is a worthy objective to create a real market, whether it becomes a global effort or just American policy, it will be fraught with loopholes and unfair practices. I am afraid it will be much harder to make work and agree upon than the general standards for global trade under the WTO.

Also importantly, cap and trade does not work directly to solve the large economic and national security problems related to excessive oil imports because it is doubtful that if the cap and trade limits are placed on the transportation sector that the fluctuating CO_2 prices would be sufficient to reduce gasoline demand meaningfully. Therefore, cap and trade will not be a sufficiently effective force to reduce oil imports to a level that can begin to restore U.S. national and economic security. On the other hand, a green tax on oil, particularly imported oil, will do just that. However, cap and trade would be compatible and effective along with a green tax.

Overarching Macro Policy Objectives

The United States is in the midst of great crises at home, as well as what most likely will become civilization's largest crises emanating from our energy, geostrategic, and climate risks, so we must be bold and embrace change as never before. We must set our eyes firmly on the goal and never waver, because the magnitude of these crises is also the foundation for opportunities of equal magnitude, but only if acted on with equal boldness. President Obama must remember that our path to failure will be the path limited by the fear of bold action.

What follows are my recommendations for massive changes in how the United States consumes energy, and the macro policies necessary to jet the GET.

As I see the future, there are two fundamental seismic policy shifts necessary for America's future economic, environmental, and national security success. One is a green consumption-based tax system initially focused on coal and oil. The second is an energy and industrial policy organized to replace at least half our vehicle fleet with natural gas fueled CNG vehicles by the year 2015. By implementing these tax, energy, and industrial policies, the United States can unleash economic expansion, regain energy independence, and be far down the road toward climate stabilization by 2015. I will tackle the subject of a green consumption-based energy tax first, followed by an energy and industrial policy organized to convert half America's vehicle fleet to natural gas by 2015, and by doing so, regain our energy independence.

A Green Consumption-Based Tax System

We need a policy that will eliminate the indirect, hidden external subsidies to coal and oil that were the subject of Chapter 9. No matter what we do, we cannot overturn the economic truth that *we will always use more of what costs less, less efficiently, and less of what costs more, more efficiently.*

The fundamental questions to ask as we face the looming three intolerables—intolerable economic, climate, and national security risks emanating from our current energy consumption rates and fuel mix—are these: What energy sources must we use less of to win our sustainable future? What must we use less of to regain economic and national security? What must we use *more* of to prevent energy-related economic and climate disasters and to become the world's energy technology leader? And how can we best accomplish these goals in turbulent and troubled economic times?

The GET gives us straightforward answers. We need to phase out the use of coal and oil that are causing the majority of our climate, economic, and national security problems, and use more gases: natural gas, wind, solar, and hydrogen. And most importantly, particularly in the midst of the U.S. financial crisis, we must drive the GET forward so that gaseous fuels replace solids and liquids, to accelerate us into the next great wave of economic growth. Let me repeat, the forthcoming wave of energy gases will unleash even greater economic growth than what we experienced in coal's Industrial Revolution and oil's post–World War II economic expansion to globalization.

In order to take full advantage of the next great economic pulse that will be fueled by the Age of Energy Gases, the United States must do all that is possible to encourage individual innovation, labor, productivity, and the growth and use of capital. In order to use less coal and oil, it seems clear that we should create a consumption-based green tax system that focuses initially on coal and oil. At the same time, in order to create incentives for labor, creativity, innovation, and invention to flourish and capital to grow and be deployed, we should eliminate all taxes on the income from our labor and the use and growth of our capital.

It is past time for a complete reform of our incomprehensibly complex, special-interests-dominated tax system. The cost for businesses, individuals, and nonprofits to comply with our tax laws and file returns has been estimated to be up to $265 billion each year.[28] U.S. taxpayers should be freed from this ludicrously wasteful burden of money and time through tax simplification. To dig ourselves out of this deep economic contraction, we need all of our labor and capital to be focused on productive efforts and investments in new opportunities. So, we must eliminate the tax laws as they currently stand and remove the tax burden from income and capital, to be replaced by a new green consumption-based tax system that will be the most macroeconomically efficient way to pay for government and at the same time drive us toward our energy and climate goals. It is a tax policy to jet the GET.

New taxes to replace these revenues could include a low flat tax or a consumption tax or both. I favor consumption taxes for three reasons. First, the mechanism for collecting sales and excise taxes is already in place. Second, sales taxes apply to everyone, foreigners and Americans, so everyone pays their fair share. The U.S. cash economy is huge—over $100 billion per year[29]—and not much of that is taxed. To balance our budget again, we need that tax revenue. Third, it is imperative for the United States to use less coal and oil, so a green consumption-based tax must be added on coal and oil that will reflect their real external costs. With the implementation of the green tax system, the government should conduct official studies on a continuing basis to determine as closely as possible the real external costs of the continuing use of coal and oil, as well as the other energy sources.

I know I will be rightfully challenged on the issue that a consumption tax is regressive. However, a consumption tax would broaden the tax base to include all Americans, the cash economy, and all foreigners purchasing goods in the United States. So, hopefully, such a broad tax base would lower the total burden on individual taxpayers. Additionally, our Social Security system or unemployment system would need to be expanded to include the idea of a "negative income tax" for the truly needy.

Some Approximate Tax Numbers

Individual federal income taxes produce approximately $1.2 trillion[30] in revenue each year. A green consumption-based tax system initially focused on coal and oil could be phased in to replace this revenue. Imported oil's external costs have been variously estimated to be from $5 to $10 per gallon.[31] At current consumption rates, a tax of $1 per gallon on gasoline, diesel, and jet fuel would produce revenues of about

$200 billion. If the tax was increased by $1 per gallon each year for five years, the revenue would be in the range of about $900 billion after adjusting for an approximately 13 percent reduction in oil products consumption after a full five years.[32]

External costs for the health effects of coal-produced electricity have been estimated to be in a wide range of from $33 to $83 per ton of coal consumed.[33] By starting a tax at $30 per ton of coal consumed, revenue would equal about $34 billion per year. If this tax were escalated to $100 per ton over a five-year period, yearly revenue would likely increase to about $113 billion. These rough calculations indicate federal revenue from coal and oil taxes to be about $234 billion per year initially, escalating to approximately $1 trillion in five years.[34] Thereafter, revenue would probably begin to fall as coal and oil are replaced by energy gases. As revenues from oil and coal taxes decline, sales or other consumption taxes could be increased as necessary.

I cite these numbers simply to show that the replacement of all income taxes could be achieved with a consumption-based green tax system. I will not attempt to define how a new green tax system will work, as I know there are plenty of great minds in Washington that can figure out the details. My goal is to lay out the philosophy of a green tax system and stimulate debate.

Finally, and most importantly, to set aside the regressive problem, any new plan would need to accommodate the poor, who need to drive but cannot afford the escalating gasoline cost or the conversion of their cars to CNG, as well as those who cannot afford the increased cost of electricity produced from coal alternatives. I believe that a system that offers assistance directly to the poor would be far superior and more economically efficient than one that creates macroeconomic distortions of the entire energy market and the building of energy inefficient infrastructure by keeping energy prices low *because* of the poor. By not charging the real full-cycle costs of coal and oil to consumers, we have polluted the country, diminished our health, and lost our national security. Just like the financial system, we have overleveraged our energy use and most of the debt has yet to come due. So, let's devise a system to care for the poor at the same time we phase in green taxes on coal and oil that represent—as closely as possible—their real external costs.

By making these bold changes in how we tax to pay for government, people will begin immediately to change their habits and to use less and less coal and oil as they turn to cleaner, less costly domestic fuels of all varieties. A real market for coal and oil that reflects their full-cycle costs will be, by far, the best and fastest way to diminish their use and accelerate the use of clean alternatives. At the same time, Americans will be able to keep the money they earn and grow their capital without tax. When the external costs of coal are charged to the consumer, wind and solar will certainly be less expensive and demand for them will continue to grow at exponential rates, so their current subsidies can be eliminated.

Need for Bold Changes and Fairness

Unfortunately for the United States, with today's political climate, troubled economic times, *and* unprecedented financial stress and credit problems, and the fact that so much brain power and economic strength is being drained by financial bailouts, Iraq, and Afghanistan, it is difficult to imagine that the necessary revolution in how the tax system works will occur without first experiencing further catastrophic disasters brought by one or all three of the three intolerables. However, a complete overhaul of how the government taxes to pay its costs is long overdue and vital for success in the twenty-first century.

Today, the United States must compete as never before. *Newsweek*'s Fareed Zakaria aptly described this new world era as the "rise of the rest" in his book *The Post-American World*.[35] Without such dramatic energy and tax changes, the United States will continue to be faced with the difficult, competitive problem of a burdensome system that taxes the income from our labor and the growth of our capital worldwide, as well as a burdensome, inefficient, unsustainable nineteenth- and twentieth-century energy system. Conversely, most wealthy foreign participants in the "rise of the rest" will be able to grow their wealth largely offshore and untaxed, increasing the ever-widening gap between the world's poor and middle class, and the super-wealthy. Over decades, this trend will make the United States less competitive in the global economy, while more and more social costs and energy externalities fall upon the American wage earner. Also, without green energy taxes, this untaxed foreign wealth will profit by participating in America's growth and by purchasing U.S. goods cheaply at less than their full cost. This is because foreign wealth will not be paying its fair share of the real external costs of energy used to create our growth or produce our goods. Without a green consumption-based tax, the external energy costs will continue to fall only upon the shoulders of Americans and inhibit our economic growth. The only way Americans can share the real costs of the use of coal and oil with all foreign participants in our economy is to create a green tax system that internalizes these costs. Otherwise, no matter who profits, these costs will continue to be borne only by Americans.

I argue that for the next 100 years, during civilization's evolution to sustainable energy systems, taxes on income and capital be abolished, and a green consumption-based tax system be phased in, focused on the two energy uses we wish to first reduce and eventually eliminate— coal and oil. Because external subsidies are the primary cause of the three intolerables, *taxes, energy, and climate are inexorably connected to one another*, as well as to future economic growth.

A green tax on coal and oil at rates estimated by government to equal the real cost of their use is fair. Why should an SUV commuter from the suburbs be subsidized by those who cannot afford SUVs and live close enough to work to walk? Obviously, such unintended, but real, consequences are unfair. Society as a whole is carrying the burden of the external costs of coal and oil. Our current policies have created the three intolerables by encouraging the inefficient use of coal and oil products. Second, to continue to tax labor and capital is to tax what we desperately need to grow and flourish, particularly as we face the necessary creative destruction of our outdated energy industries and the costs of rebuilding our entire energy infrastructure. We must not rebuild our energy infrastructure to use the same old energy sources that have brought us to the three intolerables.

Our current system of taxation was created for different times. It may have been effective for an agrarian and old industrial economy, but it is no longer socially fair or efficient. Our tax system is as outdated as our energy technologies. To compete effectively with the rise of the rest in the twenty-first century, it is my premise that the United States must make radical changes in how we tax to pay for government, as well as radical changes in the fuels we use to run our economy.

Why a Green Tax Works Better than a Carbon or CO_2 Tax

My argument is based on the fact that in order to have a real, fair, and effective market to allocate coal, oil, natural gas, wind, solar, and hydrogen needed for future growth, we must level the economic and environmental playing field with a green consumption tax. Neither a carbon tax nor a CO_2 emissions tax will level the playing field because there are large external costs related to the full-cycle consumption of the use of coal and oil that do not apply to natural gas and are not measured by the varying quantities of carbon contained in coal, oil, and natural gas or their CO_2 emissions.

First, let's compare coal to natural gas. As a solid, coal emits particles into the air that natural gas does not. Coal also emits large quantities of sulphuric acid, which creates acid rain, and coal's emissions of mercury are the world's largest.[36] Forty-nine states have issued fish consumption advisories due to high mercury concentrations in freshwater bodies throughout the United States.[37] The American Lung Association has estimated coal's emissions cause 24,000 premature deaths annually, in addition to 550,000 asthma attacks each year and 38,000 heart attacks.[38] Also, as a new report implies, the full-cycle consumption cost of coal's externalities will continue to grow as coal quality declines, requiring increased coal tonnages to produce the same amount of electricity.[39] None of these costs relate to natural gas because natural gas produces nearly none of the pollutants that create these real and large health and environmental costs to society.

A fair consumption tax for imported oil must be set higher than for the use of coal. This is because imported oil has significantly higher external costs per unit of energy, even though it contains less carbon than coal. These higher external costs are associated with the large cost of our military protecting the free flow of oil, the cost of oil-related wars, our 2008 export rate of $475 billion to pay for oil imports[40] that equaled about 70 percent of our trade deficit,[41] and the loss of those funds to the U.S. economy. Of course, the greatest immeasurable and tragic cost of oil is the cost of U.S. lives, oil's related cost of our diminished national security, and the fact that oil revenues finance our terrorist enemies.

A CO_2 or carbon tax does not level the environmental playing field between gasoline and natural gas because gasoline is the principal cause of the smog in all of our major cities. The extremely fine particulates emitted from gasoline are particularly deadly and linked to adverse pulmonary health effects.[42] The use of natural gas in vehicles would eliminate all particulates and most of gasoline's other pollution. Although very difficult to measure, analysts have estimated the external costs of gasoline refined from Mideast oil to be in a range of $5.00 to $10.00 per gallon.[43] Again, natural gas has virtually none of these external costs.

If the external costs of *foreign oil imports* averaged only $1 to $3 per gallon since 1980, then the real cost of that oil would have been not only the price consumers paid, but an additional $4 trillion to $12 trillion, none of which was paid by the gasoline consumer.[44] In the case of coal, if the external costs of all coal consumed in the United States since 1980 averaged from $10 to $30 per ton, then the real cost of that coal would have been an additional $260 to $790 billion over and above what coal-fired electric power consumers paid.[45] Even though coal has considerably more carbon than oil, its external costs are less than imported oil. Neither a carbon tax nor a CO_2 tax level the economic or environmental playing field between coal, oil, and natural gas.

In addition to the serious question of whether such a thing as clean coal is pragmatically achievable, there is one additional fact about coal versus natural gas for America's energy future. In the book *Coal: Research and Development to Support National Energy Policy*, The National Research Council of the National Academies stated that "almost certainly, coals mined in the future will be lower quality because current mining practices result in higher-quality coal being mined first, leaving behind lower-quality material, with higher ash yield, higher sulfur, and/or higher concentrations of potentially harmful elements."[46] In fact, in terms of energy content, one analyst indicates U.S. coal production peaked in 1998[47] and the increased volumes of coal necessary to meet the same energy demand was made up by increased volumes of Wyoming's lower quality subbituminous coal. For the future, this means that the increasingly larger volumes needed simply to meet today's electric needs will yield increasing levels of ash, sulphur and mercury as well as more CO_2 emissions per megawatt of electricity produced. All of these pollutants must be dealt with or the external costs of coal's use to society will continue to rise for the foreseeable future. However, none of these external costs apply to the use of increasing quantities of natural gas. In the case of natural gas, more efficient turbine designs now underway should actually lower CO_2 emissions per megawatt in the future.

Now let's look at natural gas. Natural gas contains little to nearly none of coal's and oil's non-CO_2 emissions, so the non-CO_2 external costs for the use of natural gas are minimal. One study estimated the external cost of natural gas to be about 40 cents per megawatt-hour or a tiny fraction of coal's external costs of $13 to $33 per megawatt-hour.[48] Because the use of natural gas to displace coal and oil will eliminate coal's and oil's large external costs, the use of natural gas actually has *external economic benefits* far in excess of its external costs. Natural gas's displacement of foreign oil imports has many external climate, economic, and security benefits. In addition, significant increases in the use of natural gas will also create large economic benefits because its increased use stimulates the domestic economy and creates more jobs at home.

To sum up, in order to level the economic and environmental playing field in the United States for the use of these three primary fuels, we would have to charge the consumer of imported oil a use tax that is actually in excess of a tax on coal, because even though oil has less carbon than coal, the use of imported oil has larger external costs. And because natural gas has very little non-CO_2 external costs, a system that only deals with carbon content is neither fair nor balanced. Neither a carbon tax nor a cap and trade system will economically or environmentally balance the carbon-based fuel playing field. So a green consumption tax is necessary to treat each fuel separately. Otherwise, the market will always tend to allocate more demand to the fuel with the highest external subsidies. Either a carbon tax or a cap and trade system by itself will be an energy policy designed to *favor* coal and oil over natural gas, wind, solar, and hydrogen, and will extend the use of coal and oil for decades into the future.

Our policy actions must respect that natural gas is the only domestic primary fuel that can be scaled up to reduce U.S. CO_2 emissions and foreign oil imports within the coming decade. Only policies that address the external noncarbon social costs will achieve a fair and balanced energy future. At the end of the day, it is important to remember that we can't overturn the fundamental economic law that if we want to use less of something, we should increase its price, and if we want to use more of something, we should decrease its price.

The Systemic Relationship of Tax, Energy, and Climate

Because tax, energy, and climate policies are inextricably connected within society, we must be as bold in changes to our tax policies as we are in policies to solve economic, energy, and climate problems. Our economic goal must be to accelerate the forthcoming pulse of growth that will emanate from a major energy transition so that the cost of the transition is more than offset by both the economic growth and the savings that are achieved by eliminating the external costs of the old energy systems.

I call upon President Obama to scrap our inefficient, special-interest-riddled tax system and make a grand bargain with the American people to rid them of taxes on their income and the growth of their capital and replace the revenue with a green consumption-based tax system initially focused principally upon the use of coal and oil. A green consumption-based tax system will accelerate the phasing out of coal and oil and the phasing in of alternative energy sources, while releasing the product of our capital and labor from the chains of taxation. If enacted, these inexorably interconnected tax-energy-climate policies will not only accelerate the GET to diminish the three intolerables, but they will also stimulate and accelerate civilization's next and largest-ever economic expansion that will be driven by our transition to the Age of Energy Gases.

A Call for a Twenty-First-Century Energy and Industrial Recovery Plan

The American people are counting on President Obama and Congress to create a new America. We need a vision of a new future that all

Americans can come together and rally behind. Sure, we need to do all we can to prevent another Great Depression and jump-start the U.S. economy, but we need more than that and we need action now. To ensure action, the Obama administration needs overwhelming support from the American people. Here is a proposal most Americans may enthusiastically endorse:

A $1 trillion Energy and Industrial Recovery Plan to convert and retrofit one-half of the U.S. vehicle fleet to compressed natural gas (CNG) by 2015 at little net cost to the U.S. economy. Saved payments to foreign oil producers will offset the plan's cost by 2017.[49] And we will profit from the trillions more saved over the long term. Americans paid about $4 trillion for SUVs, light trucks, and gas-guzzlers they love. In these difficult times, we shouldn't expect them to buy new, more efficient cars to replace perfectly good ones.

America's vastly abundant, clean, affordable natural gas is the only scalable alternative to gasoline and diesel that can make a big energy and environmental difference in the near-term because much of the infrastructure is already in place. America's 2.2-million-mile natural gas pipeline grid connects most metropolitan gasoline stations and industrial facilities where CNG fueling tanks can rapidly be installed. Most importantly, 63 million American homes are connected to the grid where 130 million automobiles reside and can fill up at home. Automobile dealers can maintain jobs by beginning a massive CNG retrofitting program, along with the installation of fueling appliances at those homes.

Any automobile industry bailout should require automakers to produce CNG vehicles they manufacture in Europe here in the United States as a first step toward clean, efficient vehicles. Ford, GM, and Chrysler could also retrofit their millions of unsold SUVs, light trucks, and gas-guzzlers. The Big Three should continue to develop hydrogen fuel cell vehicles and electric plug-ins. But until most electricity is produced by sources other than coal, now generating 50 percent of America's electricity, plug-in vehicles are premature because they will actually increase CO_2 emissions. The Chevy Volt only goes 40 miles before it needs gasoline, whereas a CNG retrofitted SUV will drive about 200 miles or more. The ideal transition vehicle would be Toyota's recently announced CNG/electric hybrid.

Let's look at what this plan will accomplish:

- Pay for itself many times over in reduced foreign oil payments.
- Save millions of jobs in the automobile industry.
- Reduce oil imports by between 5 and 6 million barrels per day.
- Significantly enhance energy security.
- Save trillions of dollars in payments to foreign oil producers that can instead be invested in the United States.
- Stimulate our domestic economy by increasing natural gas demand that will trigger hundreds of billions of dollars in new private-sector capital expenditures that will generate a two to three times economic multiplier.
- Add about 250,000 new jobs in the natural gas sector.
- Increase payments to U.S. farmers and landowners by tens of billions of dollars annually.
- Help the United States dodge the economically deadly peak oil bullet.
- Reduce CO_2 emissions by over 200 million tons annually.
- Eliminate much of the pollution in major metropolitan areas and reduce related health costs.
- Restore the U.S. global leadership in energy and climate and help regain soft power.

The Obama administration's plan to save the financial system and rebuild America's deteriorating infrastructure is imperative, but a $1 trillion Energy and Industrial Recovery Plan to convert and retrofit half of U.S. vehicles to CNG has a larger multiplier because it will go much further toward stimulating the economy and saving and adding U.S. jobs. And the owners of SUVs, light trucks, and gas-guzzlers will get full value from their $4 trillion investment. This plan would be a major leap toward President Obama's energy and environmental goals and would set the United States on the course for an unprecedented economic expansion.

What follows are my recommendations for the transportation sector.

Low-Hanging Fruit in the Transportation Sector

Government mandates on automobile fuel standards have worked well and should continue to be an important part of policies to accelerate the GET. Today, China already has higher gasoline efficiency standards in place than the U.S. targets for 2015.[50] The United States should lead the world in automobile efficiency and set the global standard. Therefore, U.S. mileage mandates for gasoline and diesel should be increased substantially and immediately.

America's new energy and industrial recovery plan should be organized to convert and retrofit half of all cars, trucks, and buses to compressed natural gas, CNG, principally by retrofit but also by increased production of CNG vehicles, by 2015. No other fuel can be scaled up faster to reduce our oil addiction and simultaneously diminish CO_2 emissions, smog, and other pollution in all urban areas.

Policy makers should recognize that there is no reason SUV and light-truck owners should not get full use from vehicles that have significantly depreciated in value because of high gasoline costs. The answer is to retrofit these vehicles to less-expensive, clean CNG. Americans have invested about $4 trillion in SUVs, light trucks, and gas-guzzlers,[51] and it is a tragedy for them to go on guzzling gasoline or for their owners to trade in or sell at a huge loss if gasoline becomes unaffordable, as is likely in the future. This would be a tragic loss for so many who are also struggling with home mortgage payments, losses in home values, or lost jobs.

I recommend a plan for tax credits and government guaranteed loans so that owners can retrofit their vehicles to run on 130 octane, clean CNG that usually costs less than gasoline and is produced at home and not subject to the real possibility of pocketbook-busting price increases. The plan should also cover filling appliances so if you decide to spend another $2,000 to $4,000,[52] you can fill up at home as long as you are connected to the natgas grid. Think of the time and money you will save by not going to the gasoline station. The only downside is that you would have the inconvenience of only driving about 200 to 300 miles[53] before you throw the switch on your dashboard to go back to gasoline if your conversion remained dual-fueled. Unfortunately, unlike the rest of the world, where retrofits to CNG vehicles are growing like wildfire, the high costs and time required to meet EPA and California Air Resources Board rules, regulations, and certifications are effectively prohibiting fast conversion. Today, our regulatory system is a major incentive to keep importing oil.

Effective energy and industrial policy for converting half our automobile fleet must create clear and uncomplicated national standards and regulations so that certification can be quick and low-cost and easily completed by your local mechanic or auto dealership. Tax credits and government loans or guarantees for retrofitting to either dual-fuel or dedicated CNG vehicles should be clearly established and run through 2015. I recommend that the initial tax credit and/or loan guarantee be from $3,000 for smaller cars and up to $10,000 for larger cars, light trucks, SUVs, and vans. I recommend that whatever plan the government adopts be sufficient to cover the cost of conversion.

America's 2.2-million-mile natural gas pipeline grid is already connected to 63 million homes that house about 130 million vehicles, approximately half our auto fleet, and most gasoline filling stations in metro areas, and many industrial facilities and factories are also connected to the pipeline grid. Because this large part of the infrastructure is already in place, much of the chicken-and-egg infrastructure barrier to scaling up a clean alternative fuel is eliminated with CNG. We should focus on home refueling because it is vital to the creation of a large market for both the retrofitting of up to 130 million automobiles and CNG production models. As CNG catches on, this program will help motivate the auto industry to tool up for CNG vehicles. I recommend the existing federal tax credit of $1,000 for a natural gas home fueling station be increased to $3,000 and be combined with a government loan guarantee through 2015. Additionally, there should be mandates that CNG fueling must be installed at all gasoline fueling stations on or near the natural gas pipeline grid, and ample government assistance should be provided to owners of gasoline filling stations to cover the cost of installation.

In early spring 2009, U.S. Congressmen Dan Boren and John Sullivan of Oklahoma and John Larson of Connecticut introduced legislation to extend natural gas vehicle and infrastructure tax credits, give incentives for vehicle manufacturers to build natural gas vehicles, and require the federal fleet to choose natural gas vehicles for 50 percent of its vehicle purchases.[54] As a first step, I recommend the immediate adoption of this and similar initiatives. Tax credits, government loans, or guarantees should also be available for large industries and manufacturing facilities that are on the natural gas grid to install filling facilities so workers can fill their CNG vehicles while at work. Fleets of vans, trucks, or buses could also be converted and filled at these locations.

CNG Production Models

The next step should be substantial government assistance for the U.S. automakers to tool up CNG vehicle production. Currently, Honda has the only production CNG vehicle—the Civic GX—now sold in the United States, while GM and Ford have several models that are upfitted to run on compressed natural gas. However, nearly all European automakers manufacture CNG vehicles, including BMW, Ford, GM/Opel, Mercedes, Peugeot, Porsche, Volvo, and Volkswagen.[55] These models could quickly come to the United States as the market demands. Today, there are only about 150,000 CNG vehicles in the United States,[56] compared to about 8 million around the world.[57] The number is growing rapidly outside the United States. About two years ago, there were only about 5 million CNG vehicles in the world and all the growth has come from other countries such as Pakistan, India, Bangladesh, China, Iran, and South American countries. It is time the United States becomes the world's leader in CNG vehicles (see Exhibit 12.1).

In fall 2008, President Bush signed into law a spending bill that included a $25 billion loan package for troubled automakers to produce more fuel-efficient cars and trucks. To meet CAFE standards is an important goal, but tooling up could be phased in over the longer term. In the near term, converting several of their existing models to CNG

Exhibit 12.1   Honda Civic GX Natural Gas Vehicle: About $25,000
Source: Courtesy of American Honda Motor Co. Inc.

or producing in the United States some of their current CNG models now sold in Europe would cost only a fraction of that amount for U.S. automakers. So the production of CNG models should become mandatory for the automakers that receive government assistance.

Today, there are a range of tax credits in place for purchasing a new, dedicated CNG automobile that are set to expire September 30, 2009.[58] What is needed immediately are much higher tax credits and some form of government rebate as well as loans or guarantees for CNG automobile buyers.

With these kinds of proactive policies in place to convert half of our automobile fleet to CNG and to achieve a 40 percent increase in fuel efficiency through CAFE standards by 2016, the United States can cut its oil imports from about 13 million barrels per day to about 5 million barrels per day and, by doing so, achieve a large measure of energy security.

To fuel half the U.S. fleet, including half the nation's trucks, with natural gas would require about 11 Tcf a year of new natural gas supplies.[59] I will address why I am confident we can easily meet this new demand later in this chapter.

The Approximate Costs

For half our fleet to be CNG vehicles by 2015, by far the largest percentage will be retrofitted vehicles and the balance will be new CNG production models. So let's guess that 75 percent of the 130 million automobiles at homes on the natural gas pipeline grid will be retrofitted, or about 100 million vehicles, and the other 30 million would be newly purchased CNG production models. If a tax credit was $3,000 for most retrofits and $15,000 for new CNG vehicles, then the lost revenue over the period from enactment to 2015 would be about $300 billion for retrofitting and about $450 billion for new CNG vehicles.

To install a natural gas fueling appliance in 63 million American homes, at about $4,000 each (and prices would be lower when mass produced), would cost about $250 billion. To install natural gas fueling facilities at the approximately 120,000 metropolitan gasoline filling stations estimated to be on or near the natural gas pipeline grid would cost about $70 billion more.[60] Because, like home filling, CNG fill-ing stations are fundamental to the conversion of half of our fleet, we should mandate that those stations on or close to the natural gas pipe-line grid be CNG capable by 2012. To assist their owners, we should also put in place a tax credit and government loan program to help facilitate their installation.

America's Heavy Trucks and Buses

I have concentrated so far on personal cars, light trucks, and SUVs because those are the vehicles needed by Americans for their jobs and lives. However, another sector of low-hanging fruit in transportation is the heavy trucks that move U.S. goods. Each of these heavy-hauling trucks use about 15,000 to 20,000 gallons of diesel each year.[61] Many truckers turn over their fleet every 7 to 10 years,[62] so by 2020 most of the fleet would be renewed and could be natural gas capable. Because the incremental cost of CNG or LNG capability can add as much as $40,000 to $60,000 to the cost of heavy trucks, they should be added to the government assistance program.

A company called Clean Energy Fuels is the only public company in the business of both converting vehicles to CNG and owning CNG fueling stations. Although relatively small, it is an excellent test case to show how well CNG works and how much the United States benefits. In late 2008, Clean Energy had about 175 CNG fueling stations with plans to add about 150 more, mostly in the Los Angeles region (see Chapter 10). The company has recently been working with the ports of Long Beach and Los Angeles to convert the heavy-haulers that pick up mostly Asian imports and deliver them to places like Wal-Mart distribu-tion centers around the country. Within the next five years, thousands of trucks working in and out of these two ports will operate on natu-ral gas, reducing diesel demand by about 160 million gallons per year and saving their owners about $155 million annually.[63] My point in recounting this is that we know it can be done successfully here in the United States because it *is* being done. Let's learn from Pakistan, India, Bangladesh, China, Iran, our South American neighbors, and Clean Energy Fuels and ramp up this program as part of our new energy and industrial policy. If the federal government put in place the Energy and Industrial Recovery Plan recommended herein, the combination of tax credits and government guaranteed loans could equal up to about $1 trillion over the period 2010 to 2015. But $700 billion would be saved during the same period on purchases of foreign oil and would pay trillions in dividends in the future.

Energy Independence and Climate Progress by 2015

With the successful implementation of this Energy and Industrial Recovery Plan, we will be well on the way to overcoming our climate and energy problems by 2015. Without including sizable CO_2 reductions resulting from across-the-board gains in energy efficiency, the transportation accomplishments alone will have lowered CO_2 emissions by about 225 million metric tons per year.[64] Our conversion to CNG vehicles, including heavy trucks, will have reduced foreign oil imports by 5 to 6 million barrels per day, and increased CAFE standards will save us another 2.3 million barrels per day,[65] for a total reduction in oil consumption of about 8 million barrels per day. That is equal to 40 percent of our daily use of 20 million barrels a day. Most importantly, our foreign imports will decline from about 13 million barrels per day to about 5 million barrels per day. *So by 2015, our nation will have regained most of its energy independence.* If peak oil occurs during this period as so many experts predict, and the world is facing oil shortages rationed either physically or by price, or both, another significant benefit is that *America will have dodged that deadly bullet.*

Under this plan, we would have substantially reduced U.S. payments to foreign producers from 2008's near $500 billion per year. Total savings between now and 2015[66] just from our conversion to CNG would be $700 billion, with trillions more in the decades to come. We could create a million or more jobs in the transportation and energy sectors, and we would have enriched millions of U.S. landowners by drilling for and producing their underground natural gas wealth. Most importantly, throughout this energy and industrial economic expansion, Americans would be adding to their new wealth without taxes on their income or the growth of their capital. We would be living in a reenergized, competitive America, leading the world in energy technologies, and will have regained energy independence.

How Natural Gas, Wind, and Solar Will Meet This New Demand

If either a green consumption-based tax is placed on coal or a sufficiently stringent cap and trade system is implemented, then coal will be phased out of power generation and most new electric demand will be met with natural gas, wind, and solar facilities, paid for by the private sector without the need for subsidies. If we were to mandate that no coal-fired electric plants be built without working CCS at start-up, as I recommend, then, because of the current state of CCS technology, it is doubtful that many plants could be built until after 2020. Therefore, most new electric demand in the near term will need to be met principally with natural gas, wind, solar, and nuclear. However, because of financing and siting delays, it is unlikely that nuclear power will contribute much. So at least 90 percent of new electric demand[67] will need to be met with natural gas, wind, and solar. Assuming an 85 percent to 15 percent natural gas to wind and solar sharing, the additional natural gas required to meet new demand in the power sector would be about 2 Tcf by 2015.

When the new natural gas demand from the transportation and power sectors are added together, natural gas supplies would need to increase by about 13 Tcf—from 23 Tcf in 2008 to 36 Tcf in 2015. I am confident producers could increase domestic natural gas production to the levels necessary to meet this demand. If there are shortfalls, the balance could be made up with Canadian imports, LNG shipments from around the world (the world also has an excess supply of LNG), and our large Alaskan supplies even without drilling in ANWR.

My confidence is derived from my belief in natural gas abundance set out in Chapters 6 and 7, bolstered by the new Navigant Consulting study of U.S. natural gas resources,[68] as well as, and most importantly, the actual results from U.S. shale production over the past decade. The key for the growth of shale natural gas supplies is demand and price. If natural gas prices were demand driven over the period with prices in the range of $6 to $9 per Mcf (the equivalent of $36 to $54 per barrel of oil), then it is credible to predict that the recent accelerating rate of shale production growth would continue and provide about 10 to 14 Tcf of supply by 2020.[69] That being true, shale production alone could scale up to meet demand necessary for half the vehicle fleet. U.S. non-shale natural gas from the very large and still undeveloped conventional reservoirs (off both coasts, particularly the East Coast, in the Rocky Mountains and Alaska), tight sands, coal bed methane, and vast potential supplies from our deep, largely undeveloped onshore geological basins, would offset much of the natural decline rates, as well as add additional reserves. In fact, with demand-driven prices all of this other nonshale natural gas should be able to grow its production another several Tcf in the near term.

In summary, to supply the transportation and power sectors, natural gas supplies in the United States would need to increase by about 13 Tcf by 2015. In 2008, the United States produced 20.5 Tcf[70] and imported 3.6 Tcf from Canada[71] and less than a half of a Tcf by LNG. The United States's domestic natural gas production could grow from 20.5 Tcf in 2008 to about 30 Tcf by 2015, or about 5 percent per year. This growth would come from additional shale production and additional production from nonshale after making up for the decline rates. So domestic production, excluding Alaska, could meet near 30 Tcf of the 36 Tcf per year needed for domestic consumption. The balance would be made up by Canadian imports, LNG, and from Alaska's vast supplies.

U.S. natural gas producers can meet this challenge. Natural gas is the only fuel that can be scaled up to do the job. No other alternative fuel could accomplish so much for our climate goals and energy security for less cost to our U.S. economy with so many collateral economic benefits. When the economic benefits of a million or more new jobs, reductions of payments of trillions of dollars to foreign oil producers, reductions in U.S. health costs, and all the other climate, economic, and national security benefits are added in, it is my belief that the United States will actually be making money while achieving new economic growth and a higher quality of life. In the big picture, our enormous savings on foreign oil imports will pay several times over the about $1 trillion cost of converting and retrofitting half of the U.S. automobile fleet to CNG and putting in place fuel appliances and filling stations to serve this new industry.

Over the longer term, natural gas is the bridge fuel to the hydrogen economy. As we use up America's natural gas over the next 60 to 70 years, wind, solar, and hydrogen will continue to displace natural gas and electric and hydrogen fuel cell vehicles will replace CNG. These policies will lead us naturally into the hydrogen economy. The key components of the hydrogen economy are hydrogen itself, wind, and solar, and because natural gas is compatible with wind and solar, the natural gas bridge actually works to accelerate wind and solar. Because some natural gas infrastructure works with hydrogen, natural gas is also a bridge to hydrogen itself. For instance, hydrogen can be phased into natural gas pipelines and natural gas–generating facilities to lower CO_2 emissions. In the transportation sector, Honda makes a home hydrogen appliance that supplies hydrogen made from natural gas for fuel cell vehicles. Others will soon come on the market if this becomes America's direction.

Conclusion

I cannot recommend the form of these tax, energy, and economic policies, as I think that is for our policy makers to shape, but rather, here I state the case that we can afford them and even suggest that it is probable that we cannot afford *not* to embrace them. My hope is to start the debate the United States needs in order to sort out the right path through the complexities of energy use.

President Obama must rally Americans behind this new vision for our future. I believe that in the midst of all our current troubles and chaos, Americans are hungry for and in need of a new vision. It is my great hope these ideas may be the starting point. All Americans will win big from our next Industrial Revolution and economic expansion fueled by clean energy gases. It is time for the United States to re-create itself to lead the world to a twenty-first-century energy and Industrial Revolution for the benefit of all. At no other time in history has it been so essential to jet the GET.

Chapter 13

The Age of Energy Gases: America's and China's Opportunity

The writing is on the wall. Gas will continue to replace oil. The world is now entering the "methane age."
—DR. SUBROTO, SECRETARY GENERAL, OPEC, APRIL 16, 1993

The Age of Energy Gases is in ascendance. This is the last wave of the Grand Energy Transition, the GET. It is the wave that will take us to our sustainable future. It starts principally with the world's abundant, clean supplies of natural gas, supplemented by its rapidly growing sister energy sources—wind and solar. Natural gas is a fuel that is technologically well-established, versatile, globally abundant, and ready to tackle the world's energy and climate dilemmas.

Each day, it becomes more and more apparent that our use of coal and oil in a business-as-usual scenario is unsustainable. The globalization of the world's economies and the vast quantities of the energy they require have brought us face-to-face with the fact that the three intolerables of climate, economic, and geostrategic risks are building to levels that have the capacity to severely disrupt or even end civilization as we know it. However, if 2007 to 2008 truly witnessed the tipping point for energy and climate awareness, as I believe, leading nations may well embrace the magnitude of bold change necessary to accelerate the Age of Energy Gases. The acceleration of this wave will immediately begin to displace coal and oil to alleviate, or even eliminate, the three intolerables.

The Age of Energy Gases includes all the gases that are used generally as an energy source. I include natural gas, which is mostly carbon light methane; wind, which is the Earth's atmosphere and also a gas; solar, because the sun is basically a ball of burning hydrogen gas (technically, the fusion of hydrogen gas); hydrogen gas itself; and eventually, hydrogen fusion nuclear, the sun in a box, nuclear fusion.

As previous chapters explained, natgas is our first step forward. It is our bridge fuel to a fully sustainable future. Not only is natural gas compatible with wind, solar, and hydrogen and their infrastructures, but also I believe it is a catalyst to their increased use. Unlike coal, whose continued use simply further entrenches its long resistance to displacement and tends to limit increased use of solar and wind, the use of natgas will not impede the increasing use of wind, solar, and hydrogen. Indeed, it goes hand-in-hand with their development, because natural gas generation can easily meet the demand for electricity when the wind is still and the sun is blocked by clouds.

By contrast, because coal plants are so capital-intensive—and technically and economically difficult to shut down and start up—each new, average-sized coal plant built blocks the entry of about 500 new one-megawatt wind turbines or about 45 11-megawatt solar power installations for 30 years or more.[1]

In the United States, but increasingly so in other countries, the natgas pipeline grid can rapidly facilitate more efficient, distributed natural gas generation of electricity that can be on immediate call during periods of cloud cover or calm winds. Additionally, electricity can be generated at about any point on the pipe grid either by conventional combustion generators or fuel cells, such as the very promising Bloom fuel-cell system, financed by the California venture capitalist firm Kleiner Perkins.[2] Also, hydrogen can be stripped from natural gas to use in cars with hydrogen fuel cells at homes, factories, and industrial facilities along the grid. Honda makes a home hydrogen unit that gets its hydrogen from natgas. Also, a small generator or small-scale integrated generation heating and cooling plant that produces as-needed quantities of electricity can be installed anywhere on the natural gas pipeline grid for consumers who need the certainty of continuous electric power or within the environment of a city to provide power off the electric grid along with heating and cooling for the surrounding buildings.

The increasing use of natural gas will act as a catalyst for the rapid introduction of wind, solar, and hydrogen in more ways than I can imagine. The fuels of the Age of Energy Gases are compatible and, together, create interactive synergies and smart power.

The use of natural gas does release CO_2 to the atmosphere, although its emissions are 50 percent that of coal.[3] Enhanced turbine efficiencies are increasing the megawatts of electricity from each Btu of natural gas, so CO_2 emissions per megawatt will continue to decline. Natural gas also produces about 25 to 30 percent less CO_2 than gasoline and diesel and virtually none of the other pollutants.[4] Natgas without sequestration will not become the final answer but will be the pathfinder to our totally sustainable future, in which hydrogen, wind, solar, and nuclear fusion will become the dominant energy sources. However, if sequestration becomes economic, then natural gas power plants will be almost as green and nonpolluting as wind and solar.

Importantly, natgas will also accelerate large gains in energy efficiency, particularly where there is an existing pipeline grid. For instance, it is more efficient and less polluting to produce natgas from natural gas wells and distribute it via a pipeline system for end use by a homeowner or industrial facility, than it is to mine coal from a coal mine, transport it by freight trains to a central generation facility, and transmit electricity across a vast electric grid. You simply can't easily start up and shut down large coal plants and all the mines and railroad delivery systems that supply power plants. Today, both the railroads and electric transmission systems are old, hard-pressed to maintain their current demand, and will require enormous investments to meet significant increases in demand.

For the transportation sector, the natural gas pipeline grid also makes it possible for consumers to fill up their cars and trucks with clean natural gas at home, or at work, by installing a natural gas compressor appliance, and retrofitting an auto or buying a CNG vehicle, such as the Honda Civic GX, which costs about $24,500.[5] If you could fill up with

CNG at home, or while your car is parked at work (if your workplace is on the natural gas pipeline grid), think of all the time and money you'd save by not driving to, and often waiting in line at, a gasoline station. If time is money, then CNG delivers ever-greater savings when you fill up at home.

The Silver Path

What follows is the GET solution to the energy, climate, environmental, macroeconomic, and geostrategic intolerables. If coal and oil, along with other solids and liquids, are the problem—and are creating the three intolerables—then what is the solution? There is no one solution, or as many say about energy, there is no *silver bullet*. But there is a *silver path* forward. The natural, evolutionary transition of the GET to the Age of Energy Gases is that silver path that will create for civilization its first epoch of sustainable growth and life on Earth.

Natural gas, because of its global abundance, will be our bridge fuel for this long-term transition. Natural gas is a big step toward hydrogen, as it is so much cleaner and contains so much more hydrogen than coal and oil, and because natgas infrastructure can be used to phase in hydrogen gas. Because natural gas technologies are well-developed and readily available, no other fuel can be scaled up to displace coal and oil in sufficient quantities and at a rate necessary to stabilize climate change in the next few decades. In fact, over the past decades, natural gas has grown to become a principal global energy source, meeting 24 percent, of the global mix, as compared to coal at 28 percent, oil at 36 percent and nuclear at 6 percent.[6] Certainly, the LNG (liquefied natural gas) deals in the past year or so by China, Japan, Korea, and Singapore are a good indication that the natural gas wave is gaining momentum across Asia.

Twenty-First-Century Winners

By following the natural path of technology, the world will move faster and faster into the Age of Energy Gases and our ultimate energy goal of sustainable economic growth. Energy gases will supply civilization for millennia to come, and we are already seeing the acceleration of this transition.

Countries that ride this next great wave and accelerate into the Age of Energy Gases will be the twenty-first-century winners. And in many areas of the world—Germany, Denmark, India, Israel, Singapore, Florida, California, and others—the transition to the gases is well underway. Generating capacity and investment in natural gas, wind, and solar have dramatically expanded in the past five years. Worldwide, 310,000 new megawatts of installed natural gas power is expected to be added between 2005 and 2010—a 31 percent increase,[7] 55 new megawatts of installed wind capacity were added every day in 2007,[8] and solar has only begun its exponential growth.

The Age of Energy Gases will last for millennia because the final stage will be the hydrogen economy, which will be fueled by virtually limitless energy sources (wind, solar, hydrogen, and, likely, nuclear fusion), which will allow the earth to sustain its forecast population growth, as well as the economic growth created by waves of continuing technological innovation to come.

The Hydrogen Economy

Hydrogen and the hydrogen economy should be civilization's energy end goal. Only within a hydrogen-based economy, which produces virtually no energy pollutants, can predicted levels of global population and their required increases of economic growth be sustained environmentally. The path toward civilization's ultimate goal is clearly marked by a series of energy waves that have decarbonized energy sources over the past 150 years by shifting from wood (composed principally of carbon), to coal (with a little less carbon and some hydrogen), to oil (with, again, less carbon and more hydrogen), to natgas (with even more hydrogen, composed of only one carbon and four hydrogen atoms). The transition to natural gas will be a "giant step for mankind" toward hydrogen itself, which has no carbon and which, when used as a fuel, is environmentally benign, producing only heat and water.

The hydrogen economy (wind, solar, and nuclear fusion) is an economy fueled by virtually limitless, totally clean, and fully sustainable gaseous forms of energy. Hydrogen, one of the basic elements of nature, is the universe's simplest and most abundant element, accounting for more than 90 percent of the observable universe. Hydrogen is found in all organic matter and in the water that covers 70 percent of the Earth's surface.[9] When hydrogen is burned with oxygen, only heat and water are produced.[10] Hydrogen is truly nature's sustainable energy system.

The hydrogen economy is technologically possible today. Cars, planes, and boats[11] have already been fueled with hydrogen, so the technology is basically in hand and is not something that is yet to be invented. As I said before, it is not *Star Wars* technology. What is needed is a *long-term* commitment by governments to provide research and development funding for natural gas, wind, solar, hydrogen, and hydrogen technology, including nuclear fusion, with incentives like those given in the past to coal, oil, and nuclear fission, and commitments by nations equal to or exceeding the one that put man on the moon.

As the energy waves show in Exhibits 4.1 (World Primary Energy Substitution) and 3.1 (GET Waves), the Age of Energy Gases has begun its inevitable ascension, and civilization must now accelerate this one-time Grand Energy Transition toward humanity's destiny of sustainable life and growth on Earth.

America's Politically Difficult Opportunity

In the United States, there are three major impediments to becoming a global energy leader in this inevitable evolutionary transition. Those impediments are, first, the existence of a largely coal- and oil-based energy infrastructure with enormous unamortized capital-investment; second, the depth of their political and economic vested interests; and third, our particularly American democratic political system and culture based on short-term desires and policy needs, which are not well-suited for the creation of fundamental long-term policy adjustments. In the United States, transformational long-term energy planning will be difficult without further catastrophic energy or climate crises. It took the Cold War and Sputnik to spur the United States to a decade-long plan to put a man on the moon. So, for at least the near term, I fear America may remain stuck in the straitjacket of dirty and inefficient nineteenth- and twentieth-century energy sources and their infrastructures and technologies. However, as the global economy returns to growth and oil prices return to $140 per barrel, where they were in the summer of 2008, or even skyrocket from there as a result of peak oil or terrorist attacks, or if more climate disasters occur, the United States may be ready to embrace the enormous change necessary to displace both oil as a principal transportation source and coal for electric generation.

On the other hand, change is in the air. The Obama presidential campaign engaged a new American generation that is willing to embrace major change and that has a deeply felt relationship with the environment, so with the bold and forceful leadership of President Obama, the United States may well overcome these barriers to meaningful, long-term energy changes. However, when it comes to energy and the deeply vested interests of coal and oil powerfully represented in the U.S. Congress, meaningful change will require use of the bully pulpit and the majority of the American people behind him.

For the United States to remain the economic powerhouse that it has been for the past century, it must seize today's greatest opportunity for the coming century: the opportunity to lead the world toward climate stability and the development of twenty-first-century energy technologies. With great leadership and a long-term commitment to this great and necessary human accomplishment, our youth will have the opportunity to set their sights on new educational goals of science, engineering, technology, and the environment. There can be no question that such a long-term American commitment to energy and climate solutions will be fundamental for their resolution. Because of the pervasive nature of energy in all government decisions, President Obama must elevate these issues to the highest level. And for global success in the areas of climate and energy that will also create a new, geostrategic global stability, there can be nothing better than for America to join with China in a Grand Energy Alliance (GEA). This is the topic of Chapter 14, "Crisis and Opportunity."

Because so many people in the West, and particularly the United States, seem resigned to the notion that China and its vast population is entering the Industrial Revolution with the same old nineteenth- and twentieth-century energy sources, technologies, and inefficiencies used to develop our country, there too often seems to be little hope that even if the United States did what was necessary to reduce CO_2 emissions and oil use that the world would have any chance of improvement, because China and Asia would more than offset our accomplishments. What follows is my case that Asia, led by China, may surprise us all and lead the world into the Age of Energy Gases.

China's and Asia's Opportunity

In many ways, China and Asia are showing more indications of riding the wave of energy gases than the West. Along with Asia's recent economic and technological rise, there has also been significant growth in its natural gas discoveries and use. Of course, solar is starting from a low base, but its Asian growth is phenomenal. As has often been the case, Singapore is leading the way by fueling more than 80 percent of its power generation with natural gas,[12] recently signing its first LNG contract, and planning to become a globally important physical and financial trading center for natural gas. Singapore already has in place two public hydrogen filling stations used by a number of cars and buses, as well as a plan to convert more taxis to natural gas. But the real opportunity for global leadership for the wave of energy gases rests with China.

China's leaders have used the words "peaceful rise" to describe its path toward regaining status as a global superpower. To achieve this goal over the coming decades will require that China successfully deals with many domestic and global challenges. Two of these challenges are essential to its success. First, China needs to maintain internal stability, and second, China needs to continue its international participation as a responsible stakeholder in sustaining external peace and trade. To maintain long-term internal stability will require strong and sustained economic growth, including the development of a rising middle class, as hundreds of millions of Chinese move to cities and rapidly increase their demand for more energy.

As China's economy and demand for energy continues to grow over the coming decades, the maintenance of internal stability will require the reversal of environmental degradation, caused principally by coal-fired power generation and the side effects of harm to public health and resulting higher health costs, lower levels of industrial and agricultural productivity, and diminished quality of life. Indeed, incidents of violent social backlash against the use of more coal have already occurred.[13]

China's policy makers may soon accept the fact that the real costs of burning coal, including large external costs, will be much higher than the costs of using natgas to meet its increasing demand for power. If one believes that the World Bank's report[14] on environmental costs is basically correct, then China's external costs of coal use are 5.8 percent of GDP, or US$100 billion annually, although the Chinese State Environmental Protection Agency (SEPA) says it is 3 percent,[15] or US$64 billion. A Chinese energy path based on natural gas will immediately begin to reduce coal's CO_2 emissions. Possibly more importantly, natgas eliminates the deadly sulphur, mercury, and ash pollutants that continue to limit economic growth and deteriorate Chinese quality of life. These are the deadly coal pollutants that reduce visibility, create dense fogs, poison fish and crops, reduce human productivity, and add to health care costs. They are also killing the grasslands of inner Mongolia and spawning severe dust storms that choke Beijing and have recently been found as far away as the west coast of the United States.[16]

Many in China believe that the requirements of substantial increases in energy demand to provide for the massive migration to the cities and to sustain current rates of economic growth are in direct opposition to China's equally important need to begin to clean its environment. In fact, it seems that because China's forecast demand for electricity is so large, it has little option but to forge ahead with coal generation for now, and hope for the best. But this is not truly the case. Natgas power generation, supplemented with wind and solar, can solve the demand for cleaner power and quickly begin to reverse China's environmental degradation, while lowering forecast CO_2 emissions substantially, as well as reducing the true costs of energy consumption. If China is to be welcomed internationally as a responsible stakeholder in the maintenance of external peace and stability, its leaders must see the need for a major shift in domestic energy policy. Otherwise, with a business-as-usual scenario, China's growing strategic need for oil will inevitably collide with the developed economies and their continuing addiction to oil. Both China and America must work to avoid a clash over oil supplies.

China's forecasted large increase in coal use and CO_2 emissions[17] are already in direct opposition to the increasingly emotional plea by more and more of the world's people, including growing numbers of Chinese, for relief from global climate warming. Chinese leaders know full well that China may be disproportionately impacted by climate change. Once again, natgas can substitute—for coal in power-generation, and for liquid gasoline in automobiles, trucks and buses—supplemented by wind and solar. It can be both a near-term and long-term solution to this apparent dialectic.

Because the use, source, and form of energy consumption will be a fundamental determinant of China's economic, environmental, foreign policy, and defense directions as a nation and a global player over the coming decades, China's choice of energy sources may well determine the success of its peaceful rise. I believe China's leaders understand this and will take the necessary steps to succeed.

As we enter the twenty-first century, all nations have only two energy choices: to be a follower or to be a leader. It would be a tragic, long-term macroeconomic and political mistake for China to follow the West by continuing to build its energy infrastructure with old, inefficient and dirty nineteenth- and twentieth-century coal and oil technologies. To choose to follow would be a course that will increasingly limit economic growth and will increasingly pollute its people and lands. For China to follow the West in carbon-dense energy consumption would be a path of increasing internal instability, and one that is certain to reverse recently acquired global soft power as China becomes the world's largest polluter, while competing with the West for shrinking flows of accessible oil; whereas the choice to lead the world in the development of high-tech, smart, efficient, clean twenty-first-century energy systems would provide for environmentally sustainable internal economic growth and would simultaneously reduce global strategic tensions over long-term access to oil supplies. An innovative leadership strategy will not only expand China's soft power but will also create a vast new long-term external market for newly developed twenty-first-century smart green energy technologies, and move Chinese society faster into the Age of Energy Gases.

I believe that China's best domestic and international interests are served by becoming a global energy leader and following the path to the Age of Energy Gases. Because China is a developing nation, it has the opportunity to leapfrog the West into the Age of Energy Gases. Although China correctly asserts that the industrialized nations achieved their current status without regard to CO_2 emissions and are largely responsible for bringing climate change to its current tipping point, that reality will not solve China's energy climate problems; however, it is a point America must accept in order to form any long-term energy and climate alliance with China.

For these reasons, I believe China will choose the energy path fundamental to achieving its goal of Peaceful Rise. China has an unprecedented educational, commercial, and political opportunity to establish itself as a global technological leader. China has everything to gain, both internally and internationally, by global leadership in creating and developing the most fundamentally necessary technologies for civilization's future during the twenty-first century and beyond. The technological leadership role is totally befitting a civilization that, as Cambridge University's renowned China scholar Joseph Needham asserted, created and developed at least half of the inventions and technology necessary for the modern world, including, I must add, the development of a natural gas drilling, production, and distribution industry more than 800 years ago (see Exhibit 13.1).

The arguments are compelling for natural gas to be the principal fuel for China. In 1985, I studied the potential for natural gas in China, and later reported to the Ministry of Geology and Ministry of Petroleum, predicting China's natural gas resource potential to be similar to America's, and in the range of 1,100 to 1,400 Tcf (30 to 40 trillion cubic meters).[18] I remain confident of China's natural gas potential. Natgas is an energy resource that is abundant in vast quantities, both within China and globally. However, many energy experts have historically doubted, and continue to doubt, such natgas abundance. I believe it is time for China to study the natural gas paradigm shift taking

Exhibit 13.1   Sichuan Province, China (circa 1041–1368 A.D.) This oil painting illustrates deep well drilling from the years 1041 to 1368 A.D. that was the precursor to the modern gas well.
Source: Hefner collection.

place in the United States today, described in Chapter 7, "Natural Gas Abundance," and to reevaluate its domestic potential for clean natural gas supplies.

All said, it is my forecast that China's leaders will guide the country to ride the wave of energy gases. As Chou En-Lai said, "The helmsman must guide the boat by using the waves, otherwise the boat will be submerged by the waves."[19]

Chapter 14

Crisis and Opportunity

No other alliance in human history could achieve for civilization so much for so long.
—Robert A. Hefner III, July 21, 2008

There will be nothing more transformational for civilization in the early decades of the twenty-first century than defining how we, the world's people, deal with our energy and climate crises. As I have said over and over during the past decade, how we deal with energy will either tear us apart or bring us together.

If we lack the will to work together and overcome comparatively smaller political differences to enact globally coordinated policies that confront the civilization-threatening three intolerables, then certainly we will be torn apart. We will suffer the ravages of climate change. Tens of millions of people will be displaced. We will see oil price spikes and shortages that lead to macroeconomic disruption and even the eventual breakdown of the globalized trading system. Dangerous geostrategic tensions could develop that would lead to a collapse in the existing world order. Civilization as we know it could end, and billions of the world's people would fall backward into abject poverty.

But, as always, the bigger the challenge, the bigger the opportunity. By accelerating the GET, humankind is certain to experience *once again* the largest economic expansion in all of human history. We spent much of the last half of the twentieth century getting ready. At the end of

World War II, former enemies became allies and trading partners. The United Nations and a new world order emerged. Eventually, the communist economic system failed and communists learned that real markets really work. Deng Xiaoping said, "Poverty is not socialism. To be rich is glorious."[1] He opened China's doors to the world, beginning its increasingly market-oriented, exponential growth that led the phenomenal rise of all Asia. All civilization must capture this momentum, created by the recent participation of nearly half the world's people that were formerly locked out.

Ronald Reagan went to Berlin with a clear message: "Mr. Gorbachev, tear down this wall!"[2] Soon after, energized by this hope, the people came together and did the job. The economic pulse of globalism commenced. Not long afterward, Reagan mused, "I occasionally think how quickly our differences worldwide would vanish if we were facing an alien threat from outside this world."[3] Reagan's aliens have indeed materialized—and they are us.

We travelers on Spaceship Earth have created a truly global crisis that is larger than governments, larger than international differences, larger than a nuclear Iran, larger than the Iraq and Afghanistan wars, larger than terrorism, larger than the "free Tibet" movement, and larger than Chinese and U.S. differences over Taiwan. As I see it, there is only one sure road forward that can place humanity squarely on the path to eliminating the three intolerables. That sure road can only be created by a Grand Energy Alliance (GEA) between the world's two largest energy consumers, polluters, and soon-to-be two largest economies—the United States and China.

How naturally fitting for the United States, with the most advanced technologies and largest economy, to join China, the world's former technological leader that is rapidly regaining its technological preeminence, to create the GEA. The GEA would work with all the world's nations to join forces in the propulsion of the GET. The GEA would be charged with the task to create policies and fund the development of technologies to lead humanity to sustainable life and growth on Earth by 2050.

There could be no nobler alliance, nor could any other relationship have such a positive influence for world peace and stability in the twenty-first century. Within the GEA, the 21st Century Energy

Corporation (EC21) should be organized, initially funded by the United States and China with $1 trillion. These two giants can afford an investment of this size for the most important endeavor in the history of civilization. EC21 should then invite and encourage additional financial participation by all the other nations of the world and be charged with the responsibility of creating and developing the technologies necessary for the solution of our climate and energy crises by 2050.

The joining together of the world's two "biggest brothers" would give new hope to all the world's people and unleash heightened levels of life force in all people to come together to get the job done. Richard Nixon and Mao Tze Tung both surprised the world as they put aside their historical differences to look forward and to "change the world forever." It is within such periods of great change that creativity, innovation, and invention explode to create a vast expansion of new, unforeseen opportunities. The ascendance of the Age of Energy Gases will fuel these hitherto unimagined economic gains for the global economy, just as was the case during coal's Industrial Revolution and oil's post–World War II economic explosion that led to our globalized and connected world of today.

All the tools are in hand; there is no need for *Star Wars* technology. All that is needed is the political will to break with the past and to focus on the final energy wave of the GET with our capital, and the intellect, creativity, and personal drive of the world's best minds. We must not be distracted by the myriad proposed diversions and leaps backward, constantly put forth by the vested interests of our nineteenth and twentieth century solid and liquid fuels that we "must do it all"— that we must use every energy source known to man. No, in order to win, we must narrowly focus our capital, talent, intellect, and creativity on the clean path forward to our energy goal, and ride the wave of energy gases to the hydrogen economy.

These energy and climate crises are undeniable, but never before in human history have we had more opportunity. We have created a globalized trading system in which billions more increasingly participate. The world's GDP has never been larger. About 1.5 billion people[4] are connected to one another, and most all of humanity's accumulated knowledge is available to them at nearly the speed of light, and millions more are connecting every month. The field of smart nanotechnology has only this decade exploded into use. All of its components will help run our new, smart, highly efficient and connected twenty-first-century energy system. Biotechnology is following closely on nanotech's heels. No doubt this incomprehensibly important field will also become deeply embedded in these new energy technologies.

To the youth of the world, let me say there has never been so much opportunity to succeed and make the world a better place than in the field of twenty-first-century energy technologies. This will be, by far, the world's largest growth business for the coming decades, and participation within it promises great fulfillment because your individual accomplishment will be even greater for all humanity. Opportunity lies before you like never before. Join together in your connected world so that you will have the strength and collective will to overcome any turning back or political diversion that might slow down this opportunity for you and for all humanity. We must all work together to jet the GET!

Notes

Chapter 2

1. Thomas K. McCraw, *Prophet of Innovation: Joseph Schumpeter and Creative Destruction* (Cambridge, MA, and London: Belknap Press, 2007). Joseph Schumpeter made the phrase *creative destruction* famous by using it to describe a process in which the old ways of doing things are endogenously destroyed and replaced by new ways.

2. "Naval Innovation: From Coal to Oil," *Joint Force Quarterly* (Winter 2000–2001), 52.

3. Department for Business Enterprise & Regulatory Reform, "Energy Trends and Quarterly Energy Prices" (U.K. National Statistics publication, September 2007) 34, www.berr.gov.uk/energy/statistics/publications/dukes/page39771 .html.

Chapter 3

1. Thomas Gold (1920–2004) was among the most creative and wide-ranging of scientists, the author of *Power from the Earth* and *The Deep Hot Biosphere*, as well as more than 280 papers in areas as diverse as cosmology, zoology, physics, and astronomy. A member of the U.S. National Academy of Sciences and a Fellow of the Royal Society, London, he held teaching and research posts at Cambridge, Harvard, and Cornell, where he was founder and for 20 years director of the Cornell Center for Radiophysics and Space Research.

2. Cesare Marchetti and Nebojsa Nakicenovic, *The Dynamics of Energy Systems and the Logistic Substitution Model*, RR-79-13 (Laxenburg, Austria: International Institute for Applied Systems Analysis, 1979), and Nebojsa Nakicenovic, *Patterns of Change: Technological Substitution and Long Waves in the United States*, WP-86-12 (Laxenburg, Austria: International Institute for Applied Systems Analysis, 1986).

3. Professor Carver Mead, as quoted in *Microcosm*, George Gilder (New York: Simon & Schuster, 1989), 11.

4. Energy Information Administration, *Monthly Energy Review* (July 2008), Tables 3.1 and 3.5.

5. Data from Bureau of Transportation Statistics, www.bts.gov/publications/national_transportation_statistics/html/table_04_01_html, Table 4-1: Overview of U.S. Petroleum Production, Imports, Exports, and Consumption (retrieved March 31, 2008).

6. Karen Dillon, "Rush for Coal Plants Slows to a Stagger," *The Kansas City Star* (March 13, 2009).

7. Average 2008 price of oil was $99.75 per barrel (per Bloomberg Data Services, January 5, 2009) and 2008 U.S. petroleum imports averaged 12.9 million barrels per day. Energy Information Administration, *Monthly Energy Review* (March 2009), Table 3.1, equaling a total import cost of $470 billion for 2008.

Chapter 4

1. Data figured from BP's online historical data, *BP Statistical Review of World Energy*, www.bp.com.

2. Data figured from *BP Statistical Review of World Energy* (June 2008); Cesare Marchetti and Nebojsa Nakicenovic, 1979, "The dynamics of energy systems and the logistic substitution model," RR-79-13, 73 p., International Institute for Applied Systems Analysis, Laxenburg, Austria. Also, Nebojsa Nakicenovic, 1986, "Patterns of change: Technological substitution and long waves in the United States," WP-86-13, 32 p., International Institute for Applied Systems Analysis, Laxenburg, Austria.

3. Data figured from *BP Statistical Review of World Energy* (June 2008); Cesare Marchetti and Nebojsa Nakicenovic, 1979, "The dynamics of energy systems and the logistic substitution model," RR-79-13, 73 p., International Institute for Applied Systems Analysis, Laxenburg, Austria. Also, Nebojsa Nakicenovic, 1986, "Patterns of change: Technological substitution and long waves in the United States," WP-86-13, 32 p., International Institute for Applied Systems Analysis, Laxenburg, Austria.

4. Data figured from *Oil Economists' Handbook* and *BP Statistical Review of World Energy* (June 2008).

5. Energy Information Administration, *International Energy Outlook* (2005), 3.

6. Population Reference Bureau, "World Population Estimates and Projections by Single Years, 1750–2150."

7. Henry R. Linden, "Outlook for U.S. Gas Supply Improves if Production Efforts Are Stepped Up," *Oil & Gas Journal* (February 4, 2008), 37: ". . . gas with a carbon to hydrogen atomic ratio of 1:4 compared with 1:2 for oil, 2:1 for coal, and 10:1 for wood."

8. Amory Lovins, e-mail correspondence, July 8, 2007.

9. Jesse Ausubel, as quoted in Jeremy Rifkin's *The Hydrogen Economy* (New York: Tarcher/Penguin, 2003), 179–180.

10. Roberto F. Aguilera and Roberto Aguilera, "Assessing the Past, Present, and Near Future of the Global Energy Market," *Society of Petroleum Engineers* 110215-PP (2007).

Chapter 5

1. 1,908 Tcf mean estimate from U.S. Geological Survey, *World Petroleum Assessment 2000*, Table AR-1; 1,533 Tcf from Department of Energy, Energy Information Administration, *Annual Energy Review* 2007 (2008); 1,525 Tcf from Potential Gas Committee, *Potential Supply of Natural Gas in the United States*, (September 2007), with reserves; 2,247 Tcf from Navigant Consulting, "North American Natural Gas Supply Assessment" (July 4, 2008), 8.

2. Exxon Company, U.S.A., Exploration Department, "U.S. Oil and Gas Potential" (March 1976).

3. J. D. Langston, vice president, Exploration, Exxon Company, U.S.A., "A New Look at the U.S. Oil and Gas Potential" (remarks at the Sixteenth Annual Institute on Petroleum Exploration and Economics, The Southwestern Legal Foundation, Dallas, Texas, March 10, 1976).

4. Follow-up private correspondence between Robert A. Hefner III and J. D. Langston, June 17, 1976.

5. Robert A. Hefner III, testimony before the Senate Committee on Interior and Insular Affairs (February 19, 1972, March 2, 1972, and April 10, 1972); before the Senate Committee on Commerce, Science and Transportation (November 8, 1972); before the House Subcommittee on Energy and Power, Committee on Interstate and Foreign Commerce (March 21, 1975, January 27, 1976, March 24, 1977, and May 12, 1977); before the House Committee on Ways and Means (May 24, 1977); before the Senate Committee on Energy and Natural Resources (June 13, 1977, and November 6, 1981); before the Senate Subcommittee on Antitrust and Monopoly, Committee on the Judiciary (July 15, 1977); before the House Subcommittee on Energy and the Environment, Committee on Interior and Insular Affairs (September 22, 1977); before the Senate Subcommittee on Energy Regulation, Committee

on Energy and Natural Resources (April 23, 1981, March 11, 1983, and April 26, 1984); and before the House Subcommittee on Fossil and Synthetic Fuels, Committee on Energy and Commerce (March 24, 1983, and April 14, 1983).

6. Robert A. Hefner III, Congressional testimony (November 8, 1972, March 21, 1975, March 24, 1977, May 12, 1977, May 24, 1977, and June 13, 1977).

7. Robert A. Hefner III, Congressional testimony of September 22, 1977.

8. Edward Cowan, "He May Ask for a Windfall-Profit Limit: Energy Firms Await Carter's Call for Sacrifices," *New York Times* (February 13, 1977). Article quotes John O'Leary, Administrator, Federal Energy Administration.

9. John Dingell as quoted in Richard Vietor, *Contrived Competition: Regulation and Deregulation in America* (Cambridge, MA: Harvard University Press, 1994).

10. Gordon K. Zareski, Chief, Resource Evaluation and Analysis Division, Bureau of Natural Gas, Federal Power Commission, testimony before the House Subcommittee on Energy and Power of the Committee on Interstate and Foreign Commerce (March 24, 1977, March 25, 1977, and April 5, 1977).

11. John F. O'Leary, administrator, Federal Energy Administration, testimony before the House Subcommittee on Energy and Power of the Committee on Interstate and Foreign Commerce (March 24, 1977, March 25, 1977, and April 5, 1977).

12. John D. Moody, testimony before the House Subcommittee on Energy and Power of the Committee on Interstate and Foreign Commerce (March 24, 1977, March 25, 1977, and April 5, 1977).

13. Robert A. Hefner III, testimony before the House Subcommittee on Energy and Power of the Committee on Interstate and Foreign Commerce (March 24, 1977, March 25, 1977, and April 5, 1977).

14. First said by Robert A. Hefner III before the House Subcommittee on Energy and Power, Committee on Interstate and Foreign Commerce (January 27, 1976).

15. M. King Hubbert, "Nuclear Energy and the Fossil Fuels," Publication No. 95 (Houston, Texas: Shell Development Company, Exploration and Production Research Division, June 1956).

16. "Workshop on R&D Priorities and the Gas Energy Option," Executive Summary (Aspen, Colorado: Aspen Institute, June 1978). Participants listed as: Charles J. Hitch, president, Resources for the Future; Dr. Arnold E. Safer, vice president, Economics, Irving Trust Co.; Dr. Lester B. Lave, professor of economics, Carnegie-Mellon University; Dr. William T. McCormick Jr., vice president, Policy Analysis and Government Relations, American Gas Association; Eric R. Zausner, vice president, Booz Allen Applied Research; Dr. David Sternlight, chief economist, Atlantic Richfield Co. Inc.; Dr. Herman Franssen, Director, market analysis, Office of International Affairs, Department of Energy; Dr. Harry C. Kent, director, Potential Gas

Agency, Colorado School of Mines; Robert A. Hefner III, president, GHK
Corporation; Dr. Richard Gonzales, consulting economist; Laurence I. Moss,
environmental consultant; Gerald Decker, DOW Chemical Corp.; Dr. Ron
Erickson, director, Environmental Studies Program, University of Montana;
attorney Philip J. Mause; attorney Bruce J. Terris; Dr. John H. Gibbons, direc-
tor, Environment Center, University of Tennessee; Dr. Lawrence E. Swabb
Jr., vice president, Synthetic Fuels Research, Exxon Research & Engineering
Co.; Harry Perry, Consultant, Resources for the Future; Dr. S. William
Gouse, chief scientist, The MITRE Corp.; Dr. Kenneth Street, associate
director for Fossil Energy Programs, Lawrence Livermore Laboratories; Eric
H. Reichl, president, Conoco Coal Development Co.; Dr. James M. Sharp,
president, Gulf Universities Research Consortium; Lloyd Elkins, petroleum
consultant; William F. Morse, director of research, Columbia Gas System
Service Corp.; professor Myron H. Dorfman, director for geothermal studies, University of Texas; Dr. Lincoln F. Elkins, technical advisory to general
manager, Sohio Petroleum Co.; Dr. John Foster Jr., vice president and general
manager, Energy System Group, TRW Inc.; Dr. Melvin K. Simmons, assist-
ant director for analysis and assessment, Solar Energy Research Institute;
G.H. Farbman, Westinghouse Electric Corp.; Dr. Henry J. Gomberg, president,
KMS Fusion Inc., Dr. Edward Teller, associate director emeritus, Lawrence
Livermore Laboratories; Roger W. Sant, director, Energy Conservation Policy
Center, Carnegie-Mellon Institute of Research; Dr. Gene G. Mannella,
director, Conservation Programs, Institute of Gas Technology; Dr. Robert
C. Weast, vice president, research, Consolidated Natural Gas Service Co. Inc.;
Dr. Barry Commoner, director, Center for the Biology of Natural Systems,
Washington University (St. Louis, MO); Frank M. Potter Jr., staff director,
Subcommittee on Energy & Power, House Committee on Interstate and
Foreign Commerce; Robert W. Fri, consultant; Dr. Daniel A. Dreyfus, dep-
uty staff director for legislation, Senate Committee on Energy and Natural
Resources; Dr. Philip W. White, consultant; Dr. Bernard S. Lee, president-
elect, Institute of Gas Technology; and Dr. Robert A. Charpie, president, The
Cabot Corp.

17 "Study Examines Costs of an Aging Workforce," *The American Oil & Gas Reporter* (July 2007).

18. Charles B. Wheeler, senior vice president, Exxon Co. U.S.A., testimony before the Senate Committee on Energy Regulation, Subcommittee of the Full Committee of Energy & Natural Resources (April 26, 1984).

19. Robert A. Hefner III, "The Energy Connection," *Property Journal* (Autumn 1977).

20. Robert A. Hefner III, testimony before the Senate Committee on Energy and Natural Resources, Subcommittee on Energy Regulation (April 26, 1984).

21. "Exxon says North American Gas Production Has Peaked" (June 21, 2005), www.rueuters.com.

22. Allen Baker, "ConocoPhillips' Jim Mulva Bets Big on Gas," *Petroleum News* 10, no. 51 (retrieved June 19, 2008), www.petroleumnews.com/pntruncate/540339253.shtml.

23. Energy Information Administration, *Monthly Energy Review* (various issues).

24. Navigant Consulting, *North American Natural Gas Supply Assessment* (July 4, 2008), 8.

25. "Chesapeake and Plains Kick the Haynesville Play into High Gear," *Natural Gas Week* (July 7, 2008).

26. Robert A. Hefner III, "New Thinking about Natural Gas," *The Future of Energy Gases* (U.S. Geological Survey Professional Paper; 1570, 1993).

27. "BP America Buys 25 Percent Chesapeake Stake" (September 2, 2008), http://news.moneycentral.msn.com/ticker/article.aspx?Feed=AP&Date=20080902&ID=908.

Chapter 6

1. "Energy Security in Asia: The Case for Flexibility," *World Energy* 6, no. 3 (2003), 18.

2. International Energy Agency, *World Energy Outlook* (2007), Reference Scenario.

3. Richard Denney, "Hydrogen More Myth than 'Messiah,'" *The American Oil & Gas Reporter* (October 2007); "Doing the Green Thing," Chesapeake Energy Community Ties publication (Spring 2008).

4. Chris Woodyard, "Natural-Gas Powered Cars: Who Even Knows They Exist? Clean Efficient Vehicles Have Been Ignored," *USA Today* (May 9, 2007).

5. American Gas Association, *Gas Facts: A Statistical Record of the Gas Industry* (2007), Table 8-2, Residential End-Users.

6. Vehicle count data from *Highway Statistics 2006*, "State Motor-Vehicle Registrations" (U.S. Department of Transportation, Federal Highway Administration). Data on number of SUVs and light trucks and estimates of average costs of SUVs and light trucks from private conversations with car dealership personnel.

7. Based on saving the use of approximately 5 to 6 million barrels of imported oil per day, using the March 31, 2009, strip price for the cost of oil for 2010 through 2015 (via Bloomberg), and presuming a phased-in conversion, the savings would be $700 billion.

8. "Natural Gas Found on Pluto," *BBC Online Network* (July 20, 1999), http://news.bbc.co.uk/2/hi/science/nature/399324.stm, retrieved September 12, 2008.

9. "Pluto Atmosphere Reported Observed for the First Time," *New York Times* (June 12, 1988).

10. "Methane's Abundance Fuels NASA Dream for Interplanetary Travel," *Natural Gas Week* (June 2, 2008), 7.

11. Gary Clouser, "Barnett Barrels Along," *Oil & Gas Investor Supplement* "Shale and Coalbed Methane" (January 2008), 10.

12. Richard M. Pollastro, "Total Petroleum System Assessment of Undiscovered Resources in the Giant Barnett Shale Continuous (Unconventional) Gas Accumulation, Fort Worth Basin, Texas," *AAPG Bulletin* 91, no. 4 (April 2007), 551.

13. Gary Clouser, "Barnett Barrels Along," *Oil & Gas Investor Supplement* "Shale and Coalbed Methane" (January 2008), 10. Barnett production reached 2.8 Bcf a day as of July 1, 2007. This is 5.3 percent of average daily 2007 U.S. natural gas dry gas production, as reported in EIA's *Monthly Energy Review* (May 2008), 69.

14. "A Vast Ocean of Natural Gas," *American Clean Skies* (Summer 2008), 49.

15. John-Laurent Tronche, "EnCana Moves to Shift Barnett Assets to Gas Group," *Fort Worth Business Press* (May 19, 2008); "Devon Energy in Barnett Shale," *The Oklahoman* (August 1, 2008); Chesapeake Energy, "Investor Presentation" (May 2008), 8.

16. "Chesapeake and Plains Kick the Haynesville Play into Gear," *Natural Gas Week* 24, no. 27 (July 7, 2008).

17. CHK-Chesapeake Energy Corporation Conference Call to Discuss Haynesville Shale Joint Venture, July 2, 2008.

18. E-mail communication from Joseph Gladbach, Jefferies Randall & Dewey, July 1, 2008.

19. "Natural Gas Hydrates—Vast Resource, Uncertain Future," USGS Fact Sheet FS-021-01 (March 2001).

20. Extrapolation from *BP Statistical Review of World Energy* (June 2008); BP Review of World Gas, gas conversion factors card, with approximate conversion factors on energy equivalent basis.

21. Compiled using data from Carbon Dioxide Information Analysis Center, http://cdiac.ornl.gov/ftp/ndp030/global.1751_2004.ems, using carbon/CO_2 conversion; International Energy Agency, *World Energy Outlook 2007*, Reference Scenario.

22. Shai Oster and David Winning, "China Aims to Curb Power Shortages," *Wall Street Journal* (January 24, 2008).

23. "Safety" (U.K. Natural Gas Vehicle Association), www.ngva.co.uk/index/fuseaction/site.articleDETAIL/con_id/5036.

24. U.S. Environmental Protection Agency, "Methane," www.epa.gov/methane, retrieved August 4, 2008.

25. "Common Sense on Climate Change: Practical Solutions to Global Warming" (Union of Concerned Scientists), http://www.ucsusa.org/global_warming/solutions/common-sense-on, retrieved June 18, 2008.

26. Compiled from data from Energy Information Administration, *Monthly Energy Review* (various issues).

27. "History of Natural Gas Vehicles" (Union Gas), www.uniongas.com/aboutus/aboutng/ngv/ngvhistory,asp, retrieved May 28, 2008.

28. Daniel Yergin, *The Prize: The Epic Quest for Oil, Money and Power* (New York: Simon & Schuster, 1991).

29. Communication, IHS Energy, June 11, 2008.

30. E-mail correspondence, Herman Franssen, June 4, 2008.

31. "Gas-Strapped Argentina Paying $14/MMBtu for Initial LNG Cargo," *Natural Gas Week* (April 28, 2008), 13; "A New Global Market for Natural Gas," *Seeking Alpha* (August 13, 2008), http://seekingalpha.com/article/90699-a-new-global-market-for-natural-gas.

32. Sebastian Abbot, "Gulf States Rise Higher on Oil Boom," Associated Press (May 21, 2008); "KSA—KAEC gets strong investor response," *Mist News* (May 28, 2008).

33. Carl Mortished, "Gulf States May Soon Need Coal Imports to Keep the Lights On," *The Times* (May 19, 2008).

34. "Nuclear Energy Best Option for Gulf States: Experts," *AFP* (May 27, 2008).

35. "Total Abandons SRAK in Empty Quarter," *Zawya Ltd.* (May 28, 2008).

36. "Shortfall in the Pipeline" (gulfnews.com, May 29, 2008), http://archive.gulfnews.com/articles/08/05/29/10216795.html.

37. Robert A. Hefner III, *Proposal for Cooperation between the People's Republic of China and GHK (China) Limited* (The GHK Company, 1985).

38. "PetroChina Finds Mammoth Field," *Upstream* (March 23, 2007).

Chapter 7

1. Wallace E. Pratt, "Toward a Philosophy of Oil-Finding," *Bulletin of the American Association of Petroleum Geologists* 36, no. 12 (December 1952).

2. "The Blame Game" segment from CNBC's special "America's Oil Crisis" with Maria Bartiromo, originally aired May 22, 2008, http://www.cnbc.com/id/15840232?video=750996001, retrieved July 15, 2008.

3. M. King Hubbert, "Nuclear Energy and the Fossil Fuels," Publication No. 95, Shell Development Company, Exploration and Production Research Division, Houston, Texas, June 1956.

4. Allen Baker, "ConocoPhillips' Jim Mulva Bets Big on Gas," *Petroleum News* 10, no. 51 (retrieved June 19, 2008), www.petroleumnews.com/pntruncate/540339253.shtml.

5. "Methane's Abundance Fuels NASA Dream for Interplanetary Travel," *Natural Gas Week* (June 2, 2008).

6. Fraser Cain, "Organic Molecules Seen in an Extrasolar Planet," *Universe Today*, http://www.universetoday.com/2008/03/19/organic-molecules-seen-in-an-extrasolar-planet/, retrieved August 26, 2008.

7. "Deepest Well Ever Drilled," Hart's *E&P* (March 2000).

8. "Natural Gas Hydrates—Vast Resource, Uncertain Future," USGS Fact Sheet FS-021-01 (March 2001).

9. "Chesapeake and Plains Kick the Haynesville Play into High Gear," *Natural Gas Week*, (July 7, 2008); e-mail communication, July 1, 2008, from Joseph Gladbach.

10. AAPG Memoir 78, *Giant Oil and Gas Fields of the Decade, 1990–1999* (Tulsa, OK: The American Association of Petroleum Geologists, 2003).

11. Proven reserves are those quantities of petroleum that, by analysis of geological and engineering data, can be estimated with reasonable certainty to be commercially recoverable, from a given date forward, from known reservoirs and under current economic conditions, operating methods, and government regulations. Proved reserves can be categorized as developed or undeveloped. www.spe.org, 1997 Reserves Definitions.

12. *BP Statistical Review of World Energy*, June 2008 (extrapolation).

13. Robert A. Hefner III, "New Thinking about Natural Gas," *The Future of Energy Gases* (U.S. Geological Survey Professional Paper; 1570), 1993.

14. Figured from assorted data on fields obtained 2008 from IHS Energy.

15. Energy Information Administration, "U.S. Crude Oil, Natural Gas and Natural Gas Liquids Reserves," 2007 Annual Report, Advance Summary (October 2008).

16. USGS world gas total mean estimates: 15,401 Tcf, from U.S. Geological Survey *World Petroleum Assessment 2000*, Table AR-1, "World Level Summary of Petroleum Estimates for Undiscovered Conventional Petroleum and Reserve Growth for Oil, Gas, and Natural Gas Liquids."

17. Chris Hopkins, president, Data & Consulting Services, Schlumberger Oilfield Services, from presentation, "Unconventional Gas Reservoirs" at Aspen Institute 2007 Aspen Forum on Global Energy, Economy & Security "Toward a Global Natural Gas Market," Aspen, Colorado, July 8–11, 2007.

18. Robert A. Hefner, III, "The Future for Conventional U.S. Natural Gas Supply," Aspen Institute Workshop on R&D Priorities and the Gas Energy Option, Aspen, Colorado, June 25–29, 1978.

19. "We have arrived pretty much at a consensus among responsible estimators of some 400 to 600 Trillion cubic feet as the undiscovered potential for gas in the United States," John D. Moody, Mobil Oil Corp., statement before the

Subcommittee on Energy and Power, Committee on Interstate and Foreign Commerce, U.S. House of Representatives First Session, 95th Congress (March 24, 25, and April 5, 1977), pp. 67 and 76.

20. Energy Information Administration, *Monthly Energy Review* (various issues).

21. BP *Statistical Review of World Energy* (June 2007).

22. Richard Heinberg, "Peak Coal: Sooner than You Think," *Energy Bulletin* (May 21, 2007), http://www.energybulletin.net/node/29919, retrieved August 29, 2008.

23. Energy Watch Group, "Coal: Resources and Future Production" (background paper), March 2007, EWG-Series No 1/2007, updated version July 10, 2007.

24. B. Kavalov and S. D. Peteves, "The Future of Coal," DG JRC Institute for Energy, European Commission, Joint Research Centre (February 2007).

25. Heinberg.

26. "How Much Coal Remains?" *Science* 323, (13 March 2009), pp. 1420–1421.

27. Heinberg.

28. *Id.*

29. "How Much Coal Remains?" pp. 1420–1421.

30. Energy Watch Group; Kavalov and Peteves.

31. National Research Council of the National Academies, *Coal: Research and Development to Support National Energy Policy* (Washington, D.C.: The National Academies Press, 2007).

32. *Id.*

33. Arch Coal, Inc. is involved in several lawsuits in West Virginia, including a case for property damage and personal injuries from flooding in southern West Virginia and a case involving the Coal River watershed (dismissed but appealed). They have also been named in the remaining Upper Guyandotte watershed trial group. From Arch Coal, Inc. 2007 Annual Report, pages 33–34.

34. National Research Council of the National Academies, p. 4.

35. *Id.*, p. 44.

36. *Id.*, p. 4.

37. *Id.*, p. 5.

38. Bob Moen, "USGS Revises Coal Estimates," *Casper Star-Tribune* (August 2, 2008), http://www.trib.com/articles/2008/08/04/news/wyoming/677beb14234151a687257498008.

39. National Research Council of the National Academies, p. 45 (citing Wood et al., 1983).

40. *Id.*, p. 44.

41. *Id.*, p. 44 (citing EIA, 2006a).

42. *Id.*, p. 44 (citing NMA, 2006a).

43. *Id.*, p. 69.

44. Energy Information Administration, "U.S. Crude Oil, Natural Gas and Natural Gas Liquids Reserves," 2007 Annual Report, Advance Summary (October 2008).

45. Society of Petroleum Engineers, http://www.spe.org/spe-site/spe/spe/industry/reserves/GlossaryPetroleumReserves-ResourcesDefinitions_2005.pdf

46. National Research Council of the National Academies, p. 50.

47. *Id.*, p. 50.

48. *Id.*, p. 44 (citing NMA, 2006a).

49. USGS: 1,908 Tcf mean estimate from *U.S. Geological Survey World Petroleum Assessment 2000*, Table AR-1; DOE/EIA: 1,533 Tcf—*Annual Energy Review 2007*, published 2008; Potential Gas Committee: 1,525 Tcf—from *Potential Supply of Natural Gas in the United States*, published September 2007, with reserves; Navigant Consulting: 2,247 Tcf—from "North American Natural Gas Supply Assessment," Navigant Consulting, July 4, 2008, page 8.

50. National Research Council of the National Academies, p, 4.

51. Hefner, "New Thinking about Natural Gas."

52. National Research Council of the National Academies, p. 3.

53. Richard Heinberg, "Burning the Furniture," MuseLetter #179, March 2007, http://www.richardheinberg.com/museletter/179 (retrieved August 30, 2008).

54. National Research Council of the National Academies, p. 53.

Chapter 8

1. U.S. Environmental Protection Agency, "Methane," www.epa.gov/methane/, retrieved August 4, 2008.

2. "Common Sense on Climate Change: Practical Solutions to Global Warming" (Union of Concerned Scientists). http://www.ucsusa.org/global_warming/solutions/common-sense-on- . . . (retrieved June 18, 2008).

3. *Energy Statistics Sourcebook*, 14th ed. (Tulsa, OK: PennWell, 1999).

4. Robert A. Hefner III, Oral Presentation transcript, Federal Power Commission Hearing, Docket Number R-389A (August 13, 1970).

5. Figured from Energy Information Administration, *Monthly Energy Review* (March 2009), Table 3.1 (gross imports as a percent of petroleum products supplied).

6. Gordon K. Zareski, chief, Resource Evaluation & Analysis Division, Bureau of Natural Gas, Federal Power Commission, at Hearings before the House Subcommittee on Energy & Power of the Committee on Interstate & Foreign Commerce, on Long-Term Natural Gas Policy Issues & Questions, March 24, 1977, March 25, 1977, and April 5, 1977.

7. See "Explosion of Laws; Here's What's Left of Carter's Energy Package," *U. S. News & World Report* (October 23, 1978); and Edward Walsh, "Carter Signs Natural Gas Deregulation; Energy Bill Signed, Carter Tackles Deficit," *The Washington Post* (November 10, 1978), A1. Also see Merrill Sheils et al., "Will the Gas Bill Help?" *Newsweek* (October 2, 1978), p. 103.

8. Compiled from various Energy Information Administration publications on electricity for years 1979 through 1988 and data from Edison Electric Institute.

9. Compiled from data from Carbon Dioxide Information Analysis Center, multiple Energy Information Administration sources, Edison Electric Institute.

10. Fact sheets assembled from "Super Well Study," prepared by Resource Analysis and Management Group (RAM), 1972.

11. "Worldwide Look at Reserves and Production," *Oil & Gas Journal* (December 22, 2008); Energy Information Administration, *Monthly Energy Review* (April 2009), Tables 3.1 and 11.1b.

12. "Study Examines Costs of an Aging Workforce," *The American Oil & Gas Reporter* (July 2007), 30; James Hertlein, "The Importance of Effective Succession Planning," *Oil & Gas Financial Journal* (January 2008), 52; "The Not-So-Great Crew Change," *E&P* (July 2007), 5.

Chapter 9

1. Nicholas Stern, "Stern Review on the Economics of Climate Change," 700-page report released October 30, 2006, for the British government.

2. Fiona Harvey and Jim Pickard, "Stern Underestimated Global Warming Risks," *Financial Times* (April 17, 2008); "A New Stern Report on Climate Change," *Globe-Net News* (May 8, 2008), http://www.globe-net.com/news/index.cfm?type=2&newsID=3522.

3. Compiled using data from Carbon Dioxide Information Analysis Center, http://cdiac.ornl.gov/ftp/ndp030/global.1751_2004.ems.

4. "Berlin Pressed to Restore Fuel Tax Break," *Financial Times* (June 26, 2008).

5. Walt Kelley, *Pogo: We Have Met the Enemy and He Is Us* (New York: Simon & Schuster, 1972).

6. "U.S. Gas: So Cheap It Hurts," CNNMoney.com, updated July 15, 2008.

7. *Id.*

8. "Highlights of Energy Bill Passed by Congress," *1010Wins* (December 19, 2007), http://www.1010wins.com/topic/ap_news.php?story=AP/APTV/National/f/f/FuelEconomy-Glance.

9. "Statement from World Bank China Country Director on 'Cost of Pollution in China' Report," July 11, 2007.

10. Average 2008 price of oil was $99.75 per barrel (Bloomberg online service) and U.S. petroleum imports averaged 12.87 million barrels per day (Energy Information Administration, *Monthly Energy Review* [March 2009], Table 3.1), equaling a total import cost of $469 billion for 2008.

11. "Understanding Extreme Weather and Climate Impacts in China—Q&A," Pew Center on Global Climate Change, http://www.pewclimate.org/china-extremeweather_qa (retrieved May 18, 2009).

12. Jeff Goodell, *Big Coal: The Dirty Secret behind America's Energy Future* (Boston and New York: Houghton Mifflin Company, 2006), p. 116.

13. "Greenspan Says Iraq War Is 'about Oil,'" *Toronto Vision News* (July 31, 2008), as quoted from reported excerpts of Alan Greenspan's book *The Age of Turbulence: Adventures in a New World* (New York: Penguin, 2007).

14. Cambridge Lecture, "The Great Repricing," speech by Singapore Minister for Foreign Affairs George Yeo at the Distinguished Lecture at the University of Cambridge (March 27, 2009).

15. Data figured from *BP Statistical Review of World Energy*, June 2008.

16. "Gross Domestic Product 2007," World Development Indicators database, World Bank (July 1, 2008), http://web.worldbank.org/WBSITE/EXTERNAL/DATASTATISTICS/0,,contentMDK:20 (accessed July 29, 2008).

17. Zaki Yamani (former Saudi Arabia oil minister) as quoted in *Yamani*, 1988.

18. Edmund Conway, "Stern Favours World Carbon Tax," *Telegraph.co.uk* (January 25, 2007), http://www.telegraph.co.uk/money/main.jhtml?xml=/money/2007/01/24/bcnstern24.xml (accessed September 4, 2008).

19. Government data reported by Xinhua news said China's wind power generation rose 95.2 percent to 5.6 billion Kw hours in 2007, from a year previous. The report said China had wind-power facilities with a combined installed capacity of 6.05 million kW at the end of 2007, up from 2.67 million kW in 2006. The country achieved the goal set for 2010 three years ahead of schedule. Vestas Wind System A/S' Chief Executive Officer Ditlev Engel says China may become the world's leading market for wind-power generation within five years.

20. Michael Graham Richard, "Chinese Fuel Economy Laws" (July, 25, 2005), www.treehugger.com/files/2005/07/Chinese_fuel_ec.php (accessed May 27, 2008); "Fuel Economy Standard Will Be 31.6 mpg," Associated Press (April 22, 2008), www.msnbc.msn.com/id/24258714/print/1/displaymode/1098/ retrieved 5/27/08.

21. Coal's percentage of world energy consumption had declined to about 27 percent by 1977, and then went back up to about 29 percent by 1985. Data figured from BP's online historical data, Statistical Reviews of World Energy, www.bp.com.

22. Compiled from data from Carbon Dioxide Information Analysis Center, multiple Energy Information Administration sources, Edison Electric Institute.

23. "Outfront: Short Circuit—Brownout," *Forbes* (June 30, 2008).

24. National Defense Council Foundation, "The Hidden Cost of Oil" (retrieved February 4, 2008), www.setamericafree.org/saf_hiddencostofoil010507.pdf.

25. U.S. total oil import numbers, 1980 through 2007, from Energy Information Administration, *Monthly Energy Review* (August 2008), Table 3.1, and (December 2001), Table 3.1b. Total import numbers (in barrels/day) multiplied by 365 to get barrels/year, multiplied by 42 to get gallons/year, times estimated external cost of $3 per gallon.

26. Thomas K. McCraw, *Prophet of Innovation: Joseph Schumpeter and Creative Destruction* (Cambridge, MA, and London, England: The Belknap Press of Harvard University Press, 2007).

27. Goodell, p. 254.

Chapter 10

1. "Driving in Los Angeles County," http:/wikiktravel.org/en/Driving_in_Los_Angeles_County (retrieved August 15, 2008).

2. When retrofits are mass produced, costs should not exceed these levels.

3. A natural gas home-fill appliance now costs $4,000, but mass production should reduce the cost by at least 50 percent.

4. Norman L. Miller et al., "Climate, Extreme Heat, and Electricity Demand in California," *Journal of Applied Meteorology and Climatology* 47, no. 6 (June 1, 2008); "Projected California Warming Creates Cycle of More Heat Waves, Energy Use for 21st Century," *Targeted News Service* (July 10, 2008).

5. "California World's Sixth-Largest Economy? Not Anymore," *International Herald Tribune* (January 12, 2007). California's economy is the eighth largest economy in the world.

Chapter 11

1. "What's News?" *Wall Street Journal* (February 27, 2008).

2. Viren Doshi, Gary Schulman, and Daniel Gabaldon (consultants from Booz Allen Hamilton, Inc.), "Lights! Water! Motion!" (retrieved May 6, 2008), *Strategy+Business*, http://www.strategy-business.com/press/article/07104?gko=a8c38-1876-23502998.

3. Kristin M. Hall, "Spill from Coal Plant May Have Permanently Altered Landscape in Eastern Tennessee," Newsday.com (December 30, 2008).

4. "Better Energy," *Discover* (May 2008), pp. 29–30.

5. Jeff Goodell, *Big Coal: The Dirty Secret behind America's Energy Future* (Boston, MA, and New York: Houghton Mifflin Company, 2006), pp. 131, 139.

6. American Lung Association, "Power Plants and Air Pollution" (retrieved April 30, 2008), www.lungusa.org/site/pp.asp?c=dvLUK9O0E&b.

7. Carbon Dioxide Information Analysis Center, "Global CO_2 Emissions from Fossil-Fuel Burning, Cement Manufacture, and Gas Flaring: 1751–2004" (retrieved July 20, 2007), http://cdiac.ornl.gov/ftp/ndp030/global.1751_2004, ems.

8. Natural Resources Defense Council, "Mercury Contamination in Fish," http://www.nrdc.org/health/effects/mercury/sources.asp, retrieved May 6, 2008.

9. Massachusetts Institute of Technology, "The Future of Coal: An Interdisciplinary MIT Study," Summary Report, page IX, 2006.

10. Energy Information Administration, *Monthly Energy Review* (April 2008), Table 3.1, showing total crude oil production.

11. Andrew C. Revkin, "A 'Bold' Step to Capture an Elusive Gas Falters," *New York Times* (February 3, 2008).

12. Goodell, p. 254.

13. Energy Information Administration, *Electric Power Annual 2006*, Table 2.2, "Existing Capacity by Energy Source, 2006," citing generator nameplate capacity for coal at 335,830 megawatts; Energy Information Administration, "Assumptions to the Annual Energy Outlook 2007," Table 39: Cost and Performance Characteristics of New Central Station Electricity Generating Technologies. Using base overnight costs and assuming natural gas replaces 85 percent of coal generator capacity, and wind and solar each replace 7.5 percent of coal generator capacity.

14. David Leonhardt, "What $1.2 Trillion Can Buy," *New York Times* (January 17, 2007).

15. "Coal-to-Liquid Fuel Plant Opportunity Fact Sheet," "Coal-to-Liquid Technology Fact Sheet," and "CTL Carbon Sequestration," (retrieved May 5, 2008), www.airforce.mil (Malmstrom Air Force Base Web site).

16. "Will Air Force coal-to-fuel plan fly?" MSNBC.com (May 1, 2008), http://www.msnbc.msn.com/id/23811258/print/1/displaymode/1098/, retrieved May 5, 2008.

17. Guy Chazan, "A Gamble in Qatar: Royal Dutch Shell is making a huge—and risky—bet on technology that transforms natural gas to diesel fuel," *Wall Street Journal*, February 9, 2009.

18. *Id.*

19. Amanda Griscom Little, "Take a Peak," *Grist Environmental News & Commentary*, (November 3, 2005), interview with Matthew Simmons; http://www.grist.org/news/maindish/2005/11/03/simmons/, retrieved September 3, 2008.

20. "ExxonMobil Corporation Announces Estimated Record 2007 Results," *Business Wire* (February 1, 2008); "Chevron Issues Interim Update for Fourth Quarter 2007," *Business Wire* (January 10, 2008); ConocoPhillips 2007 Annual Report, p.11; Shell "Oil & Gas—Operational Data," (retrieved May 6, 2008), http://www.shell.com/home/content/investor-en/financial_information; BP p.l.c. Group Results, Fourth Quarter and Full Year 2007, February 5, 2008.

21. Matthew R. Simmons, *Twilight in the Desert: The Coming Saudi Oil Shock and the World Economy* (Hoboken, NJ: John Wiley & Sons, 2006).

22. Matthew R. Simmons, "2008—A Wild Ride for Oil Markets," *World Oil* (February 2009).

23. Michael Wang, "Well-to-Wheels Analysis of Vehicle/Fuel Systems," Center for Transportation Research, Argonne National Laboratory, Workshop on Modeling the Oil Transition, Washington, DC, April 20–21, 2006, p. 4.

24. Sheila McNulty, "Green Leaves, Black Gold," *FT Magazine*, FT.com (December 15, 2007), http://www.cbsnews.com/stories/2006/01/20/60minutes/main1225184.shtml.

25. "Peak Opportunity! Earth Liberation and the Oil Endgame," *Alternative Press Review*, http://www.altpr.org/modules/php?op=modload&name=Sections&file=index&req=viewarti . . . , retrieved September 5, 2008.

26. John Lippert and Alan Ohnsman, "End of the Oil Age," *Bloomberg Markets* (March 2008).

27. Andrew Nikiforuk, "Liquid Asset; Could the Oil Sands, Canada's Greatest Economic Project, Come Undone Simply Because No One Thought about Water?" *The Globe and Mail* (March 28, 2008).

28. Douglas Martin, "An Audience with Mr. Exxon," *New York Times* (August 9, 1981).

29. "Rush to Drill for Oil Shale Unwise," *The Denver Post* (June 13, 2008).

30. Energy Information Administration, Country Page, Canada, Oil, http://eia.doe.gov/cabs/Canada/oil.html.

31. Michael E. Webber, "Energy versus Water: Solving Both Crises Together," *Scientific American*, Special Edition (October 22, 2008), http://www.sciam.com/article.cfm?id=the-future-of-fuel.

32. "Three Gorges Dam Relocation Funding Misused," *China in Transition*, http://josieliu.blogspot.com/2007/01/three-gorges-dam-relocation-funding.html, retrieved September 3, 2008.

33. "Glen Canyon Dam Generates Less than 1% of the Power on the Western Power Grid," http://www.glencanyon.org/aboutgci/faq.php.

34. European Commission, "Report on the Green Paper on Energy" (2005), http://www.jet.efda.org/documents/ad-hoc/2005-green-paper-report-en.pdf, p. 8.

35. *Id.*, p. 23.

36. Figured from *BP Statistical Review of World Energy*, June 2007.

37. Yuka Hayashi, "As Nuclear Power Gains Global Appeal, Japan Is Hit by Setbacks," *Wall Street Journal* (July 9, 2008).

38. Graham Allison, "Graham Allison Commentary: Nuclear Attack a Worst-Case Reality?" *Washington Times* (April 23, 2008).

39. American Institute of Physics, "Committee Examines Future Cost of Nuclear Waste Storage," *AIP Bulletin of Science Policy News*, FYI no. 110 (November 7, 2007).

40. H. Josef Hebert, "Nuclear Waste Disposal Will Cost US $96B," *Forecast Earth* (August 6, 2008), http://climate.weather.com/articles/nuclearwaster080608.html, retrieved August 25, 2008.

41. Don Warlick, "Energy Bill Provides Kick-Start to Biofuels," *Oil & Gas Financial Journal* (January 2008), p. 37.

42. "Consider Shifting Energy Sources," *E&P* (January 2008), p. 101.

43. Total 2007 U.S. CO_2 fossil fuel emissions are 5.984 billion metric tons, of which 2.583 billion metric tons are petroleum emissions (Energy Information Administration, "U.S. Carbon Dioxide Emissions from Energy Sources 2007 Flash Estimate," http://www.eia.doe.gov/oiaf/1605/flash/flash.html (July 1, 2008). The U.S. petroleum supply of about 20 million barrels per day (Energy Information Administration, *Monthly Energy Review* (September 2008), Table 3.1, Petroleum Overview) produced 2.583 billion metric tons of CO_2 in 2007; the 5.75 million barrels of oil per day saved by using CNG (or 28.75 percent of the 20 million barrels per day) produce 743 million metric tons of CO_2 per year. CNG could save about 30 percent of the 743 million metric tons or a savings of about 223 million metric tons per year.

44. U.S. oil imports total 13 million barrels per day (Energy Information Administration, *Monthly Energy Review* (September 2008), Table 3.1, Petroleum Overview); converting 130 million U.S. vehicles to CNG would save 5.75 million barrels per day; so, with a phased-in CNG conversion plan and using the Bloomberg March 31, 2009, strip prices for crude oil from 2010 through 2015, savings by 2015 would be $700 billion.

45. American Wind Energy Association, "Another Record Year for New Wind Installations" (retrieved May 6, 2008), www.awea.org; American Wind Energy

Association, "2008: Another Record Year for Wind Energy Installations" (retrieved May 18, 2009), www.awea.org/pubs/factsheets.html.

46. Jack Money, "Can Pickens Plan End Oil Addiction?" *The Oklahoman* (July 9, 2008); "Oil Billionaire Pickens Puts His Money on Wind Power," CNN.com/technology (July 8, 2008), http://www.cnn.com/2008/TECH/science/07/08/pickens.plan/, retrieved July 9, 2008.

47. http://www.wind-energie.de/en/wind-energy-in-germany/ (retrieved May 6, 2008).

48. "U.S. Becomes Top Producer of Wind Power," *China Economic Net* (August 4, 2008).

49. K. Zweibel, J. Mason & V. Fthenakis, "By 2050 Solar Power Could End U.S. Dependence on Foreign Oil and Slash Greenhouse Gas Emissions," *Scientific American* (January 2008).

50. Travis Bradford, *Solar Revolution: The Economic Transformation of the Global Energy Industry* (Cambridge, MA: MIT Press, 2006), p. 18.

51. Francois Isaac de Rivaz, of Switzerland, constructed the first internal combustion engine, powered by a mixture of hydrogen and oxygen, in 1806.

52. "Hydrogen Fuel Cells," K-Gray Engineering Pathway Digital Library (retrieved August 26, 2008), http://www.engineeringpathway.com/ep/learning_resource/summary/;jsessionid=VC5DT.

53. Mary Bellis, "Hydrogen Fuel Cells: Innovation for the 21st Century," About.com, http://inventors,about.com/od/fstartinventions/a/Fuel_Cells.htm, retrieved July 30, 2008.

54. Grid-Lok SMT Support Systems, "Fuel Cell Auto Sets Speed Record," U.S. Tech Interactive (September 2007), http://www.us-tech.com/RelId/635638/ISvars/default/September_2007 - Fuel_Cell_Aut.html, retrieved August 25, 2008.

55. "Tupolev Tu-154," Wikipedia, http://en.wikipedia.org/wiki/Tupolev_Tu-154, retrieved August 25, 2008.

56. "Boeing Tests HALE Hydrogen Propulsion System Based on 2.3-Liter Ford Hydrogen Engine," originally published October 25, 2007, reprinted in *Green Car Congress* (July 30, 2008), www.greencarcongress.com/2007/10/boeing-tests-ha.html.

57. Tyler Hamilton, "Hydrogen Economy Could Fuel a Nuclear Renaissance," *Toronto Star* (October 22, 2007), thestar.com, price extrapolated from numbers in article.

58. Energy Information Administration weekly report, July 24, 2008.

59. Bloomberg Data Services, March 31, 2009.

60. ITER, "Introduction," http://www.iter.org/a/index_nav_1.htm.

61. JET, "Fusion as a Future Energy Source," http://www.jet.efda.org/pages/fusion-basics/fusion6.html.

62. Jeremy Rifkin, *The Hydrogen Economy: The Creation of the Worldwide Energy Web and the Redistribution of Power on Earth* (New York: Jeremy P. Tarcher/Penguin, 2003).

Chapter 12

1. "Rig Count Falls by 46 in Nation," *The Oklahoman* (March 28, 2009): "The number of rigs actively exploring for oil and natural gas in the United States dropped by 46 this week to 1,039 . . . A year ago, the rig count stood at 1,808."

2. "Who Gives First if Summer Gas Market Collapses?" *Natural Gas Week* (March 30, 2009), quoting Raymond James analyst Marshall Adkins: "Even with our bearish rig count assumptions (we assume a 65% peak-to-trough gas rig decline, or over 1,000 rigs cut from the nearly 1,600 gas rig count peak) . . . "

3. Consolidated Statements of Operations, for year ended December 31, 2008, for Devon Energy Corporation and Subsidiaries and Chesapeake Energy Corporation and Subsidiaries.

4. U.S. petroleum imports for January and February 2009 are estimated at about 12.5 million barrels per day. December 2008 petroleum imports were 12.6 million barrels per day, per Energy Information Administration's *Monthly Energy Review* (March 2009), Table 3.1; Nymex Bloomberg average crude price: $43.78 for month of January 2009 and $39.26 for month of February 2009.

5. John Porretto, "Hard Times Mean New Opportunities for Big Oil," *The Washington Post* (March 29, 2009).

6. President Ronald Reagan, Inaugural Address, January 20, 1981. "In this present crisis, government is not the solution to our problem; government is the problem."

7. "About Natural Gas," American Gas Association (April 23, 2008), www.aga.org/Kc/aboutnaturalgas/. "Natural gas is delivered to customers through a safe, sound, 2.2-million-mile underground pipeline system . . . "

8. Energy Information Administration, *Electric Power Annual 2007* (January 2009), Table 2.2.

9. *Id.*

10. "Energy Security in Asia: The Case for Flexibility," *World Energy* 6, no. 3 (2003), 18.

11. "Energy Bill Provides Kick-Start to Biofuels," *Oil & Gas Financial Journal* (January 2008), Table 2, p. 37.

12. Karen Dillon, "Rush for Coal Plants Slows to a Stagger," *The Kansas City Star* (March 13, 2009).

13. Energy Information Administration, *Electric Power Annual 2006*, Table 2.6; Energy Information Administration, *Electric Power Annual 2007* (published January 2009), Table 2.6.

14. "Idaho Power Selects Langley Gulch Natural Gas-Fired Combined-Cycle Combustion Turbine Power Plant from Baseload Resource Request for Proposals," *PR Newswire* (U.S.) (March 9, 2009).

15. National Mining Association, "Trends in U.S. Coal Mining, 1923–2007," www.nma.org/pdf/c_trends_mining.pdf (retrieved May 21, 2009).

16. National Research Council of the National Academies, *Coal: Research and Development to Support National Energy Policy* (Washington, D.C.: The National Academies Press, 2007), p. 57.

17. The Energy Policy Act of 2005 included more than $9 billion in subsidies for the coal industry (Taxpayers for Common Sense, "Coal Subsidies: Energy Policy Act of 2005" [May 26, 2008], http://www.taxpayer.net/search_by_category.php?action=view&proj_id=556&category=E, retrieved October 1, 2008); and the current U.S. economic recovery package will provide $2.4 billion to coal interests (H. Josef Hebert, "U.S. Official Announces Billions for Clean Coal," Associated Press [May 18, 2009]).

18. Amory B. Lovins et al., *Winning the Oil Endgame: Innovation for Profits, Jobs, and Security* (Rocky Mountain Institute, 2005), p. vii.

19. *Id.*, p. ix.

20. Diana Farrell and Jaana K. Remes, "How the World Should Invest in Energy Efficiency," *McKinsey Quarterly* (July 2008).

21. Steve Lohr, "A McKinsey Study Says the Market Alone Can't Cut Carbon," *International Herald Tribune* (May 17, 2007), http://www.iht.com/articles/2007/05/17/business/greenhomes.php, retrieved September 24, 2008.

22. National Research Council of the National Academies, *Coal: Research and Development to Support National Energy Policy* (Washington, D.C.: The National Academies Press, 2007), p. 3.

23. "Taxpayers for Common Sense is an independent and non-partisan voice for taxpayers working to increase transparency and expose and eliminate wasteful and corrupt subsidies, earmarks, and corporate welfare." http://www.taxpayer.net.

24. Taxpayers for Common Sense, "End the Clean Coal Program" (February 15, 2002), http://www.taxpayer.net/search_by_category.php?action=view&proj_id=684&category=E, retrieved October 1, 2008.

25. Taxpayers for Common Sense, "Coal Subsidies: Energy Policy Act of 2005" (May 26, 2008), http://www.taxpayer.net/search_by_category.php?action=view&proj_id=556&category=E, retrieved October 1, 2008.

26. "Sunset for Synfuels Corp.?" *The Energy Daily* (January 4, 1984). "If the board asks Congress to shut the SFC down at the end of 1984, it would leave some $5 billion of the SFC's original $15 billion appropriation unspent." Synfuels was established in 1980. $10 billion in 1980 dollars equals $26 billion in 2008 dollars (according to the Federal Reserve Bank of Minneapolis inflation calculator).

27. American Petroleum Institute, "Fact Sheet: The Facts about Non-Producing Federal Leases" (June 13, 2008).

28. "In 2005 individuals, businesses and nonprofits will spend an estimated 6 billion hours complying with the federal income tax code, with an estimated compliance cost of over $265.1 billion." Scott A. Hodge, J. Scott Moody, and Wendy P. Warcholik, Ph.D., "The Rising Cost of Complying with the Federal Income Tax," The Tax Foundation Special Report No. 138, Executive Summary (January 10, 2006), http://www.taxfoundation.org/news/show/1281.html, retrieved September 12, 2008.

29. National Taxpayer Advocate, "2007 Annual Report to Congress," Volume One, page 35, http://www.irs.gov/pub/irs-utl/arc_2007_vol_1_cover_msps.pdf, retrieved September 4, 2008.

30. *Economic Report of the President* (February 2008), Table B-80.

31. Milton Copulos, "National Defense Council Foundation: Issue Alert, the Hidden Cost of Oil, an Update" (January 8, 2007), http://ndcf.dyndns.org/ndcf/home.htm, retrieved August 7, 2008. The "total of all oil-related external or 'hidden' costs . . . is equivalent to adding $8.35 to the price of a gallon of gasoline . . . " International Center for Technology Assessment, "The Real Price of Gasoline, Report No. 3—An Analysis of the Hidden External Costs Consumers Pay to Fuel Their Automobiles," November 1998.

32. Base numbers for oil products currently supplied from Energy Information Administration, *Monthly Energy Review* (July 2008), Table 3.5.

33. Jeff Goodell, *Big Coal: The Dirty Secret behind America's Energy Future* (Boston: Houghton Mifflin, 2006), p. 116, says "According to ExternE, factoring in just the public health effect of air pollution from U.S. coal plants would add an average of about $13 per megawatt-hour to the price of coal-fired power . . . For the big dirties, added costs could be as high as $33 per megawatt-hour." Using 12,500 Btu/lb. and an average heat rate (Btu/kWh) of 9918, at $33/MWh, the proportional, order of magnitude, cost per ton would be $83; at $13/MWh, the proportional cost per ton would be $33.

34. Compiled using coal consumption data from Energy Information Administration, *Monthly Energy Review* (July 2008), Table 6.1, base numbers for oil products currently supplied from Energy Information Administration, *Monthly Energy Review* (July 2008), Table 3.5.

35. Fareed Zakaria, *The Post-American World* (New York: W.W. Norton & Company Inc., 2008), Chapter 1 "The Rise of the Rest."

36. Natural Resources Defense Council, "Know Where It's Coming From, Issues: Health, Mercury Contamination in Fish," http://www.nrdc.org/health/effects/ mercury/sources.asp, retrieved August 30, 2008.

37. "Top Ten Reasons Coal Is Dirty," www.coal-is-dirty.com/the-coal-hard-facts, retrieved August 27, 2008.

38. "Top 5 'Clean Coal' Myths," www.coal-is-dirty.com/top-5-clean-coal-myths, retrieved August 27, 2008.

39. National Research Council of the National Academies, *Coal: Research and Development to Support National Energy Policy* (Washington, D.C.: The National Academies Press, 2007).

40. Average 2008 price of oil was $99.75 per barrel (per Bloomberg Data Services, January 5, 2009) and 2008 U.S. petroleum imports averaged 12.9 million barrels per day (Energy Information Administration, *Monthly Energy Review* [March 2009], Table 3.1), equaling a total import cost of $470 billion for 2008.

41. Martin Crutsinger, "Trade Deficit Drops to $39.9 Billion [in December]; Lowest in 6 Years," *Houston Chronicle* from Associated Press (February 11, 2009), saying "for the year [2008], the deficit shrank by 3.3 percent to $677.1 billion."

42. B. Stringer and L. Kobzik, "Environmental Particulate-Mediated Cytokine Production in Lung Epithelial Cells (Abstract)," CAT.INIST, http://cat.inist .fr/?aModele=afficheN&cpsidt=2392763, retrieved August 30, 2008.

43. Milton Copulos, "National Defense Council Foundation: Issue Alert, the Hidden Cost of Oil, an Update" (January 8, 2007), http://ndcf.dyndns.org/ ndcf/home.htm, retrieved August 7, 2008; International Center for Technology Assessment, "The Real Price of Gasoline, Report No. 3—An Analysis of the Hidden External Costs Consumers Pay to Fuel Their Automobiles" (November 1998).

44. U.S. total oil import numbers, 1980 through 2007, from Energy Information Administration, *Monthly Energy Review* (August 2008), Table 3.1, and (December 2001), Table 3.1b. Total import numbers (in barrels/day) multiplied by 365 to get barrels/year times 42 to get gallons/year times estimated external cost of $1 to $3 per gallon.

45. Goodell, p. 116: "According to a ten-year study known as ExternE . . . factoring in just the public health effects of air pollution from U.S. coal plants would add an average of about $13 per megawatt-hour to the price of coal-fired power . . . For the big dirties, added costs could be as high as $33 per megawatt-hour." Using 12,500 Btu/lb. and an average heat rate (Btu/kWh) of 9918, at $33/MWh, the proportional, order of magnitude, cost per ton, would be $83; at $13/MWh, the proportional cost per ton would be $33. Numbers then figured for $10 to $30 external costs per ton of coal. U.S. coal consumption

numbers, 1980 through 2007, from Energy Information Administration, *Annual Energy Review* (2007), Table 7.3.

46. National Research Council of the National Academies, *Coal: Research and Development to Support National Energy Policy* (Washington, D.C.: The National Academies Press, 2007), p. 53.

47. Richard Heinberg, "Burning the Furniture," MuseLetter #179 (March 2007), http://www.richardheinberg.com/museletter/179, retrieved August 30, 2008.

48. Goodell, p. 116.

49. Bloomberg Data Services, March 31, 2009, strip price for crude oil from 2010 to 2015.

50. Michael Graham Richard, "Chinese Fuel Economy Laws," 070.25.05, www.treehugger,com/files/2005/07/chinese_fuel_ec.php, retrieved May 27, 2008; "Fuel Economy Standard Will Be 31.6 mpg," Associated Press (April 22, 2008), www.msnbc.msn.com/id/24258714/print/1/displaymode1098/, retrieved May 27, 2008.

51. Vehicle count data from U.S. Department of Transportation, Federal Highway Administration, *Highway Statistics 2006*, "State Motor-Vehicle Registrations." Data on number of SUVs and light trucks and estimates of average costs of SUVs and light trucks from private conversations with car dealership personnel.

52. A natural gas home-fill appliance now costs $4,000, but mass production should reduce the cost by at least 50 percent.

53. E-mail correspondence with James N. Harger, senior vice president, Marketing & Sales, Clean Energy Fuels, August 5, 2008.

54. "Proposed Bill Would Give Major Boost to NGVs in Federal Fleets," *Natural Gas Week* (April 6, 2009).

55. E-mail correspondence with James N. Harger, August 5, 2008.

56. Alex Halperin, "Pickens' Gas IPO Runs on Fumes," *Business Week Online* (May 28, 2007).

57. Bill Siuru, "Can You Convert to Natural Gas?" Ron Cogan's Green Car. com, http://www.greencar.com/features/natural-gas-conversions/, retrieved August 12, 2008.

58. E-mail correspondence with Todd R. Campbell, October 2, 2008.

59. Additional natural gas consumption to supply 130 million U.S. vehicles with CNG: 130 million vehicles represents 53 percent of the total U.S. vehicle fleet of 244 million vehicles (U.S. Department of Transportation, Federal Highway Administration, *Highway Statistics 2006*, "State Motor-Vehicle Registrations"); 244 million vehicles use about 11.5 million barrels of oil per day (for gasoline and diesel); 130 million vehicles would therefore use about 6 million barrels

of oil per day; 1 barrel of oil equals between about 5.06 to 5.8 Mcf equivalent for CNG; 6 million barrels of oil per day equals 2,190 million barrels of oil per year, or, at equivalency rates, over about 11 Tcf per year. Natural gas consumption in the U.S. for 2007 was 23 Tcf (Energy Information Administration, Monthly Energy Review (September 2008), Table 4.1, Natural Gas Overview, so an additional approximate 11 Tcf for CNG use would require consumption to grow to about 34 Tcf, an approximate 48 percent growth, which, over 12 years would be a near 4 percent growth rate per year.

60. E-mail correspondence with Rich Kolodziej, president, NGVAmerica, September 25, 2008. There are about 190,000 gasoline-fueling stations in the United States. It is thought about 130,000 to 140,000 of these are in metropolitan locations, with about 90 percent of metropolitan stations—or about 120,000—having natural gas service or natural gas service in the street. The cost to install CNG fueling facilities to a gasoline filling station is believed to be about $500,000 to $750,000, so the total cost would range between about $60 billion to $90 billion.

61. E-mail correspondence with Todd R. Campbell, October 2, 2008.

62. *Id.*

63. *Id.*

64. Total 2007 U.S. CO_2 fossil fuel emissions are 5.984 billion metric tons, of which 2.583 billion metric tons are petroleum emissions and 2.154 billion metric tons are coal emissions (Energy Information Administration, "U.S. Carbon Dioxide Emissions form Energy Sources 2007 Flash Estimate," http://www.eia.doe.gov/oiaf/1605/flash/flash.html [July 1, 2008]). The U.S. petroleum supply of about 20 million barrels per day (Energy Information Administration, *Monthly Energy Review* [September 2008], Table 3.1, Petroleum Overview), produced 2.583 billion metric tons of CO_2 in 2007; the 5.75 million barrels of oil per day saved by using CNG (or 28.75 percent of the 20 million barrels per day) produce 743 million metric tons of CO_2 per year. CNG could save about 30 percent of the 743 million metric tons, or a savings of about 225 million metric tons per year.

65. Nelson D. Schwartz, "Who Else Can Pile on for a Federal Rescue?" *New York Times* (September 9, 2008), citing the "energy bill signed last year to raise corporate average fuel economy standards for cars and trucks by 40 percent by 2020." All U.S. vehicles use about 11.5 million barrels of oil per day (for gasoline and diesel); if half of all vehicles used CNG, a 40 percent efficiency savings on the remaining half of all vehicles (which use 5.75 million barrels of oil per day) would imply savings of about 2.3 million barrels of oil per day. (New fuel efficiency measures were proposed by President Obama in May 2009—to be effective by 2016.)

66. U.S. oil imports total 13 million barrels per day (Energy Information Administration, *Monthly Energy Review* [September 2008], Table 3.1, Petroleum Overview); converting 130 million U.S. vehicles to CNG would save 5.75 million barrels per day. With a phased-in CNG conversion plan and using the Bloomberg March 31, 2009, strip prices for crude oil from 2010 to 2015, savings by 2015 would be $700 billion.

67. Electricity consumption is projected to grow from 3,814 billion kWh in 2006 to 4,972 billion kWh in 2030, increasing at an average annual rate of 1.1 percent (Energy Information Administration, *Annual Energy Outlook*, 2008, reference case). A growth rate of about 1.1 percent per year would indicate growth from 2009 to 2015 of some 300 billion kWh.

68. Navigant Consulting, "North American Natural Gas Supply Assessment," July 4, 2008.

69. E-mail correspondence and personal communication with Rick Smead, director, Navigant Consulting, September 26, 2008 and October 3, 2008. Current natural gas shale production is between 5–6 Bcf/day [which equals 1.8 to 2.2 Tcf/year]; natural gas shale production could grow to 27 Bcf/day by the early 2020s up to 39 Bcf/day [which equals 10 to 14 Tcf/year].

70. Energy Information Administration, Monthly Energy Review (March 2009), Table 4.1, Natural Gas Overview.

71. Energy Information Administration, Monthly Energy Review (March 2009), Table 4.2, Natural Gas Trade by Country.

Chapter 13

1. In 2007, there were 645 coal-fired plants in the U.S. (Keith O. Rattie, "The Role of Natural Gas in a Carbon-Constrained World," *Landman Magazine* [November/December 2007]); existing generator nameplate capacity for coal in the U.S. is 336,040 megawatts (Energy Information Administration, *Electric Power Annual 2007*, Table 2.2 "Existing Capacity by Energy Source, 2007," published January 2009), indicating the average-sized coal plant in the U.S. is just over 500 megawatts.

2. Adam Lashinsky, "Kleiner Bets the Farm" (paper presented at Fortune Brainstorm TECH, July 24, 2008). http://money.cnn.com/2008/07/08/technology/Kleiner_bets_the_farm_Lashinsky.fortune/i . . . , retrieved October 7, 2008.

3. "Energy Security in Asia: The Case for Flexibility," *World Energy* 6, no. 3 (2003), 18.

4. As compared to gasoline, CNG reduces carbon monoxide emissions 90 percent to 97 percent, reduces carbon dioxide emissions 25 percent, emits virtually no particulate matter, and eliminates evaporative emissions. "Natural

Gas Vehicle Emissions" (U.S. Department of Energy, Energy Efficiency and Renewable Energy, Alternative Fuels & Advanced Vehicles Data Center), http://www.eere.energy.gov/afdc/vehicles/natural_gas_emissions.html, retrieved June 12, 2008.

5. "Though Best of Show, Honda GX NGV Still Sputters; Volvo in Wings," *Natural Gas Week* (March 10, 2008).

6. Compiled using data from *BP Statistical Review of World Energy* (June 2008).

7. Energy Information Administration, *International Energy Outlook 2008*, Table H3.

8. Janet L. Sawin, "Wind Power Continues Rapid Rise" (Vital Signs Online), www.worldwatch.org.

9. "Hydrogen Futures: Toward a Sustainable Energy System" (Worldwatch Institute Paper 157, August 2001).

10. "Hydrogen as an Energy Carrier," April 10, 2007, www.hydrogenassociation. org/general/faqs.asp.

11. "Hydrogen Ferry to Serve Amsterdam Commuters," February 14, 2007, http://www.edie.net/news/news_story.asp?id=12617&channel=0, retrieved August 29, 2008.

12. Country Analysis Briefs—Singapore (Energy Information Administration), http://www.eia.doe.gov/emeu/cabs/Singapore/NaturalGas.html, retrieved April 25, 2008.

13. Jonathan Watts, "Chinese Militia Open Fire on Demonstrators Opposing Coal Plant," *The Guardian* (December 9, 2005).

14. "Statement from World Bank China Country Director on 'Cost of Pollution in China' Report" (July 11, 2007).

15. "Official: China Needs to Look Back at Environment before Leap" (SEPA, September 12, 2006), http://english.sepa.gov.cn/zwxx/hjyw/200609/t20060912_92681.htm.

16. The EPA has estimated that, on some days, about 25 percent of the pollution in Los Angeles comes from China. Thomas L. Friedman, "The Greening of Geopolitics," *New York Times Magazine* (April 15, 2007).

17. Elisabeth Rosenthal, "China Increases Lead as Biggest Carbon Dioxide Emitter," *New York Times*, June 14, 2008. Rosenthal says, "China has clearly overtaken the United States as the world's leading emitter of carbon dioxide," citing the Netherlands Environmental Assessment Agency report; "China: Developed Nations Should Take Lead in Emissions Fight," *Wall Street Journal* (April 26, 2007), which says China is predicted to overtake the United States as the world's biggest source of greenhouse gasses this year [2007].

18. Robert A. Hefner III, *Proposal for Cooperation between the People's Republic of China and GHK (China) Limited* (Oklahoma City, OK: The GHK Company, 1985).

19. "The helmsman must guide the boat by using the waves" quote attributed to Chou En-Lai, who told this to Henry Kissinger in explaining his decision to transfer power to Mao (David A. Heenan and Warren Bennis, *Co-Leaders: The Power of Great Partnerships*, Hoboken, NJ: John Wiley & Sons, 1999).

Chapter 14

1. Mary-Anne Toy, "Watching the Dragon Gain Its Fire," *The Sydney Morning Herald* (November 24, 2008).

2. President Ronald Reagan, Speech at the Brandenburg Gate commemorating the 750th anniversary of Berlin, June 12, 1987.

3. President Ronald Reagan, Address to the 42nd Session of the United Nations General Assembly in New York, September 21, 1987.

4. "Internet World Stats, Usage and Population Statistics," http:/www.internet-worldstats.com/stats.htm, retrieved July 21, 2008.

Glossary

associated natural gas Associated natural gas is the natural gas produced by the oil industry when it produces oil. All oil accumulations contain natural gas. Natural gas is often equal to 20 to 30 percent of the oil in place in what the industry calls oil fields. Because for decades natural gas has been considered a by-product of oil, without much value, it has been flared away during the production of many of the world's largest oil fields. In NASA's night pictures of the world, three of the brightest places on Earth are associated natural gas flares from oil fields in Siberia, Saudi Arabia, and West Africa.

BOE Barrels of oil equivalent (BOE). This term was created by the oil industry so natural gas could be measured in the oil industry's economically important unit, barrels of oil. Today in the United States, many of us in the natural gas exploration and production business have begun to measure oil in MCFE, or thousand cubic feet of natural gas equivalent.

CO_2 CO_2, carbon dioxide, is one carbon atom and two oxygen atoms. It is produced by the burning of carbon-based fuels. It lasts in the atmosphere for about a century and is the principal greenhouse gas that leads to global warming. About 80 percent of the world's CO_2 emissions from energy use come from coal and oil.

coal Coal is a carbon-heavy fuel. Coal is mostly hardened carbon formed from plant matter buried to depths that produce sufficient heat and pressure over long geologic periods. In the past, coal was thought to be the world's most abundant hydrocarbon, but this book makes the case that natural gas may in fact be more abundant than coal. Natural gas is almost always found to coexist with coal and was probably formed in large quantities along with coal. Coal use produces about 36 percent of the world's CO_2 emissions from energy use.

CNG Compressed natural gas (CNG) is natural gas that has been placed under pressure in a tank or vessel so that more energy can be packed in a smaller space. CNG is mostly used in cars, trucks, and buses. When CNG is used instead of gasoline or diesel, engine life is extended, CO_2 emissions are reduced by about 30 percent, and other pollution such as smog is virtually eliminated.

fossil fuel Fossil fuel is a terrible term. It is used as a catchall term for the three principal hydrocarbon fuels; coal, oil, and natural gas. It is nice sounding but, unfortunately, it distorts the understanding of energy at the very time we need the utmost clarity to solve our energy problems. I say this because carbon heavy coal and oil are our principal energy problems and carbon light natural gas is one of our principal solutions. Coal and oil are producing about 80 percent of the world's CO_2 emissions from energy consumption. Additionally, oil use is creating intolerable economic and geostrategic problems. Natural gas, also included in the catchall "fossil fuels," is the *one* clean, affordable domestic fuel that is scalable and can displace the use of coal and oil in the near and medium term. Also, as explained in the text, a lot of natural gas isn't even fossil. So, I plead with everyone who reads this book, but particularly the world's journalists, to stop using the term that mixes our energy problems with one of our principal energy solutions.

gas In the United States, *gas* has become a confusing term because it is commonly used to mean what we use to fuel our cars, which is actually liquid gasoline and not gas at all. In this book, I will use either the term gasoline or petrol interchangeably. The only other time you will see the word *gas* is when it is appropriate to say "oil and gas," meaning the natural gas that is a "gas" produced along with oil. As an example of this confusion, CNN did a story called "We are running out of gas." The title was totally confusing and gave the wrong impression to many. What they really meant is that we are running out of oil, which refines into gasoline.

GET GET is the acronym for the Grand Energy Transition. The GET is a one-time evolutionary step for humankind that will take us from unsustainable to sustainable life and growth on Earth. The GET is the liquid transition between polluting solid sources of energy and virtually limitless, clean gaseous energy sources. The GET is driven by the cumulative effect of the hundreds of trillions of energy choices made by the world's 6.8 billion people each year. Because of the enormous number of energy choices that accumulate to determine the world's energy mix, I liken the process to the evolutionary process that Darwin described as natural selection.

hydrogen The name stems from the fact that water is generated by its combustion. So within its name is the reason why hydrogen is civilization's cleanest fuel. When produced from water, hydrogen becomes a fully environmentally benign fuel—from water to water. Hydrogen in its natural state is a gas and, therefore, part of the Age of Energy Gases. Hydrogen is the simplest element—first in the atomic table—and its chemical symbol is simply H. Over 70 percent of the mass of the universe is hydrogen, and it can become a virtually limitless energy source on Earth. It will grow to become the principal fuel for civilization's sustainable life and growth on Earth.

Mcf, Mmcf, Bcf, and Tcf In the United States, natural gas is measured in units of Mcf, Mmcf, Bcf, and Tcf. Mcf stands for one thousand cubic feet and contains one million Btus of heat value. The volume of production from natural gas wells is often measured in millions of cubic feet per day, or 1,000 Mcf, often designated as Mmcf. Similarly, Bcf means a billion cubic feet and equals 1,000 Mmcf. Tcf means a trillion cubic feet and equals 1,000 Bcf. In the balance of the world, natural gas is usually measured in the metric system by cubic meters. 1 cubic meter equals 35.3 cubic feet.

natural gas Natural gas (natgas) as used in this book refers to methane. Methane is a hydrocarbon, and its chemical symbol is CH_4. It is one carbon and four hydrogen atoms. In the United Kingdom and former British colonies, the general term for natural gas is methane, pronounced "mee-thane." This book makes the case that natural gas is the world's most abundant hydrocarbon and could exceed the Btus of energy of all the world's coal and oil combined.

NGV A natural gas vehicle (NGV) is any car, bus, or truck that runs on CNG.

LNG Liquefied natural gas (LNG) is natural gas that is in liquid form as a result of being cooled to very low temperatures and usually under added pressure to assist with liquification. LNG is used in order to pack more energy in a smaller container. The term *LNG* usually means the liquid natural gas that is transported across oceans in cryogenic tankers and bought and sold between nations. Most LNG is regasified at terminals along the coast and then goes into the domestic pipeline grid as ordinary natural gas. Trucks, buses, cars, and aircraft can run on LNG.

natural gas industry The natural gas "industry" is not really an industry. Rather, it is generally the sum of many fragmented businesses. Natural gas production, gathering, transportation, marketing, and distribution are often performed by entirely different companies with different objectives and profit motives. This means there has never been a united lobbying front for the natural gas "industry."

oil Although oil means many things and is used in many ways, in this book, the term *oil* means the fuel produced by the petroleum industry that today meets 36 percent of the world's demand for energy and 90 percent of the transportation sector's demand. Oil is the principal liquid transition fuel of the GET that will take civilization from dirty, finite, unsustainable solid fuels to its destiny of sustainable life and growth on Earth, fueled by virtually limitless, clean energy gases. Oil's percentage of the energy mix peaked in 1973, when it met 48 percent of the world's energy needs, and has subsequently declined to about 36 percent. The era of oil is in its twilight.

oil and gas The term is misleading as it leads to the presumption that they are more or less the same. I have used the conventional term sparsely and only to indicate the common misunderstanding of the oil and gas industry. Unfortunately, the term *oil and gas* is so often used that it leads to the mistaken belief that if oil is reaching its peak, natural gas must also be reaching its peak. Nothing could be further from the truth.

oil and gas industry There is no such thing. There is an integrated oil production, transportation, refining, distribution, and marketing industry. However, it is true that the oil industry produces large amounts of natural gas because natural gas is always found with oil, but the oil industry rarely transports and hardly ever distributes natural gas.

petrol Petrol is a shortened form of petroleum and is used in the United Kingdom and many of the former British colonies to refer to gasoline. You can generally count on gasoline being called petrol anywhere you drive on the left-hand side of the road.

petroleum Petroleum is aptly formed from the Latin words for rock and oil. Today it is defined by Webster's as "an oily, flammable, bituminous liquid." A more common word for petroleum is oil, the source of one of the world's principal fuels and largest industry. As you read this book, you will see that the key word in petroleum's definition is *liquid*.

solar Solar energy of course comes from the sun, which is mostly a big ball of burning hydrogen gas. The enormous quantity of solar energy that bathes the Earth each day is sufficient to meet all the world's energy needs for over one year. Solar energy is a part of the Age of Energy Gases and its use is exploding into the world's energy mix at exponential rates of growth. We should consider the sun our solar system's public power plant.

standard of living and quality of life In today's world, many people do not differentiate between these two terms. However, as I use them, *standard of living* has more to do with income level and wealth, and *quality of life* is the intangible quality of how we live and the environment within which we live. In my use of these terms, there is a dialectic tension between each meaning. For example, one may give up some of the finer things in life to seek fortune, or vice versa.

wind The Earth's atmosphere is a gas, so wind is a part of the Age of Energy Gases. Wind is the movement of the Earth's atmosphere driven by the daily heating and cooling of the Earth as it rotates in and out of the sun's daily solar energy. Wind is a nearly limitless energy source whose growth will continue at an exponential rate for decades.

Recommended Reading

A Thousand Barrels a Second: The Coming Oil Break Point and the Challenges Facing an Energy Dependent World, Peter Tertzakian, McGraw-Hill.

Beyond Oil: The View from Hubbert's Peak, Kenneth S. Deffeyes, Hill and Wang.

Big Coal: The Dirty Secret Behind America's Energy Future, Jeff Goodell, Houghton Mifflin Company.

China Shifts Gears: Automakers, Oil, Pollution, and Development, Kelly Sims Gallagher, MIT Press.

Climatic Cataclysm: The Foreign Policy and National Security Implications of Climate Change, Kurt M. Campbell, Editor, Brookings Institution Press.

Coal: Research and Development to Support National Energy Policy, National Research Council of The National Academies, The National Academies Press.

E=mc²: A Biography of the World's Most Famous Equation, David Bodanis, St. Martin's Press.

Earth the Sequel: The Race to Reinvent Energy and Stop Global Warming, Fred Krupp & Miriam Horn; W.W. Norton and Company.

Energy at the Crossroads: Global Perspectives and Uncertainties, Vaclav Smil, MIT Press.

Energy in Nature and Society: General Energetics of Complex Systems, Vaclav Smil, MIT Press.

Energy Revolution: Policies for a Sustainable Future, Howard Geller, Island Press, New York.

Global Warming: Understanding the Forecast, Andrew Revkin, Abbeyville Press Publishers, New York.

Gusher of Lies: The Dangerous Delusions of Energy Independence, Robert Bryce, Public Affairs, New York.

Harnessing Hydrogen: The Key to Sustainable Transportation, James S. Cannon, Inform Inc., New York.

"How the World Should Invest in Energy Efficiency" (McKinsey & Company report), Diana Farrell and Jaana K. Remes, July 2008, The McKinsey Quarterly (Website registration is necessary to read report. Go to www .mckinseyquarterly.com/Energy_Resources_Materials).

Hydrogen as a Future Energy Carrier, Andreas Zuttel, Andreas Borgschulte and Louis Schlapbach, editors, John Wiley & Sons Inc.

Hydrogen-Hot Stuff Cool Science, Discover the Future of Energy, 2nd Edition, Rex A. Ewing, PixyJack Press.

Leveling the Carbon Playing Field: International Competition and U.S. Climate Policy Design, Trevor Houser, Rob Bradley, Britt Childs, Jacob Werksman, and Robert Heilmayr, World Resources Institute.

Lives Per Gallon: The True Cost of Our Oil Addiction, Terry Tamminen, Island Press, Washington.

Nuclear Terrorism: The Ultimate Preventable Catastrophe, Graham Allison, Holt Paperbacks,

Oil on the Brain: Petroleum's Long, Strange Trip to Your Tank, Lisa Margonelli, Broadway Publishing.

Out of Gas: The End of the Age of Oil, David Goodstein, W. W. Norton and Co., New York.

Over a Barrel: A Simple Guide to the Oil Shortage, Tom Mast, Hayden Publishers.

Pathways to a Hydrogen Future, Thomas E. Drennan and Jennifer E. Rosthal, Elsevier Science.

Power from the Earth, Thomas Gold, J.M. Dent & Sons Ltd., London.

Power to the People: How the Coming Energy Revolution Will Transform an Industry, Change Our Lives, and Maybe Even Save the Planet, Vijay Vaitheeswaran, Farrar, Strauss and Giroux, New York.

Sleeping With the Devil: How Washington Sold Our Soul For Saudi Crude, Robert Baer, Three Rivers Press, New York.

Solar Revolution: The Economic Transformation of the Global Energy Industry, Travis Bradford, MIT Press.

Stan Ovshinsky and the Hydrogen Economy: Creating a Better World, George S. Howard, Academic Publications, Indiana.

Strategic Ignorance: Why the Bush Administration Is Recklessly Destroying a Century of Environmental Progress, Carl Pope and Paul Rauber, Sierra Club Books.

The Anxious Economy, Ezra Solomon, W.H. Freeman & Company, New York.

The Bottomless Well: The Twilight of Fuel, the Virtue of Waste, and Why We Will Never Run Out of Energy, Peter Huber and Mark Mills, Basic Books, Perseus Books Group, New York.

The Deep Hot Biosphere, Thomas Gold, Springer-Verlag, New York.

The Empty Tank: Oil, Gas, Hot Air, and the Coming Global Financial Catastrophe, Jeremy Leggett, Random House, New York.

The End of Oil: On the Edge of a Perilous New World, Paul Roberts, Houghton Mifflin Company.

The Future of Energy Gases, U.S. Geological Survey Professional Paper 1570, David G. Howell, Editor (articles include "New Thinking About Natural Gas" by Robert A. Hefner III and "The Origin of Methane in the Crust of the Earth" by Thomas Gold).

The Global Deal: Climate Change and the Creation of a New Era of Progress and Prosperity, Lord Nicholas Stern, PublicAffairs.

The Hydrogen Age: Empowering a Clean-Energy Future, Geoffrey Holland and James Provenzano, Gibbs Smith Publishing.

The Hydrogen Economy: The Creation of the Worldwide Energy Web and the Redistribution of Power on Earth, Jeremy Rifkin, Jeremy P. Tarcher/Penguin, Penguin Group.

The Last Oil Shock: A Survival Guide to the Imminent Extinction of Petroleum, David Strahan; John Murray Publishing, London.

The Power of Progress: How America's Progressives Can (Once Again) Save Our Economy, Our Climate, and Our Country, John Podesta, Crown Publishing.

The Prize: The Epic Quest for Oil, Money & Power, Daniel Yergin, Free Press Simon & Schuster.

The River Runs Black: The Environmental Challenge to China's Future, Elizabeth C. Economy, Cornell University Press, Ithaca & London.

Thicker than Oil: America's Uneasy Partnership with Saudi Arabia, Rachel Bronson, Oxford University Press.

Tomorrow's Energy: Hydrogen Fuel Cells, and the Prospects for a Cleaner Planet, Peter Hoffmann, MIT Press.

Turnaround: Stories of Behind the Scenes, Political Washington, A Great American Industry, and Fun Along the Way, George H. "Bud" Lawrence, New Forums Press Inc.

Twilight in the Desert: The Coming Saudi Oil Shock and the World Economy, Matthew R. Simmons, John Wiley & Sons, Inc.

Winning the Oil End Game, Amory B. Lovins, E. Kyle Datta, Odd-Even Bustnes, Jonathan G. Koomey, Nathan J. Glasgow, Rocky Mountain Institute.

Zoom: The Global Race to Fuel the Car of the Future, Iain Carson and Vijay Vaitheeswaran, Hachette Book Group USA.

About the Author

Robert A. Hefner III is founder and owner of GHK Exploration, a private natural gas company headquartered in Oklahoma City. He pioneered ultradeep natural gas exploration and production. GHK led the development of innovative technology needed to successfully drill and produce many of the world's deepest and highest-pressure natural gas wells, setting many industry world records along the way.

In the 1970s, Hefner was a leader in the industry's successful efforts to deregulate the price of natural gas. These technological and political accomplishments led to the development of vast new domestic natural gas resources. Since the 1980s, Hefner has pursued his interest in China in the areas of energy, foreign affairs, and contemporary Chinese art (www.hefnercollection.com). He is a Fellow of the Royal Geographical Society of London, a Fellow National in the Explorers Club, a member of Singapore's International Advisory Panel (IAP) on Energy, and a member of the International Council at the Belfer Center at Harvard. He is an advisory director of the Center for a New American Security (CNAS) and has established the Hefner Initiative on Energy and National Security at CNAS.

Hefner and his wife, MeiLi, initiated and support the Hefner China Fund, which has brought rising young Chinese government officials to study in the fields of energy, culture, and foreign policy at Harvard's Kennedy School of Government and the National University of Singapore's Lee Kuan Yew School of Public Policy. He holds a bachelor's degree in petroleum geology from the University of Oklahoma.

Index